HTML5 Games Development by Example

Example

Beginner's Guide

Create six fun games using the latest HTML5, Canvas, CSS, and JavaScript techniques

Makzan

BIRMINGHAM - MUMBAI

HTML5 Games Development by Example
Beginner's Guide

First published: August 2011

Production Reference: 1180811

Published by Packt Publishing Ltd.
Livery Place
35 Livery Street
Birmingham B3 2PB, UK.

ISBN 978-1-849691-26-0

www.packtpub.com

Cover Image by Girish Suryawanshi (girish.suryawanshi@gmail.com)

Credits

Author

Makzan

Reviewers

Matteo Ferretti

Henk Jurriens

William Malone

Acquisition Editor

David Barnes

Development Editor

Neha Mallik

Technical Editors

Pallavi Kachare

Azharuddin Sheikh

Copy Editor

Neha Shetty

Project Coordinator

Zainab Bagasrawala

Proofreader

Joanna McMahon

Indexer

Rekha Nair

Graphics

Geetanjali Sawant

Production Coordinators

Melwyn D'sa

Adline Swetha Jesuthas

Cover Work

Melwyn D'sa

Preface

HTML5 promises to be the hot new platform for online games. HTML5 games work on computers, smartphones, and tablets, including iPhones and iPads. Be one of the first developers to build HTML5 games today and be ready for tomorrow!

This book will show you how to use the latest HTML5 and CSS3 web standards to build card games, drawing games, physics games, and even multiplayer games over the network. With this book, you will build six example games with clear systematic tutorials.

HTML5, CSS3, and the related JavaScript API are the latest hot topics in web. These standards bring us the new game market, HTML5 Games. With the new power from them, we can design games with HTML5 elements, CSS3 properties, and JavaScript to play in browsers.

This book is divided into nine chapters with each one focusing on one topic. We will create six games and specifically learn how we draw game objects, animate them, add audio, connect players, and build a physics game with a Box2D physics engine.

What this book covers

Chapter 1, *Introducing HTML5 Games*, introduces the new features from HTML5, CSS3, and related JavaScript API. It also demonstrates what games we can make with these features and its benefits.

Chapter 2, *Getting Started with DOM-based Game Development*, kick-starts the game development journey by creating a traditional Ping Pong game in DOM and jQuery.

Chapter 3, *Building Memory Matching Game in CSS3*, walks through the new features from CSS3 and discusses how we can create a memory card matching game in DOM and CSS3.

Chapter 4, *Building Untangle Game with Canvas and Drawing API*, introduces a new way to draw games and interact with them in a web page with the new Canvas element. It also demonstrates how to build a puzzle solving game with Canvas.

Chapter 5, Building a Canvas Game Masterclass, extends the untangle game to show how we can draw gradients and images using Canvas. It also discusses sprite sheet animations and multi-layer management.

Chapter 6, Adding Sounds Effects to Your Games, adds sound effects and background music to the game by using the `Audio` element. It discusses the audio format capability among web browsers and creates a keyboard-driven music game by the end of the chapter.

Chapter 7, Using Local Storage to Store Game Data, extends the CSS3 memory matching game to demonstrate how we can use the new Local Storage API to store and resume game progress and best records.

Chapter 8, Building a Multiplayer Draw-and-Guess Game with WebSockets, discusses the new WebSockets API which allows browsers to establish a persistent connection with the socket server. This allows multiple players to play the game together in real time. A draw-and-guess game is created at the end of chapter.

Chapter 9, Building a Physics Car Game with Box2D and Canvas, teaches how to integrate a famous physics engine, Box2D, into our Canvas games. It discusses how to create physics bodies, apply force, connect them together, associate graphics with the physics, and finally create a platform card game.

What you need for this book

You need the latest modern web browsers, a good text editor, and a basic HTML, CSS, and JavaScript knowledge.

Who this book is for

This book is for game designers who have a basic understanding of HTML, CSS, and JavaScript and want to create Canvas or DOM-based games that run on browsers.

Conventions

In this book, you will find several headings appearing frequently.

To give clear instructions of how to complete a procedure or task, we use:

Time for action – heading

1. Action 1
2. Action 2
3. Action 3

Instructions often need some extra explanation so that they make sense, so they are followed with:

What just happened?

This heading explains the working of tasks or instructions that you have just completed.

You will also find some other learning aids in the book, including:

Pop quiz – heading

These are short multiple choice questions intended to help you test your own understanding.

Have a go hero – heading

These set practical challenges and give you ideas for experimenting with what you have learned.

You will also find a number of styles of text that distinguish between different kinds of information. Here are some examples of these styles, and an explanation of their meaning.

Code words in text are shown as follows: "We will start our HTML5 game development journey from index.html."

A block of code is set as follows:

```
// starting game
var date = new Date();
audiogame.startingTime = date.getTime();

// some time later
var date = new Date();
var elapsedTime = (date.getTime() - audiogame.startingTime)/1000;
```

When we wish to draw your attention to a particular part of a code block, the relevant lines or items are set in bold:

```
function setupLevelData()
{
    var notes = audiogame.leveldata.split(";");

    // store the total number of dots
    audiogame.totalDotsCount = notes.length;

    for(var i in notes)
    {
        var note = notes[i].split(",");
        var time = parseFloat(note[0]);
        var line = parseInt(note[1]);
        var musicNote = new MusicNote(time,line);
        audiogame.musicNotes.push(musicNote);
    }
}
```

Any command-line input or output is written as follows:

```
$ ./configure
$ sudo make install
```

New terms and **important words** are shown in bold. Words that you see on the screen, in menus or dialog boxes for example, appear in the text like this: "You will get an introduction page of the multiuser sketchpad. Right click on the **Launch Experiment** option and choose **Open link in new window**".

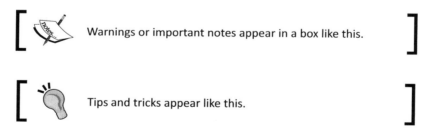

[Warnings or important notes appear in a box like this.   ]

[Tips and tricks appear like this.   ]

Reader feedback

Feedback from our readers is always welcome. Let us know what you think about this book—what you liked or may have disliked. Reader feedback is important for us to develop titles that you really get the most out of.

To send us general feedback, simply send an e-mail to feedback@packtpub.com, and mention the book title via the subject of your message.

If there is a book that you need and would like to see us publish, please send us a note in the **SUGGEST A TITLE** form on www.packtpub.com or e-mail suggest@packtpub.com.

If there is a topic that you have expertise in and you are interested in either writing or contributing to a book, see our author guide on www.packtpub.com/authors.

Customer support

Now that you are the proud owner of a Packt book, we have a number of things to help you to get the most from your purchase.

Downloading the example code for this book

You can download the example code files for all Packt books you have purchased from your account at http://www.PacktPub.com. If you purchased this book elsewhere, you can visit http://www.PacktPub.com/support and register to have the files e-mailed directly to you.

Errata

Although we have taken every care to ensure the accuracy of our content, mistakes do happen. If you find a mistake in one of our books—maybe a mistake in the text or the code—we would be grateful if you would report this to us. By doing so, you can save other readers from frustration and help us improve subsequent versions of this book. If you find any errata, please report them by visiting http://www.packtpub.com/support, selecting your book, clicking on the **errata submission form** link, and entering the details of your errata. Once your errata are verified, your submission will be accepted and the errata will be uploaded on our website, or added to any list of existing errata, under the Errata section of that title. Any existing errata can be viewed by selecting your title from http://www.packtpub.com/support.

Piracy

Piracy of copyright material on the Internet is an ongoing problem across all media. At Packt, we take the protection of our copyright and licenses very seriously. If you come across any illegal copies of our works, in any form, on the Internet, please provide us with the location address or website name immediately so that we can pursue a remedy.

Please contact us at `copyright@packtpub.com` with a link to the suspected pirated material.

We appreciate your help in protecting our authors, and our ability to bring you valuable content.

Questions

You can contact us at `questions@packtpub.com` if you are having a problem with any aspect of the book, and we will do our best to address it.

Introducing HTML5 Games

Hyper-Text Markup Language, HTML, has been shaping the Internet in the last few decades. It defines how content is structured in web and the linkage between related pages. HTML keeps evolving from version 2 to HTML 4.1, and later XHTML 1.1. Thanks to those web applications and social network applications, HTML is now on the way to HTML5.

Cascading Style Sheet (CSS) *defines how web pages are presented visually. It styles all HTML elements and the styles of their states, such as hover and active.*

JavaScript is the logic controller of the web page. It makes the web page dynamic and provides client-side interaction between the page and users. It accesses the HTML through **Document Object Model (DOM***). It re-styles the HTML elements by applying different CSS styles.*

These three receipts bring us the new game market, HTML5 Games. With the new power from them, we can design games with HTML5 elements, CSS3 properties, and JavaScript to play in the browsers.

In this chapter, we shall:

- ◆ Discover new features in HTML5
- ◆ Discuss what makes us so excited around HTML5 and CSS3
- ◆ Take a look at what others are playing with HTML5 on game designing
- ◆ Preview what games we are going to build in later chapters

So let's get started.

Discovering new features in HTML5

There are many new things introduced in HTML5 and CSS3. Before getting our hands dirty in creating the games, let's take an overview of the new features and see how we can use them to create games.

Canvas

Canvas is an HTML5 element that provides drawing shapes and bitmap manipulation functions in low level. We can imagine the Canvas element as a dynamic image tag. The traditional `<img>` tag shows a static image. Whether the image is dynamically generated or statically loaded from the server, the image is static and will not be changed. We can change the `<img>` tag to another image source or apply styles to the image, but we cannot modify the image bitmap context itself.

On the other hand, Canvas is like a client-side dynamic `<img>` tag. We can load images inside it, draw shapes there, and interact with it by JavaScript.

Canvas plays an important role in HTML5 game development. It is one of our main focuses in this book.

Audio

Background music and sound effects are often an essential element in game design. HTML5 comes with native audio support by the `audio` tag. Thanks to this feature, we do not require the proprietary Flash Player to play sound effects in our HTML5 games. We will discuss the usage of the `audio` tag in Chapter 6, *Building Music Games with HTML5 Audio Elements*.

GeoLocation

GeoLocation lets the web page retrieve the latitude and longitude of the user's computer. This feature may not have been so useful years ago when everyone was using the Internet with their desktop PC. There are not many things that we need the road level location accuracy of the user. We can get the rough location by analyzing the IP address.

These days, more and more users are going on the Internet with their powerful smartphones. Webkit and other modern mobile browsers are in everyone's pocket. GeoLocation lets us design mobile applications and games to play with the location.

Location-based services have been used in several social networking applications such as foursquare (`http://foursquare.com`) and Gowalla (`http://gowalla.com`). The success of this type of location-based social community creates a trend of using location services with our smartphone.

WebGL

WebGL extends the Canvas element by providing a set of 3D graphics API in the web browser. The API follows the standard of OpenGL ES 2.0. The WebGL provides a real 3D rendering place for 3D HTML5 games. However, not all browsers natively support the WebGL yet at the time of writing this book. Currently only Mozilla Firefox 4, Google Chrome, and a nightly build of WebKit browser support it natively.

The technique of creating games for WebGL is quite different from usual HTML5 game developments. Creating games in WebGL requires handing the 3D models and use of API similar to the OpenGL. Therefore, we will not discuss the WebGL game development in this book.

The following screenshot from Google Body (`http://bodybrowser.googlelabs.com`) demonstrates how they use WebGL to show a 3D human body that responds to the user's input:

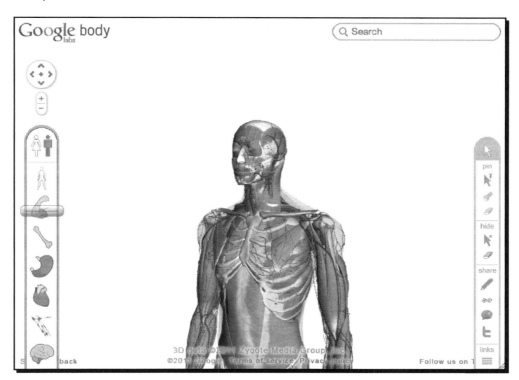

 The LearningWebGL (`http://learnwebgl.com`) provides a collection of tutorials on getting started with WebGL. It is a good starting point if you want to learn more on using it.

WebSocket

WebSocket is part of the HTML5 spec for connecting the web page to a socket server. It provides us with an event-driven connection between the browser and server. That means the client does not need to poll the server for new data every short period. The server will push updates to the browsers whenever there is any data to update. One benefit of this feature is that the game players can interact with each other almost in real time. When one player does something and sends data to the server, the server will broadcast an event to every other connected browser to acknowledge what the player just did. This creates the possibility of creating multiplayer HTML5 games.

Due to a security issue, WebSocket is now temporary disabled by Mozilla Firefox and Opera. Safari and Chrome may also drop the support on WebSocket until the issue is fixed. You can learn more on this issue by visiting the following link: `http://hacks.mozilla.org/2010/12/websockets-disabled-in-firefox-4/`.

Local Storage

HTML5 provides a persistent data storage solution to web browsers.

Local Storage stores key-value paired data persistently. The data is still there after the browser terminates. Moreover, the data is not limited to be accessible only to the browsers that created it. It is available to all browser instances with the same domain. Thanks to Local Storage, we can easily save game status, such as progress and earn achievements, locally in web browsers.

HTML5 also provides Web SQL Database. It is a client-side relational database and is currently supported by Safari, Chrome, and Opera. With the database storage, we can not only store key-value paired data but also complicated relational structures that support SQL queries.

Local Storage and Web SQL Database are useful for us to save game state locally when creating games.

Besides Local Storage, some other storage approaches are now being supported by web browsers. These include Web SQL Database and IndexedDB. These approaches support querying the stored data with condition and thus are more powerful for supporting a complicated data structure.

You can find more information on using the Web SQL Database and IndexedDB in the following link from Mozilla: `http://hacks.mozilla.org/2010/06/comparing-indexeddb-and-webdatabase/`.

Offline application

Normally we need an Internet connection to browse web pages. Sometimes we can browse cached offline web pages. These cached offline web pages usually expire quickly. With the next offline application introduced by HTML5, we can declare our cache manifest. It is a list of files that will be stored for later access without an Internet connection.

With the cache manifest, we can store all the game graphics, game control JavaScript files, CSS stylesheets, and the HTML files locally. We can pack our HTML5 games as an offline game on the desktop or the mobile device. Players can play the games even in airplane mode.

The following screenshot from the Pie Guy game (`http://mrgan.com/pieguy`) shows an HTML5 game in iPhone without an Internet connection. Note the little airplane symbol indicating the offline status:

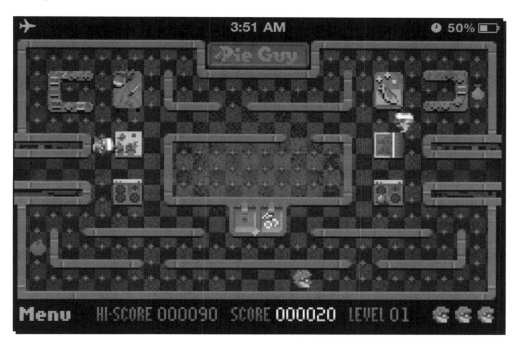

Discovering new features in CSS3

CSS is the presentation layer as HTML is the content layer. It defines how the HTML looks. We cannot miss the CSS when creating games with HTML5, especially for DOM-based games. We may purely use JavaScript to create and style the games with a Canvas element. But we need CSS when creating DOM-based HTML5 games. Therefore, let's take a look at what is new in CSS3 and how we can use the new properties to create games.

Instead of directly drawing and interacting on the Canvas drawing board, new CSS3 properties let us animate the DOM in different ways. This makes it possible to make more complicated DOM-based browser games.

CSS3 transition

Traditionally, the style changes immediately when we apply a new style to an element. CSS3 transition applies tweening during the style changes of the target elements.

For example, we have a blue box here and want to change it to red when we do a mouseover. We will use the following code snippets:

HTML:

```
<a href="#" class="box"></a>
```

CSS:

```
a.box {
  display:block;
  width: 100px;
  height: 100px;
  background: #00f; /* blue */
  border: 1px solid #000;
}
a.box:hover {
  background: #f00;
}
```

The box changes to red immediately when we do a mouseover. With CSS3 transition applied, we can tween the styles with a specific duration and the easing value:

```
a.box {
  -webkit-transition: all 5s linear;
}
```

Downloading the example code for this book

You can download the example code files for all Packt books you have purchased from your account at http://www.PacktPub.com. If you purchased this book elsewhere, you can visit http://www.PacktPub.com/support and register to have the files e-mailed directly to you.

The following screenshot shows the box hover effect with the transition applied:

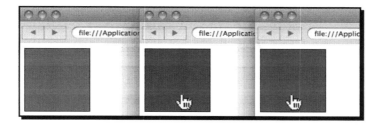

Since the CSS3 spec is still in draft and not yet fixed, the implementation from different browser vendors may have some minor differences to the W3C spec. Therefore, browser vendors tend to implement their CSS3 properties with a vendor prefix to prevent conflict.

Safari and Chrome use the `-webkit-` prefix. Opera uses the `-o-` prefix. Firefox uses the `-moz-` prefix and IE uses the `-ms-` prefix. It is a little complex now to declare a CSS3 property, such as box-shadow, with several lines of the same rule for several browsers. We can expect the prefix to be eliminated after that property spec is fixed.

I will just use the `-webkit-` prefix in most examples to prevent putting so many similar lines in the book. It is more important to get the concept instead of reading the same rules with different vendors prefixed here.

CSS3 transform

CSS3 transform lets us scale the elements, rotate the elements, and translate their position. CSS3 transform is divided into 2D and 3D.

We can reposition an element with translate:

```
-webkit-transform: translate(x,y);
```

or scale the element with scale transformation:

```
-webkit-transform: scale(1.1);
```

We can also scale and rotate the elements with CSS3 transform and combine other transformations:

```
a.box {
  -webkit-transition: all 0.5s linear;
  -webkit-transform: translate(100px,50px);
}
a.box:hover {
  -webkit-transform: translate(100px,50px) scale(1.1) rotate(30deg);
}
```

The following screenshots show the CSS3 transform effect when we do a mouseover:

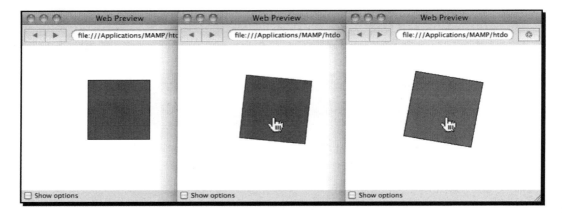

CSS3 transform 3D further extends the spaces into three axes and it currently works only on Safari and Mobile Safari. The following screenshot from `WebKit.org` shows a 3D card flipping effect when we do a mouseover:

CSS3 animation

CSS3 transition is one type of animation. It declares the tweening animation between two styles of the elements.

CSS3 animation is one step further. We can define key frames of an animation. Each key frame contains a set of properties that should change at that moment. It is like a set of CSS3 transitions applied in sequence to the target element.

The AT-AT Walker (`http://anthonycalzadilla.com/css3-ATAT/index-bones.html`) shows a nice demo on creating a skeleton bone animation with CSS3 animation key frames, transform, and transition:

Learning more detail of new HTML5 and CSS3 features

HTML5Rocks (`http://html5rocks.com`) from Google provides a solid quick start guide on new HTML5 elements and CSS3 properties.

Apple also showcases how appealing it can be by using HTML5 in the WebKit-based browser in their homepage (`http://apple.com/html5`).

CSS3 Info (`http://www.css3.info`) is a blog with the latest CSS3 news. It is a good place to get the latest CSS3 spec status, compatible list, and basic CSS3 codes.

The benefit of creating HTML5 games

We explored several key new features from HTML5 and CSS3. With these features, we can create HTML5 games on browsers. But why do we need to do that? What is the benefit of creating HTML5 games?

No third-party plugin required

With the native support of all those features in modern browsers, we do not require the users to pre-install any third-party plugin in order to play. These plugins are not standard. They are proprietary and usually require an extra plugin installation that we may not be able to install.

Supporting iOS devices without plugin

Millions of Apple iOS devices around the world do not support third-party plugins such as Flash Player. Despite whatever reason Apple does not allow Flash Player running on their Mobile Safaris, HTML5 and related web standard is what they get in their browsers. We can reach this user base by creating HTML5 games that optimize for mobiles.

Breaking the boundary of usual browser games

In traditional game designing, we build games within a boundary box. We play video games on a television. We play Flash games in web browsers with a rectangle boundary.

With creativity, we are not bound in a rectangle game stage any more. We can have fun with all the page elements and we can even use many browser windows to compose a game. Furthermore, we can even just use the URL bar to create a game (`http://probablyinteractive.com/url-hunter`). It may sound confusing, but it is because not many web pages have done this yet.

Photojojo (`http://photojojo.com/store/awesomeness/cell-phone-lenses`), an online photography store, provides a fun Easter egg feature on their store page. There is a switch button on the page with a caption **Do not pull**. When the user clicks on it, an orange arm appears from the top with frame-by-frame animation. It holds the web page like a holding cloth and pulls the whole page up to create a funny scroll-down effect. This is not a game, but it is fun enough to demonstrate how we can break the boundary.

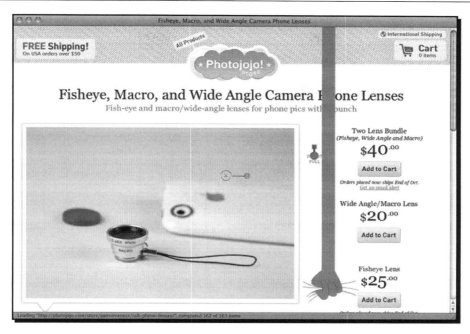

Here is another example named Twitch (`http://reas.com/twitch/`) from Chrome Experiments. It is a collection of mini games where the player has to carry the ball from the starting point to the end point. The fun part is that each mini game is a small browser window. When the ball reaches the destination point of that mini game, it is transferred into the newly created mini game browser to continue the journey. The following screenshot shows the whole map of Twitch with the individual web browser:

Building HTML5 games

Thanks to the new features from HTML5 and CSS3, we can now create an entire game in the browser. We can control every element in the DOM. We can animate each document object with CSS3. We have Canvas to dynamically draw things and interact with them. We have an audio element to handle the background music and sound effects. We also have Local Storage to save game data and WebSocket to create a real time multiplayers game. Most modern browsers are already supporting these features. It is now time to build HTML5 games.

What others are playing with HTML5

It is a good chance to study how different HTML5 games perform by watching other HTML5 games made with different techniques.

Matching game

The Match game (`http://10k.aneventapart.com/Uploads/300/`) demonstrates a beautiful matching game with CSS3 animation and other visual enhancements. The game starts when you press the 3D-like CSS button. The cards present at the back and the front side are flipped using 3D rotation. The front side patterns are fetched dynamically from an online gallery.

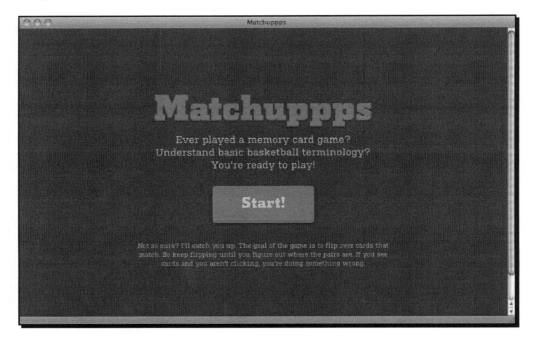

Sinuous

Sinuous (`http://10k.aneventapart.com/Uploads/83/`), winner of the 10K Apart, shows us how a simple game idea with proper implementation can get people addicted to it. The player controls the big dots in the space with the mouse. The aim is to move the dots to avoid the flying comets. It sounds easy and simple, but it is definitely addictive and a just-one-more-try game. The game is created with a Canvas tag. Players can also play this game with their webkit-enabled mobile devices, such as iPhone, iPad, and Android.

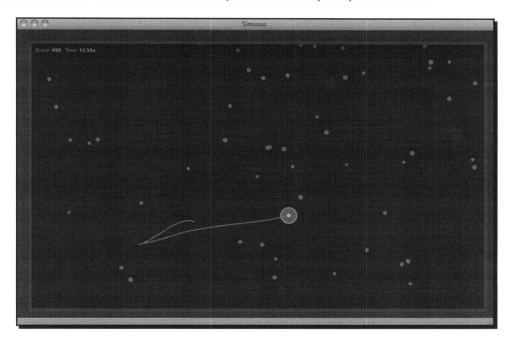

Asteroid-styled bookmarklet

Erik, a web designer from Sweden, created an interesting bookmarklet. It is an asteroid-styled game for any web page. Yes, any web page. It shows an abnormal way to interact with any web page. It creates a plane on the website you are reading from. You can then fly the plane using arrow keys and fire bullets using the space bar. The fun part is that the bullets will destroy the HTML elements on the page. Your goal is to destroy all the things on the web page you choose. This bookmarklet is another example of breaking the boundary of usual browser games. It tells us that we can think outside the box while designing HTML5 games.

The bookmarklet is available for installation at `http://erkie.github.com/`.

The following screenshot shows the plane destroying the content on the web page:

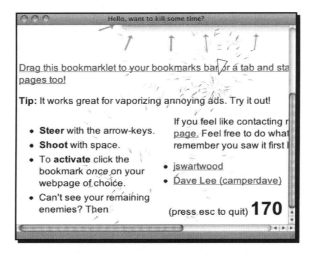

Quake 2

Google demonstrates a WebGL HTML5 port of the first person shooter game, Quake 2. Players move around using the WSAD key and shoot enemies with their mouse. Players can even play with each other in real time by using WebSocket. According to Google, the frame-per-seconds of the HTML5 Quake 2 can be up to 60 fps.

The Quake 2 port is available on Google Code at `http://code.google.com/p/quake2-gwt-port/`.

RumpeTroll

RumpeTroll (`http://rumpetroll.com/`) is an experiment of the HTML5 community where everyone gets connected via WebSocket. We can give our creatures names and move around through mouse clicks. We can also type anything to start a chat. Moreover, we can see what others are doing in real time, thanks to the WebSocketInsert.

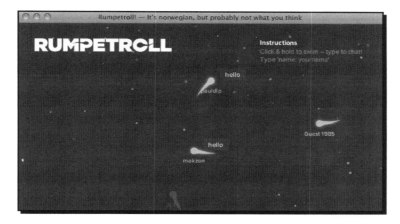

Scrabb.ly

Scrabb.ly (`http://scrabb.ly`) is a multiplayer crossword board game which won the popularity prize in the Node.js Knockout contest. It connects users together with HTML5 WebSocket. This online board game is DOM-based and driven by JavaScript.

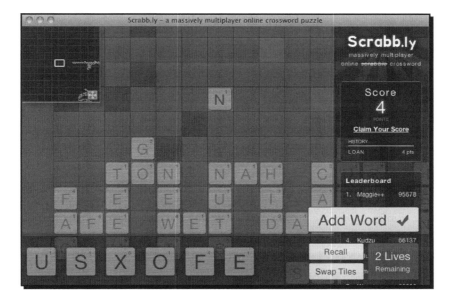

Node.js (`http://nodejs.org`) is an event-driven server-side JavaScript. It can be used as a server connecting concurrent WebSocket clients.

Aves Engine

Aves Engine is an HTML5 game development framework developed by dextrose. It provides tools and API for game developers building their own isometric browser game world with the map editor. The following screenshot captured from the official demonstration video shows how it creates an isometric world:

The engine also takes care of the 2.5 dimension isometric coordinate system, collision detection, and other basic virtual world features. This game engine even works well on mobile devices such as iPad and iPhone. The Aves Engine has gained a lot of attention since its debut and is now acquired by Zynga Game Network Inc, a big social game company.

The video demonstration of the Aves Engine is available on YouTube at the following link:

`http://tinyurl.com/dextrose-aves-engine-sneak`

Browsing more HTML5 games

These examples are just a selected few. The following sites provide updates on HTML5 games created by others:

◆ Canvas Demo (`http://canvasdemo.com`) collects a set of applications and games using the HTML5 Canvas tag. It also provides a bunch of Canvas tutorial resources. It is a good place to start learning Canvas.

◆ HTML5 games (`http://html5games.com`) collect many HTML5 games and organizes them into categories.

◆ Mozilla Labs hosted a HTML5 game design contest in early 2011 and many great games were submitted to the contest. The contest is now over and the list of all the entries is at the following link: `https://gaming.mozillalabs.com/games/`.

◆ The HTML5 Game Jam (`http://www.html5gamejam.com/games`) is an HTML5 event and the website lists a collection of fun HTML5 games and also some useful resources.

What we are going to create in this book

In the following chapters, we are going to build six games. We are going to first create a DOM-based Ping Pong game that can be played by two players in the same machine. Then we will create a memory matching game with CSS3 animation. Later, we will use Canvas to create an untangle puzzle game. Next, we will build a music game with audio elements. Then we will create a multiplayer draw and guess game with WebSocket. Lastly, we will use the Box2D JavaScript port to create a prototype of a physics car game. The following screenshot is of the memory matching game that we will build in *Chapter 3, Building a Memory Matching Game in CSS3*

Summary

We learned a lot in this chapter about basic information of HTML5 games.

Specifically, we covered:

◆ New features from HTML5 and CSS3. We had a glimpse of what techniques we will use to create our games in later chapters. Canvas, audio, CSS animation, and more new features were introduced. We will have many new features to play with.

◆ The benefit of creating HTML5 games. We discussed why we want to create HTML5 games. We want to meet the web standard, meet the mobile devices, and break the boundary of a game.

◆ HTML5 games that others are playing. We listed several existing HTML5 games that were created with different techniques that we will use. We can test those games before creating our own.

◆ We also previewed the games that we are going to build throughout the book.

Now that we've learned about some background information of HTML5 games, we're ready to create our first DOM-based JavaScript-driven game in the next chapter.

2
Getting Started with DOM-based Game Development

We have had an idea about what we are going to learn in the whole book in Chapter 1, Introducing HTML5 Games. From this chapter, we will go through a lot of learning-by-doing sections and we will focus on one topic in each section. Before digging deeply into the cutting edge CSS3 animations and HTML5 Canvas game, let's start with traditional DOM-based game development. We will warm up with some basic techniques in this chapter.

In this chapter, we will be:

- Preparing the development tools
- Setting up our first game—Ping Pong
- Learning basic positioning with the jQuery JavaScript library
- Getting keyboard inputs
- Creating the Ping Pong game with scoring

The following screenshot shows the game we will get after this chapter. It is a Ping Pong game played by two players with one keyboard simultaneously:

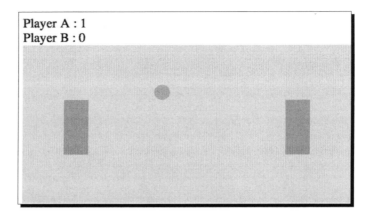

So, let's get on with making our Ping Pong.

Preparing the development environment

The environment for developing HTML5 games is similar to designing websites. We need web browsers with the required plugin and a good text editor. Which text editor is good is a never-ending debate. Each text editor comes with its own strength, so just pick your favorite one. For the browser, we will need a modern browser that supports the latest HTML5, CSS3 spec, and provides us with handy tools for debugging.

There are several modern browser choices on the Internet now. They are Apple Safari (`http://apple.com/safari/`), Google Chrome (`http://www.google.com/chrome/`), Mozilla Firefox (`http://mozilla.com/firefox/`), and Opera (`http://opera.com`). These browsers support most features we discuss in the examples in the whole book. We will use Google Chrome to demonstrate most examples in the book because it runs fast and smooth with CSS3 transition and Canvas.

Preparing the HTML documents for a DOM-based game

Every website, web page, and HTML5 game starts with a default HTML document. Moreover, the document starts with a basic HTML code. We will start our HTML5 game development journey from `index.html`.

Time for action – Installing the jQuery library

We will create our HTML5 Ping Pong game from scratch. It may sound as if we are going to be preparing all the things ourselves. Luckily, at least we can use a JavaScript library to help us. **jQuery** is the **JavaScript library** we will be using in the whole book. It will help us in simplifying our JavaScript logic:

1. Create a new folder named `pingpong`.

2. Create a new folder named `js` inside the `pingpong` directory.

3. Now it's time to download the jQuery library. Go to `http://jquery.com/`.

4. Select **Production** and click on **Download jQuery**.

5. Save `jquery-1.4.4.min.js` in the `js` folder we created in step 2.

6. Create a new document named `index.html` and save it in the first game folder.

7. Open `index.html` in text editor and insert an empty HTML template:

```html
<!DOCTYPE html>
<html lang="en">
<head>
  <meta charset="utf-8">
  <title>Ping Pong</title>
</head>
<body>
  <header>
    <h1>Ping Pong</h1>
  </header>
  <footer>
    This is an example of creating a Ping Pong Game.
  </footer>
</body>
</html>
```

8. Include the jQuery JavaScript file by adding the following line before the closing of the body tag:

```html
<script src="js/jquery-1.4.4.min.js"></script>
```

9. Finally, we have to ensure that jQuery is loaded successfully. We place the following code before the close of the body tag and after the jQuery:

```
<script>
$(function(){
  alert("Welcome to the Ping Pong battle.");
});
</script>
```

10. Save the index.html and open it in the browser. We should see the following alert window showing our text. This means our jQuery is correctly set up:

What just happened?

We just created a basic HTML5 page with jQuery and ensured that the jQuery is loaded correctly.

New HTML5 doctype

The DOCTYPE and meta tags are simplified in HTML5.

In HTML4.01, we declare doctype as the following code:

```
<!DOCTYPE HTML PUBLIC "-//W3C//DTD HTML 4.01//EN" "http://www.w3.org/
TR/html4/strict.dtd">
```

It is a long line of code, right? While in HTML5, the doctype declaration cannot be simpler:

```
<!DOCTYPE html>
```

We even do not have the HTML version in the declaration. This implies that HTML5 will support all existing content of previous HTML versions. Future HTML versions will also support the existing content of HTML5.

The simplification also comes to meta tag. We define the charset of the HTML by using the following short line now:

```
<meta charset=utf-8>
```

Header and footer

HTML5 comes with many new features and improvements, one of them is semantics. HTML5 adds new elements to improve the **semantics**. We just used two, header and footer. Header gives a heading introduction to the section or the entire page. Therefore, we put the h1 title inside header. Footer, same as its name, contains the footer information of the section or the page.

 A semantic HTML means that the markup itself provides meaningful information to the content instead of only defining the visual outlook.

Best practice to place the JavaScript code

We put the JavaScript code right before the closing </body> tag and after all the content in the page. There is a reason for putting the code there instead of putting it inside the <head></head> section.

Normally, browsers load content and render them from top to bottom. If the JavaScript code is put in the head section, then the content of document will not be loaded until all JavaScript code is loaded. Actually, all rendering and loading will be blocked if the browsers load a JavaScript code in the middle of the page. This is the reason why we want to put the JavaScript code at the bottom when possible. In this way, we can deliver the content with higher performance.

At the time of writing this book, the latest jQuery version is 1.4.4. That is why the jQuery file in our code examples is named jquery-1.4.4.min.js. This version number will be different, but the usage should be the same unless there is a big change in jQuery without backward compatibility.

Running our code after the page is ready

We need to ensure that the page is ready before our JavaScript code is executed. Otherwise, we may get an error when we try to access an element that is not yet loaded. jQuery provides us with a way to execute the code after the page is ready. It is the following code:

```
jQuery(document).ready(function(){
  // code here.
});
```

Actually, what we just used is the following codes:

```
$(function(){
  // code here.
});
```

The $ sign is a shortcut for jQuery. When we are calling $ (something), we are actually calling jQuery(something).

$ (function_callback) is another shortcut for the ready event.

It is identical to the following:

```
$ (document).ready(function_callback);
```

Also, identical to:

```
jQuery(document).ready(function_callback);
```

Pop quiz

1. Which is the best place to put JavaScript code?

    a.   Before the `<head>` tag

    b.   Inside the `<head></head>` elements

    c.   Right after the `<body>` tag

    d.   Right before the `</body>` tag

Setting up the Ping Pong game elements

We have the preparation ready and it is time to set up the Ping Pong game.

Time for action – Placing Ping Pong game elements in DOM

1.   We will continue from our jQuery installation example. Open the index.html in a text editor.

2.   Then, create the following playground and game objects with DIV nodes in the body. There are two paddles and one ball inside the playground. Moreover, the playground is inside the game:

```
<div id="game">
  <div id="playground">
    <div id="paddleA" class="paddle"></div>
    <div id="paddleB" class="paddle"></div>
    <div id="ball"></div>
  </div>
</div>
```

3. We now have the game objects' structure ready and it is time to apply styles to them. Put the following styles inside the `head` element:

```css
<style>
  #playground{
    background: #e0ffe0;
    width: 400px;
    height: 200px;
    position: relative;
    overflow: hidden;
  }
  #ball {
    background: #fbb;
    position: absolute;
    width: 20px;
    height: 20px;
    left: 150px;
    top: 100px;
    border-radius: 10px;
  }
  .paddle {
    background: #bbf;
    left: 50px;
    top: 70px;
    position: absolute;
    width: 30px;
    height: 70px;
  }
  #paddleB {
    left: 320px;
  }
</style>
```

4. In the last section, we put our JavaScript logic right after the jQuery inclusion. We will put it in a separate file as our code is getting large. Therefore, create a file named `html5games.pingpong.js` inside the `js` folder.

5. We prepared the JavaScript file. Now it is time to link them to our HTML file. Put the following code in `index.html` before the `</body>` tag:

```
<script src="js/jquery-1.4.4.js"></script>
<script src="js/html5games.pingpong.js"></script>
```

6. We will place the game logic inside the `html5games.pingpong.js`. Our only logic now is the following paddle's initialization code:

```
// code inside $(function(){} will run after the DOM is loaded and
ready
$(function(){
  $("#paddleB").css("top", "20px");
  $("#paddleA").css("top", "60px");

});
```

7. We will test the setup in a browser. Open the `index.html` file in a browser and we should see a screen similar to the one shown in the following screenshot:

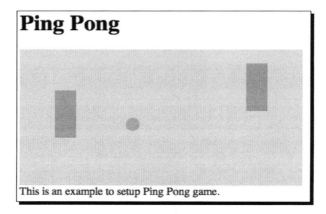

This is an example to setup Ping Pong game.

What just happened?

We have put two paddles and a ball in the Ping Pong game. We also used jQuery to initialize the position of the two paddles.

Introducing jQuery

jQuery is a JavaScript library that is designed for easily navigating the DOM elements, manipulating them, handling events, and creating an asynchronies remote call.

It contains two major parts: **selection** and **modification**. Selection uses CSS selector syntax to select all matched elements in the web page. Modification actions modify the selected elements, such as add, remove children, or style. Using jQuery often means chaining selection and modifications actions together.

For example, the following code selects all elements with box class and sets the CSS properties:

```
$(".box").css({"top":"100px","left":"200px"});
```

Understanding basic jQuery selectors

jQuery is about selecting elements and performing actions on them. We need a method to select our required elements in the entire DOM tree. jQuery borrows the selectors from CSS. The selector provides a set of patterns to match elements. The following table lists the most common and useful selectors that we will use in this book:

Selector pattern	Meaning	Examples
$("Element")	Selects all elements with the given tag name	$("p") selects all the p tags. $("body") selects the body tag.

$("#id")	Selects the element with the given ID of the attribute	Provides the following code:
		
		`<div id="box1"></div>`
		`<div id="box2"></div>`
		
		$("#box1") selects the highlighted element.

$(".className")	Selects all elements with the given class attribute	Provides the following code:
		
		`<div class="apple"></div>`
		`<div class="apple"></div>`
		`<div class="orange"></div>`
		`<div class="banana"></div>`
		
		$(".apple") selects the highlighted elements with class set to apple.

$("selector1, selector2, selectorN")	Selects all elements that match the given selector	Provides the following code:
		
		`<div class="apple"></div>`
		`<div class="apple"></div>`
		`<div class="orange"></div>`
		`<div class="banana"></div>`
		
		$(".apple, .orange") selects the highlighted elements that class is set to, either apple or orange.

Understanding the jQuery CSS function

The jQuery `css` is a function to get and set the CSS properties of the selected elements.

Here is a general definition of how to use the `css` function:

```
.css(propertyName)
.css(propertyName, value)
.css(map)
```

The `css` function accepts several types of arguments as listed in the following table:

Function type	Arguments definitions	Discussion
`.css(propertyName)`	`propertyName` is a CSS property	The function returns the value of the given CSS property of the selected element.
		For example, the following code returns the value of the `background-color` property of the `body` element:
		`$("body").css("background-color")`
		It will only read the value and not modify the property value.
`.css(propertyName, value)`	`propertyName` is a CSS property,	The function modifies the given CSS property to the given value.
	`value` is a value to set for the property	For example, the following code sets the background color to red of all elements with `box` class:
		`$(".box").css("background-color","#ff0000")`
`.css(map)`	`map` is a set of property-value pairs to update	This function is useful for setting multiple CSS properties to the same selected elements at the same time.
		For example, the following code sets both left and top CSS properties to the selected element with ID `box1`:

		`$("#box1").css({`
		`    "left" : "40px",`
		`    "top" : "100px"`
		`})`

Benefits of using jQuery

There are several advantages of using jQuery over pure JavaScript, which are as follows:

◆ Using jQuery requires shorter code to select DOM nodes and modify them

◆ Shorter code results in more clear code for reading, it is important in game development that usually contains a lot of code

◆ Writing shorter code increases the development speed

◆ Using the jQuery library enables the code to support all major browsers without extra tweaks; jQuery wraps the pure JavaScript code and deals with cross browser capability by itself

Manipulating game elements in DOM with jQuery

We initialized the paddles game elements with jQuery. We will do an experiment on how we use jQuery to place the game elements.

Time for action – Changing position of elements with jQuery

Let's inspect our Ping Pong game element with a grid background:

1. We will continue with our Ping Pong example.

2. I have prepared a grid image. Download the `pixel_grid.jpg` image from the following URL:

   `http://gamedesign.cc/html5games/pixel_grid.jpg`

3. Create a folder named `images` in the example directory.

4. Place the `pixel_grid.jpg` into the images folder. This image helps us inspect the pixel displacement later.

5. Next, open the `index.html` file in a text editor.

6. Modify the `background` property of the `playground` DIV to include the pixel grid image like the following:

```
#playground{
   background: #e0ffe0 url(images/pixel_grid.jpg);
   width: 400px;
   height: 200px;
   position: relative;
   overflow: hidden;
}
```

7. Now on opening the `index.html` in web browser we should have the following screenshot. The game elements are overlaid on top of a grid image so we can see where the elements are placed:

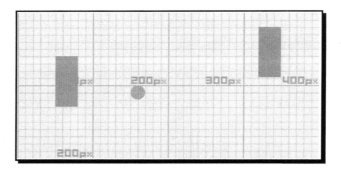

What just happened?

We began the example by placing an image called `pixel_grid.jpg`. This is an image I created for easy debugging purposes. The image is divided into small grids. Every 10 x 10 grid forms a big block with 100 x 100 pixels. By placing this image as background of the DIV, we put a ruler that enables us to measure the position of its children DIVs on the screen.

Understanding the behavior of absolute position

When a DOM node is set to be the `absolute` position, the left and top properties can be treated as a **coordinate**. We can treat the left/top properties into X/Y coordinates with Y positive pointing down. The following graphs show the relationship. The left side is the actual CSS value and the right side is the coordinate system in our mind when programming the game:

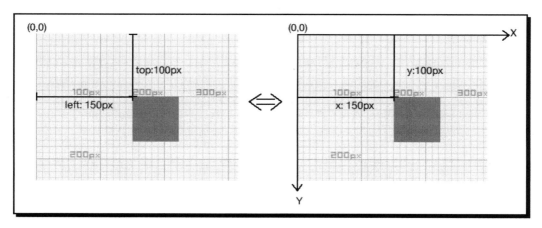

By default, the left and top properties refer to the top left edge of the web page. This reference point is different when any parent of this DOM node has a `position` style set explicitly. The reference point of the left and top properties becomes the top left edge of that parent.

This is why we need to set the playground with relative position and all game elements inside with absolute position. The following code snippet from our example shows their position values:

```
#playground{
  position: relative;
}
#ball {
  position: absolute;
}
.paddle {
  position: absolute;
}
```

Pop quiz

1. Which jQuery selector is to be used if you want to select all header elements?

    a. $("#header")

    b. $(".header")

    c. $("header")

    d. $(header)

Getting a keyboard input from players

This book is about game development. We can think about game development as the following loop:

1. A game state is visually displayed.
2. Players input their commands.
3. The game runs according to the players' input under the designed game mechanics.
4. Loop the process again from step 1.

We learned how to display game objects with CSS and jQuery in previous sections. The next thing we need to create in the game is getting input from the players. We will discuss the keyboard input in this chapter.

Time for action – Moving DOM objects by a keyboard input

We are going to create a traditional ping pong game. There are two paddles on the left and right side. A ball is placed in the middle of the playground. Players can control the left paddle and move it up and down by using *w* and *s* keys, and use *arrow-up* and *down* keys for the right paddle. We will focus on the keyboard input and leave the ball movement for the later section:

1. Let's continue with our `pingpong` directory.

2. Open the `html5games.pingpong.js` file which will contain our game logic. Our only logic now is to listen to the key down event and move the corresponding paddles up or down. Replace the content in the file with the following code:

```
var KEY = {
  UP: 38,
  DOWN: 40,
  W: 87,
  S: 83
}

$(function(){
  // listen to the key down event
  $(document).keydown(function(e){
    switch(e.which){
      case KEY.UP: // arrow-up
        // get the current paddle B's top value in Int type
        var top = parseInt($("#paddleB").css("top"));
        // move the paddle B up 5 pixels
        $("#paddleB").css("top",top-5);
        break;
      case KEY.DOWN: // arrow-down
        var top = parseInt($("#paddleB").css("top"));
        // move the paddle B down 5 pixels
        $("#paddleB").css("top",top+5);
        break;
      case KEY.W: // w
        var top = parseInt($("#paddleA").css("top"));
        // move the paddle A up 5 pixels
$("#paddleA").css("top",top-5);
        break;
      case KEY.S: // s
var top = parseInt($("#paddleA").css("top"));
// move the paddle A drown 5 pixels
$("#paddleA").css("top",top+5);
```

```
        break;
    }
  });
});
```

3. Let's test the paddle control of the game. Open the `index.html` in Google Chrome. Try pressing the *w* key, the *s* key, and *arrow-up* and *down*. The two paddles should be able to move up or down according to the input, but they cannot move at the same time now.

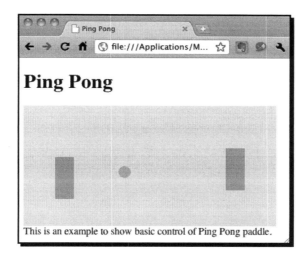

What just happened?

Let's take a look at the HTML code we just used. The HTML page contains header, footer information, and a DIV with ID `game`. The game node contains a child named playground. The playground contains three children, two paddles, and the ball.

We often start the HTML5 game development by preparing a well-structured HTML hierarchy. The HTML hierarchy helps us group similar game objects (which are some DIVs) together. It is a little like grouping assets into a movie clip in Adobe Flash if you have ever made animations with it. We may also consider it as layers of game objects for us to select and style them easily.

Understanding a key code

Every key on the keyboard is assigned a number. By getting that number, we can find out which key is pressed. We listen to the jQuery `keydown` event listener. The event fires with the `event` object containing the **key code**. We can obtain the key code by calling the `which` function to the key down `event` object.

You can try adding a console log function inside the `keydown` event listener and observe the representing integer of each key:

```
$(document).keydown(function(e){
  console.log(e.which);
});
```

Making constants more readable

In our example, we use the key code to check whether the player hits the keys we are interested in. Take the arrow-up key as an example. Its key code is 38. We can simply compare the key code with the number directly, as follows:

```
$(document).keydown(function(e){
    switch(e.which){
    case 38:
      // do something when pressed arrow-up
  }
}
```

However, this is not a recommended practice because it makes the game code more difficult to maintain. Imagine later if we want to map the action from the arrow-up key to another key. We may not be sure whether 38 means the arrow-up. Instead, we can give the constant a meaningful name with the following code:

```
var KEY = {
  UP: 38,
  DOWN: 40,
  W: 87,
  S: 83
}
// listen to the key down event
$(document).keydown(function(e){
switch(e.which){
  case KEY.UP:
    // do something when pressed arrow-up
  }
}
```

By giving 38 a name `KEY.UP`, we can be sure that the block of code is mapped to the arrow-up key and so we can modify it without doubt when maintaining the game.

Converting strings to numbers with parseInt function

In most cases, we apply the left and top CSS styles to DOM elements by using the format such as **100px**. We specify the unit when setting the property. It is the same when we get the value of the property. When we call `$("#paddleA").css("top")`, we get the value of **100px** instead of **100**. This gives us a problem when we want to perform an arithmetic operation on the value.

In the example, we want to move up the paddle by setting the paddle `top` property to its current position minus five pixels. Let us assume paddle A has the `top` property set to 100px now. If we use the following expression to add five pixels, it fails and returns `100px5`:

```
$("#paddleA").css("top") + 5
```

It is because JavaScript executes the `css` function and gets "100px". Then it appends "5" to the "100px" string.

We need a method to convert the "100px" string before doing any mathematical operation.

JavaScript provides us with the `parseInt` function.

Here is a general definition of how to use the `parseInt` function:

```
parseInt(string, radix)
```

The `parseInt` function takes one required argument and one option:

Argument	Definition	Discussion
String	The string to be parsed	The function parses the first number of the string. It will return NaN, Not a Number, if the given string cannot be converted into a number.
		It will parse the string starting with "0x" in hexadecimal by default.
		Take the following code as examples:
		`parseInt("100px")` returns 100.
		`parseInt("5cm")` returns 5.
		`parseInt("0xF")` returns 15.
Radix	Optional. A number to indicate which number system to be used	The second argument forces the `parseInt` function to parse the string in a given number system.
		For example:
		`parseInt("0x10")` returns 16
		`parseInt("0x10",10)` returns 0
		`parseInt("FF",16)` returns 255

Executing JavaScript expressions directly in the Console panel

You should also know that you can execute JavaScript expressions by directly typing it into the console window. The console window is a tool from the Developer Tool in Google Chrome. (There are also other similar tools in other web browsers). We can open the console by clicking on **Wrench Icon | Tools | Developer tools | Console**.

It is a handy way to quickly test a simple expression when you are not sure whether it works during development. The following screenshot tests the return value of the two `parseInt` expressions:

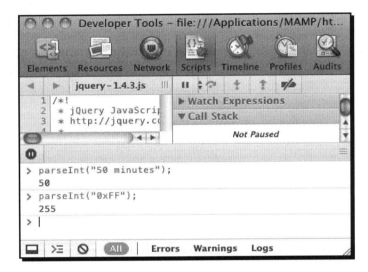

Have a go hero

Converting strings to integers can be tricky sometimes. Do you know what is the `parseInt` result of *10 seconds 20*? How about *10x10* and *$20.5*?

It is time to open the console panel and try converting some strings into numbers.

Checking the console window

We are writing more complicated logic code now. It is good practice to keep an eye on the console of the Developers Tools. If the code contains any error or warning, the error message will appear there. It reports any error found and the line of code that contains the error. It is very useful and important to have the console window open when testing the HTML5 games. I have seen many times that people get stuck and have no idea as to why the code is not working. The reason is that they have a typo or syntax error and they did not check the console window until fighting with the code for hours.

The following screenshot shows that there is an error in line 25 of the `html5games.pingpong.js` file. The error message is **Invalid left-hand side in assignment**. After inspecting the code, I found that I wrongly used an equal sign (=) when setting the CSS `top` property in jQuery:

```
$("#paddleA").css("top"=top+5);

// instead of the correct code:
// $("#paddleA").css("top", top+5);
```

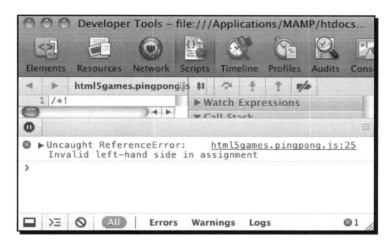

Supporting multiple keyboard input from players

The previous input method only allows one input at a time. The keyboard input is also not so smooth. Imagine now that two players are playing the Ping Pong game together. They cannot control the paddle well because their inputs interrupt the others. In this section, we are going to modify our code to make it support multiple keyboard inputs.

Time for action – Listening to keyboard input with another approach

We will use another approach to handle the key down event. This approach will be a lot smoother and supports multiple inputs at the same time:

1. Open the `html5games.pingpong.js` we used in the last section.

2. Delete all the code we coded there. It is simpler to start from scratch.

3. We will need a global variable of array to store the key pressed status. Enter the following code in the opened JavaScript file:

```
var pingpong = {}
pingpong.pressedKeys = [];
```

4. The next thing is the code is executed once the page is loaded and ready. It will listen and mark the pressed key. Put the following code in the JavaScript file after the two lines we just coded there:

```
$(function(){
  // set interval to call gameloop every 30 milliseconds
  pingpong.timer = setInterval(gameloop,30);

  // mark down what key is down and up into an array called
"pressedKeys"
  $(document).keydown(function(e){
    pingpong.pressedKeys[e.which] = true;
    });
    $(document).keyup(function(e){
      pingpong.pressedKeys[e.which] = false;
  });
});
```

5. We have stored the key which is pressed. What we are missing is actually moving the paddles. We set a timer to continuously call a function to move the paddles. Paste the following code in the `html5games.pingpong.js` file:

```
function gameloop() {
  movePaddles();
}

function movePaddles() {
  // use our custom timer to continuously check if a key is
pressed.
  if (pingpong.pressedKeys[KEY.UP]) { // arrow-up
    // move the paddle B up 5 pixels
    var top = parseInt($("#paddleB").css("top"));
    $("#paddleB").css("top",top-5);
  }
  if (pingpong.pressedKeys[KEY.DOWN]) { // arrow-down
    // move the paddle B down 5 pixels
    var top = parseInt($("#paddleB").css("top"));
    $("#paddleB").css("top",top+5);
  }
```

```
    if (pingpong.pressedKeys[KEY.W]) { // w
      // move the paddle A up 5 pixels
      var top = parseInt($("#paddleA").css("top"));
      $("#paddleA").css("top",top-5);
    }
    if (pingpong.pressedKeys[KEY.S]) { // s
      // move the paddle A down 5 pixels
      var top = parseInt($("#paddleA").css("top"));
      $("#paddleA").css("top",top+5);
    }
  }
```

6. Let's test what we just coded. Save all the files and open `index.html` in the web browser.

7. Try pressing the keys to control both paddles. The two paddles should move smoothly and respond at the same time without interruption.

What just happened?

We have used another approach to capture the keyboard input. Instead of doing the action once after the key press is detected, we store which keys are pressed and which are not. Afterwards, we use a JavaScript interval to check the pressed keys every 30 milliseconds. This approach enables us to know all the keys pressed at the time and so we can move both paddles at the same time.

Declaring global variables in a better way

Global variables are variables that can be accessed globally in the entire document. Any variable that is declared outside any function is a global variable. For instance, in the following example code snippets, a and b are global variables while c is a **local variable** that only exists inside the function:

```
var a = 0;
var b = "xyz";
function something(){
  var c = 1;
}
```

Since global variables are available in the entire document, it may increase the change of variable name conflicts if we integrate different JavaScript libraries into the web page. As good practice, we should put all global variables we use into an object.

In the *Time for action* section, we have a global array to store all pressed keys. Instead of just putting this array in global scope, we created a global object named `pingpong` and put the array inside it:

```
var pingpong = {}
pingpong.pressedKeys = [];
```

In the future, we may need more global variables and we will put them all inside the `pingpong` object. This reduces the chance of name conflict to only one name, `pingpong`.

Creating a JavaScript timer with setInterval function

The pressed keys are stored in the array and we have a timer to loop and check the array periodically. This can be done by the `setInterval` function in JavaScript.

Here is the general definition of the `setInterval` function:

```
setInterval(expression, milliseconds)
```

The `setInterval` takes two required arguments:

Argument	Definition	Discussion
expression	The function call back or code expression to be executed	The expression can be a reference of function call back or an inline code expression. The inline code expression is quoted and reference of function call back is not.
		For example, the following code calls the `hello` function 100 milliseconds:
		``` setInterval(hello,100); ```
		The following code calls the `hi` function with parameters every 100 milliseconds:
		``` setInterval("hi('Makzan')",100); ```
milliseconds	The duration between every execution of the expression, in milliseconds	The unit of the interval is in milliseconds. Therefore, setting it to 1000 means running the expression every second.

Understanding Game Loop

We have a timer to execute some game-related code every 30 milliseconds, so this code is executed 33.3 times per second. In game development, this is called **Game Loop**.

There are several common things we will execute inside a game loop:

◆ Processing user input, which we just did

◆ Updating game objects' status, including position and appearance

◆ Checking game over

What is actually executing in the game loop differs in different types of games but the purpose is the same. The game loop is executed periodically to help run the game smoothly.

Moving a DOM object with JavaScript Interval

Imagine now we can make the little red ball move around in the playground. The ball will bounce away when it hits the paddles. The player will lose a score when the ball passes the paddle and hits the playground edge behind the paddle. All these actions are manipulating the position of the DIVs inside the HTML page by jQuery. To complete this Ping Pong game, our next step is to move the ball.

Time for action – Moving the ball with JavaScript Interval

We just learnt and used the `setInterval` function to create a timer. We will use the timer to move the ball a little bit every 30 milliseconds. We are going to also change the direction of the ball movement once it hits the playground edge. Let's make the ball move now:

1. We will use our last example, listening to multiple keyboard inputs, as the starting point.

2. Open the `html5games.pingpong.js` file in the text editor.

3. We are now moving the ball and we need to store the ball status globally. We will put the ball-related variable inside the `pingpong` object:

```
pingpong.ball = {
  speed: 5,
  x: 150,
  y: 100,
  directionX: 1,
  directionY: 1
}
```

4. In every game loop, we used to move the paddles. Now we will move the ball as well. Add a moveBall function call to the gameloop function:

```
function gameloop() {
  moveBall();
  movePaddles();
}
```

5. It is time to define the moveBall function. The function is divided into four parts, it gets the current ball position, checks the boundaries of the playground, changes the direction of the ball when hitting the boundaries and actually moves the ball after all these calculations. Let's put the following moveBall function definition in the JavaScript file:

```
function moveBall() {
  // reference useful variables
  var playgroundHeight = parseInt($("#playground").height());
  var playgroundWidth = parseInt($("#playground").width());
  var ball = pingpong.ball;

  // check playground boundary
  // check bottom edge
   if (ball.y + ball.speed*ball.directionY > playgroundHeight)
  {
    ball.directionY = -1;
  }
  // check top edge
  if (ball.y + ball.speed*ball.directionY < 0)
  {
    ball.directionY = 1;
  }
  // check right edge
  if (ball.x + ball.speed*ball.directionX > playgroundWidth)
  {
    ball.directionX = -1;
  }
  // check left edge
  if (ball.x + ball.speed*ball.directionX < 0)
  {
    ball.directionX = 1;
  }
  ball.x += ball.speed * ball.directionX;
  ball.y += ball.speed * ball.directionY;

  // check moving paddle here, later.
```

```
// actually move the ball with speed and direction
$("#ball").css({
  "left" : ball.x,
  "top" : ball.y
});
}
```

6. We have prepared the code to move the ball every 30 milliseconds. Save all files and open `index.html` in Google Chrome to test it.

7. The paddles work just as in the last example and the ball should be moving around the playground.

What just happened?

We just successfully made the ball move around the playground. We have a loop to run routine game logic every 30 milliseconds. Inside that game loop, we move the ball five pixels at a time.

There are three properties of the ball, speed, and direction X/Y. The speed defines how many pixels the ball moves in each step. The direction X/Y is either 1 or -1. We move the ball with the following equation:

```
new_ball_x = ball_x_position + speed * direction_x
new_ball_y = ball_y_position + speed * direction_y
```

The direction value is multiplied by the movement. When the direction is 1, the ball moves to the positive direction of the axis. When the direction is -1, the ball moves to the negative direction. By toggling the X and Y directions, we can move the ball in four directions.

We compare the ball's X and Y with the four edges of the playground DIV element. This checks whether the ball's next position is beyond the boundary and then we toggle the direction between 1 and -1 to create the bouncing effect.

Beginning collision detection

We have checked the boundary of the playground when moving the ball in the previous section. Now we can control the paddles with the keyboard and watch the ball moving around the playground. What is missing now? We cannot interact with the ball. We control the paddles but the ball just passes through them as if they are not there. It is because we missed the collision detection between the paddles and the moving ball.

Time for action – Hitting the ball with the paddles

We will use a similar approach of checking the boundary to check the collision:

1. Open the `html5games.pingpong.js` file we used in the previous section.

2. In the `moveball` function, we have already reserved the place to put the collision detection code there. Find the line with `// check moving paddle here`.

3. Let's put the following code there. The code checks whether the ball is overlapping with either paddle and bounces the ball away when they overlap:

```
// check left paddle
var paddleAX = parseInt($("#paddleA").css("left"))+parseInt($("#paddleA").css("width"));
var paddleAYBottom = parseInt($("#paddleA").css("top"))+parseInt($("#paddleA").css("height"));
var paddleAYTop = parseInt($("#paddleA").css("top"));
if (ball.x + ball.speed*ball.directionX < paddleAX)
{
  if (ball.y + ball.speed*ball.directionY <= paddleAYBottom &&
    ball.y + ball.speed*ball.directionY >= paddleAYTop)
  {
    ball.directionX = 1;
  }
}

// check right paddle
var paddleBX = parseInt($("#paddleB").css("left"));
var paddleBYBottom = parseInt($("#paddleB").css("top"))+parseInt($("#paddleB").css("height"));
var paddleBYTop = parseInt($("#paddleB").css("top"));
if (ball.x + ball.speed*ball.directionX >= paddleBX)
{
  if (ball.y + ball.speed*ball.directionY <= paddleBYBottom &&
    ball.y + ball.speed*ball.directionY >= paddleBYTop)
  {
    ball.directionX = -1;
  }
}
```

4. We will also need to reset the ball in the middle area after the ball hits the left or right edge of the playground. Remove the bouncing ball code in the `check right` and `check left` code section and paste the following code there:

```
// check right edge
```

```
if (ball.x +ball.speed*ball.directionX > playgroundWidth)
{
  // player B lost.
  // reset the ball;
  ball.x = 250;
  ball.y = 100;
  $("#ball").css({
    "left": ball.x,
    "top" : ball.y
  });
  ball.directionX = -1;
}
// check left edge
if (ball.x  + ball.speed*ball.directionX < 0)
{
  // player A lost.
  // reset the ball;
  ball.x = 150;
  ball.y = 100;
  $("#ball").css({
    "left": ball.x,
    "top" : ball.y
  });
  ball.directionX = 1;
}
```

5. Test the game in a browser and the ball will now bounce away after hitting the left or right paddle. It will also reset to the center of the playground when hitting the left or right edge.

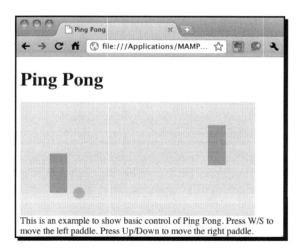

What just happened?

We have modified the ball checking to make it bounce away when overlapping with the paddles. Moreover, we reposition the ball in the center of the playground when hitting the left and right edge.

Let's see how we check the collision between the ball and the left paddle.

At first, we check whether the ball's X position is less than the left paddle's right edge. The right edge is the `left` value plus the `width` of the paddle.

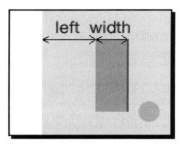

Then we check whether the ball's Y position is between the top edge and bottom edge of the paddle. The top edge is the `top` value and the bottom edge is the `top` value plus the `height` of the paddle.

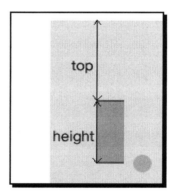

We bounce the ball away if the ball's position passes both checks. This is how we check it and it is just a basic collision detection.

We determine that the two objects are overlapped by checking their position and width/ height. This type of collision detection works well in rectangle objects but is not good for circles and other shapes. The following screenshot illustrates the issue. The collision areas shown in the following graph are false positive. Their bounding box collides but the actual shapes do not overlap each other.

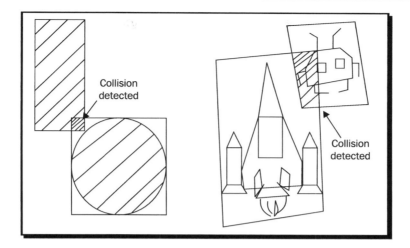

For special shapes, we will need more advanced collision detection techniques that we will discuss later.

Have a go hero

We check three edges of the paddles to determine whether the ball overlaps with them. If you play the game and observe the ball bouncing carefully, you will find that it is not perfect now. The ball may bounce while behind the paddles. Think about the reason and modify the code to make a better collision detection with the ball and the paddles.

Showing text dynamically in HTML

We have the basic game mechanics implemented in the previous sections. Our Ping Pong game is missing a scoring board now showing both players' scores. We discussed how to use jQuery to modify the CSS styles of the selected elements. Can we also alter the content of the selected elements with jQuery? Yes, we can.

Time for action – Showing the score of both players

We are going to create a text-based scoreboard and update the scores when either player scores a goal:

1. We are making improvements on our existing game so we use the last example as the starting point.

2. Open the index.html in the text editor. We are going to add the scoreboard DOM elements.

3. Add the following HTML code before the `game` DIV inside `index.html`:

```
<div id="scoreboard">
  <div class="score">Player A : <span id="scoreA">0</span></div>
  <div class="score">Player B : <span id="scoreB">0</span></div>
</div>
```

4. Let's move onto the JavaScript part. Open the `html5games.pingpong.js` file.

5. We need two more global variables to store the players' scores. Add their score variables inside the `pingpong` global object:

```
var pingpong = {
  scoreA : 0,   // score for player A
  scoreB : 0    // score for player B
}
```

6. We had a place to check if player B lost. We incremented the player A's score there and updated the scoreboard with the following code:

```
// player B lost.
pingpong.scoreA++;
$("#scoreA").html(pingpong.scoreA);
```

7. We have similar code as in step 6 to update player B's score when player A lost:

```
// player A lost.
pingpong.scoreB++;
$("#scoreB").html(pingpong.scoreB);
```

8. It is time to test our latest code. Open the `index.html` in a web browser. Try playing by controlling both paddles and lose some points. The scoreboard should be counting the scores correctly:

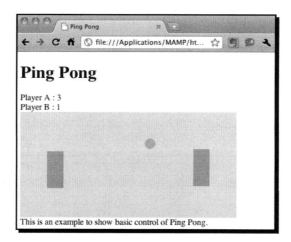

What just happened?

We just used another common jQuery function: `html()` to alter the content of the game on the fly.

The `html()` function gets or updates the HTML content of the selected element. Here is a general definition of the `html()` function:

```
.html()
.html(htmlString)
```

When we use the html ( ) function without an argument, it returns the HTML content of the first match element. When we use it with an argument, it sets the HTML content to all matched elements with the given HTML string.

For example, provide the following HTML structure:

```
<p>My name is <span id="myname" class="name">Makzan</span>.</p>
<p>My pet's name is <span id="pet" class="name">
```

Both the following jQuery calls return Makzan:

```
$("#myname").html(); // returns Makzan
$(".name").html();   // returns Makzan
```

However, in the following jQuery call, it sets all matched elements to the given HTML content:

```
$(".name").html("<small>Mr. Mystery</small>")
```

Executing the jQuery command makes the following HTML result:

```
<p>My name is <span id="myname" class="name"><small>Mr. Mystery</
small></span></p>
<p>My pet's name is <span id="pet" class="name"><small>Mr. Mystery</
small></span></p>
```

Have a go hero – Winning the game

We have the scoring now. See whether you can modify the game to make it stop after any player gets 10 points. Then show a win message.

You might also want to try styling the game to make it more appealing. How about giving the scoreboard and playground some image backgrounds? Replacing the paddles with two goalkeeper characters?

Summary

We learned a lot in this chapter about basic techniques of creating a simple Ping Pong game with HTML5 and JavaScript.

Specifically, we covered:

◆ Creating our first HTML5 game—Ping Pong

◆ Using jQuery to manipulate DOM objects

◆ Getting keyboard inputs with multiple keys down support

◆ Detecting collisions with the bounding box

We also discussed how to create a game loop and move the ball and paddles.

Now that we've warmed up by creating a simple DOM-based game, we are ready to create more advanced DOM-based games with new features from CSS3. In the next chapter, we will create games with CSS3 animation, transition, and transformation.

3

Building a Memory Matching Game in CSS3

CSS3 introduces many exciting features. In this chapter, we will explore and use some of them to create a matching memory game. The CSS3 styles how the game objects look and animate while the jQuery library helps us define the game logic.

In this chapter, we will:

◆ Transform a playing card with animation

◆ Flip a playing card with new CSS3 properties

◆ Create the whole memory matching game

◆ And embed a custom web font to our game

So let's get on with it.

Moving game objects with CSS3 transition

We had a glimpse of the CSS3 transition module and transformation module in *Chapter 1, Introducing HTML5 Games,* when we were overviewing the new CSS3 features. We often want to animate the game objects by easing the properties. Transition is the CSS property designed for this purpose. Imagine we have a playing card on the web page and want to move it to another position in five seconds. We had to use JavaScript and setup timer and write our own function to change the position every several milliseconds. By using the `transition` property, we just need to specify the start and end styles and the duration. The browser does all the easing and in-between animations, magically.

Let's take a look at some examples to understand it.

Time for action – Moving a playing card around

In this example, we will place two playing cards on the web page and transform them to a different position, scale, and rotation. We will tween the transformation by setting the transition:

1. Create a new folder with three files in the following hierarchy. The css3transition. css and index.html is empty now and we will add the code later. The jquery-1.6.min.js is the jQuery library that we have used in the previous chapter.

2. We are using two playing card graphic images in this example. The images are available in the code bundle or you can download them from http:// gamedesign.cc/html5games/css3-basic-transition/images/AK.png and http://gamedesign.cc/html5games/css3-basic-transition/ images/AQ.png.

3. Create a new folder named images and place the two card images inside.

4. The next thing is to code the HTML with two card DIV elements. We will apply CSS transition style to these two cards elements when the page is loaded:

```
<!DOCTYPE html>
<html lang="en">
<head>
  <meta charset="utf-8">
  <title>Getting Familiar with CSS3 Transition</title>
  <link rel="stylesheet" href="css/css3transition.css" />
</head>
<body>
  <header>
```

```
      <h1>Getting Familiar with CSS3 Transition</h1>
    </header>

    <section id="game">
      <div id="cards">
        <div id="card1" class="card cardAK"></div>
        <div id="card2" class="card cardAQ"></div>
      </div> <!-- #cards -->
    </section> <!-- #game -->
    <footer>
      <p>This is an example of transitioning cards.</p>
    </footer>
<script src="js/jquery-1.6.min.js"></script>
<script>
$(function(){
  $("#card1").addClass("moveAndScale");
  $("#card2").addClass("rotateRight");
});
</script>
</body>
</html>
```

5. It is time to define the visual styles of the playing cards via CSS. It contains basic CSS 2.1 properties and CSS3 new properties. The new CSS3 properties are highlighted:

```
body {
  background: #aaa;
}
/* defines styles for each card */
.card {
  width: 80px;
  height: 120px;
  margin: 20px;
  background: #efefef;
  position: absolute;
  -webkit-transition: all 1s linear;
}
/* set the card to corresponding playing card graphics */
.cardAK {
  background: url(../images/AK.png);
}
.cardAQ {
  background: url(../images/AQ.png);
}
```

```
/* rotate the applied DOM element 90 degree */
.rotateRight {
    -webkit-transform: rotate3d(0,0,1,90deg);
}
/* move and scale up the applied DOM element */
.moveAndScale {
    -webkit-transform: translate3d(150px,150px,0) scale3d(1.5, 1.5,
1);
}
```

6. Let's save all the files and open the `index.html` in the browser. The two cards should animate as shown in the following screenshot:

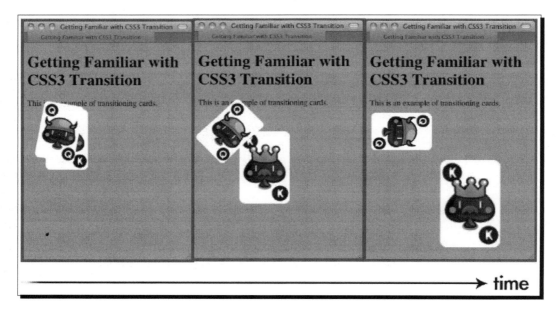

What just happened?

We just created two animation effects by using the CSS3 transition to tween the `transform` property.

> Please note that the new CSS3 transition and transform properties are not yet finalized. Web browsers support these drafted but stable properties with a vendor prefix. In our example to support Chrome and Safari, we used the `-webkit-` prefix. We can use other prefixes in the code to support other browsers, such as `-moz-` for Mozilla and `-o-` for Opera.

Here is the usage of CSS transform:

```
transform: transform-function1  transform-function2;
```

The arguments of the `transform` property are functions. There are two sets of functions, 2D `transform` function and 3D. **CSS transform** functions are designed to move, scale, rotate, and skew the target DOM elements. The following shows the usage of the transforms functions.

2D transforms functions

The 2D `rotate` function rotates the element clockwise on a given positive argument and counter-clockwise on the given negative argument:

```
rotate(angle)
```

The translate function moves the element by the given X and Y displacement:

```
translate (tx, ty)
```

We can translate the X or Y-axis independently by calling the `translateX` and `translateY` function as follows:

```
translateX(number)
translateY(number)
```

The `scale` function scales the element by the given `sx`, `sy` vector. If we only pass the first argument, then `sy` will be of the same value as `sx`:

```
scale(sx, sy)
```

In addition, we can independently scale the X and Y-axis as follows:

```
scaleX(number)
scaleY(number)
```

3D transforms functions

The 3D rotation function rotates the element in 3D space by the given [x, y, z] unit vector. For example, we can rotate the Y-axis 60 degrees by using `rotate3d(0, 1, 0, 60deg)`:

```
rotate3d(x, y, z, angle)
```

We can also rotate one axis only by calling the following handy functions:

```
rotateX(angle)
rotateY(angle)
rotateZ(angle)
```

Similar to the 2D `translate` function, `translate3d` allows us to move the element in all three axes:

```
translate3d(tx, ty, tz)
translateX(tx)
translateY(ty)
translateZ(tz)
```

Also, the `scale3d` scales the element in the 3D spaces:

```
scale3d(sx, sy, sz)
scaleX(sx)
scaleY(sy)
scaleZ(sz)
```

The `transform` functions we just discussed are those that are common and we will use them many times. There are several other `transform` functions not discussed. They are `matrix`, `skew`, and `perspective`.

If you want to find the latest CSS transforms working spec, you can visit the W3C website with the following addresses. CSS 2D Transforms Modules (`http://dev.w3.org/csswg/css3-3d-transforms/`) and the 3D Transforms Modules (`http://www.w3.org/TR/css3-2d-transforms/`).

Tweening the styles by using CSS3 transition

There are tons of new features in CSS3. Transition module is one among them that affects us most in game designing.

What is **CSS3 transition**? W3C explains it in one sentence.:

> *CSS transitions allows property changes in CSS values to occur smoothly over a specified duration.*

Normally, when we change any properties of the element, the properties are updated to the new value immediately. Transition slows down the changing process. It creates smooth in-between easing from the old value towards the new value in the given duration.

Here is the usage of the `transition` property:

```
transition: property_name duration timing_function delay.
```

Argument	Definition
property_name	The name of the property where the transition applies. It can be set to all.
Duration	The duration the transition takes.
Timing_function	The timing function defines the interpolation between the start and end value. The default value is ease. Normally we will use ease, ease-in, ease-out, and linear.
Delay	The delay argument delays the start of the transition by the given seconds.

We can put several transition properties in one line. For example, the following code transits the opacity in 0.3 seconds and background color in 0.5 seconds:

```
transition: opacity 0.3s, background-color 0.5s
```

We can also define each transition property individually by using the following properties:

transition-property, transition-duration, transition-timing-function and transition-delay.

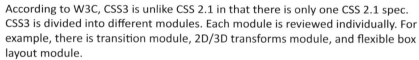

Modules of CSS3

According to W3C, CSS3 is unlike CSS 2.1 in that there is only one CSS 2.1 spec. CSS3 is divided into different modules. Each module is reviewed individually. For example, there is transition module, 2D/3D transforms module, and flexible box layout module.

The reason of dividing the spec into modules is because the working progress pace of each part of the CSS3 is not the same. Some CSS3 features are rather stable, such as border radius, while some have not yet settled down. By dividing the whole spec into different parts, it allows the browser vendor to support modules that are stable. In this scenario, slow pace features will not slow down the whole spec. The aim of the CSS3 spec is to standardize the most common visual usage in web designing and this module fits this aim.

Have a go hero

We have translated, scaled, and rotated the playing cards. How about we try changing different values in the example? There are three axes in the rotate3d function. What will happen if we rotate the other axis? Experiment with the code yourselves to get familiar with the transform and transition modules.

Creating a card-flipping effect

Imagine now we are not just moving the playing card around, but we also want to flip the card element, just like we flip a real playing card. By using the `rotation transform` function, it is now possible to create the card-flipping effect.

Time for action – Flipping a card with CSS3

We are going to start a new project and create a card-flipping effect when we click on the playing card.:

1. Let's continue on our previous code example.

2. The card now contains two faces, a front face and a back face. Replace the following code into the `body` tag in the HTML:

```
<section id="game">
  <div id="cards">
    <div class="card">
      <div class="face front"></div>
      <div class="face back cardAK"></div>
    </div> <!-- .card -->
    <div class="card">
      <div class="face front"></div>
      <div class="face back cardAQ"></div>
    </div> <!-- .card -->
  </div> <!-- #cards -->
</section> <!-- #game -->
<script src="js/jquery-1.6.min.js"></script>
```

3. Then change the CSS external link to the `css3flip.css` file:

```
<link rel="stylesheet" href="css/css3flip.css" />
```

4. Now let's add the styles to the `css3flip.css`:

```
#game {
  background: #9c9;
  padding: 5px;
}
/* Define the 3D perspective view and dimension of each card. */
.card {
  -webkit-perspective: 600;
  width: 80px;
  height: 120px;
}
```

5. There are two faces on each card. We are going to rotate the face late. Therefore, we define how the face transits by CSS3 `transition` property. We also hide the back face visibility. We will look at the detail of this property later:

```
.face {
  border-radius: 10px;
  width: 100%;
  height: 100%;
  position: absolute;
  -webkit-transition: all .3s;
  -webkit-backface-visibility: hidden;
}
```

6. Now it is time to style each individual face. The front face has a higher z-index than the back face:

```
.front {
  background: #966;
  z-index: 10;
}
.back {
  background: #eaa;
  -webkit-transform: rotate3d(0,1,0,-180deg);
  z-index: 8;
}
```

7. When we flip the card, we rotate the front face to back and back face to front. We also swap the z-index of the front and back face:

```
.card-flipped .front {
  -webkit-transform: rotate3d(0,1,0,180deg);
  z-index: 8;
}
.card-flipped .back {
  -webkit-transform: rotate3d(0,1,0,0deg);
  z-index: 10;
}
.cardAK {
  background: url(../images/AK.png);
}
.cardAQ {
  background: url(../images/AQ.png);
}
```

8. Next, we will add logic after loading the jQuery library to toggle the card-flipped status when clicking on the card:

```
<script>
$(function(){
  $("#cards").children().each(function(index) {
    // listen the click event on each card DIV element.
    $(this).click(function() {
      // add the class "card-flipped".
      // the browser will animate the styles between current state
        and card-flipped state.
      $(this).toggleClass("card-flipped");
    });
  });
});
</script>
```

9. The styles and the scripts are now ready. Let's save all the files and preview it in our web browser. Click the playing card to flip it over and click again to flip back.

What just happened?

We have created a card-flipping effect toggled by a mouse click. The example made use of several CSS transforms properties and JavaScript for handling the mouse click event.

Toggling class with jQuery toggleClass function

We apply the class `card-flipped` to the card element when the mouse is clicked on the card. On the second click, we want to remove the applied card-flipped style so the card flips back again. This is called **toggling a class** style.

jQuery provides us with a handy function named `toggleClass` to add or remove classes automatically, depending on whether the class is applied or not.

To use the function, we simply pass the classes that we want to toggle as an argument.

For example, the following code adds or removes the `card-flipped` class to an element with ID `card1`:

```
$("#card1").toggleClass("card-flipped");
```

The `toggleClass` function accepts toggle from more than one class at the sample time. We can pass in several class names and separate them by using space. Here is an example of toggling two classes at the same time:

```
$("#card1").toggleClass("card-flipped scale-up");
```

Controlling the visibility of overlapped elements by z-index

Normally, all elements in a web page are distributed and presented without overlapping. Designing a game is a different story. We always need to deal with overlapped elements and hide them (or part of them) on purpose. `z-index`, a CSS 2.1 property, helps us to control the visibility behaviors when more than one element is overlapped.

In this example, we have two faces for each card, the front and the back face. The two faces are placed in the exact position. They overlap each other. The **Z-index** property defines which element is on top and which is behind. The elements with a higher z-index go in front of elements with a lower z-index. When they overlap, the one with the higher z-index will cover the one with the lower z-index. The following screenshot demonstrates the z-index behavior:

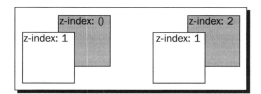

In the card-flipping example, we swapped the z-index of both faces to ensure the corresponding face is on top of the other in both the normal state and the flipped state. The following code shows the swapping.

When in a normal state, the front face has a higher z-index:

```
.front {
  z-index: 10;
}
.back {
  z-index: 8;
}
```

While in a flipped state, the front face changes to a lower z-index than the back face. The back face now covers the front face:

```css
.card-flipped .front {
  z-index: 8;
}
.card-flipped .back {
  z-index: 10;
}
```

Introducing CSS perspective property

CSS3 lets us present elements in 3D. We have been able to transform the elements in 3D space. The `perspective` property defines how the 3D perspective view looks. You can treat the value as far as you are looking at the object. The closer you are, the more perspective distortion there is on the viewing object.

 While writing this book, only Safari supported the 3D perspective feature. Chrome supports 3D transform while not supporting the `perspective` property. Therefore, we will have the best effect in Safari and an acceptable effect in Chrome.

The following two 3D cubes demonstrate how different perspective values change the perspective view of the element:

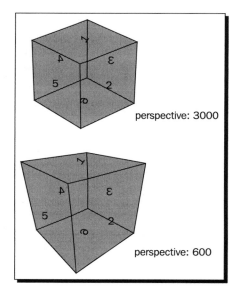

perspective: 3000

perspective: 600

You can view this experiment by going to the following address in Safari:

`http://gamedesign.cc/html5games/perspective-cube/`

Have a go hero

The cube is created by putting six faces together with 3D transforms applied to each face. It used the techniques we've discussed. Try to create a cube and experiment with the `perspective` property.

The following web page gives a comprehensive explanation on creating the CSS3 cube, and also discusses controlling the rotation of the cube through the keyboard:

`http://www.paulrhayes.com/2009-07/animated-css3-cube-interface-using-3d-transforms/`

Introducing backface-visibility

Before the backface-visibility is introduced, all elements on the page present their front face to the visitor. Actually, there was no concept of the front face or back face of the element because it was the only choice. While CSS3 introduces the rotation in three axes, we can rotate an element so that its face is on the back. Try looking at your palm and rotating your wrist, your palm turns and you see the back of your palm. This happens to the rotated elements too.

CSS3 introduces a property named `backface-visibility` to define whether we can see the back face of the element or not. By default, it is visible. The following screenshots demonstrate the two different behaviors of the `backface-visibility` property.

 At the time of writing this book, only Apple Safari supported the `backface-visibility` property.

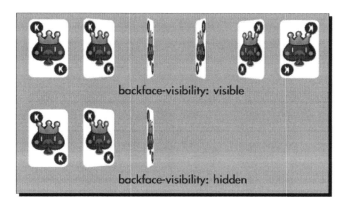

backface-visibility: visible

backface-visibility: hidden

[You can read more detailed information about different properties and functions in CSS 3D transforms on the official Webkit blog: `http://webkit.org/blog/386/3d-transforms/`.]

Creating a card matching memory game

We have gong through some CSS basic techniques. Let's make a game with the techniques. We are going to make a card game. The card game makes use of transform to flip the card, transition to move the card, JavaScript to hold the logic, and a new HTML5 feature called custom data attribute. Don't worry, we will discuss each component step by step.

Downloading the sprites sheet of playing cards

In the card-flipping example, we were using two different playing card graphics. Now we prepare the whole deck of playing card graphics. Although we only use six playing cards in the matching game, we prepare the whole deck so we can reuse these graphics in other playing card games that we may create.

There are 52 playing cards in a deck and we have one more graphic for the backside. Instead of using 53 separated files, it is good practice to put separated graphics into one big sprite sheet file. The term sprite sheet was from an old computer graphics technique that loaded one graphics texture into memory and displayed part of the graphics.

One benefit of using a big sprite sheet instead of separated image files is that we can reduce the amount of **HTTP requests**. When the browser loads the web page, it creates a new HTTP request to load each external resource, including JavaScript files, CSS files, and images. It takes quite a lot of time to establish a new HTTP request for each separated small file. Combining the graphics into one file, largely reduces the amount of requests and thus improves the responsiveness of the game when loading in the browser.

Another benefit for placing graphics into one file is to avoid the overhead of the file format header. The size of a 53 images sprite sheet is less than the sum of 53 different images with the file header in each file.

The following deck of playing cards graphics is drawn and aligned in Adobe Illustrator. You can download it from `http://gamedesign.cc/html5games/css3-matching-game/images/deck.png`.

The following article explains in detail why and how we can create and use the CSS sprite sheet:

`http://css-tricks.com/css-sprites/`

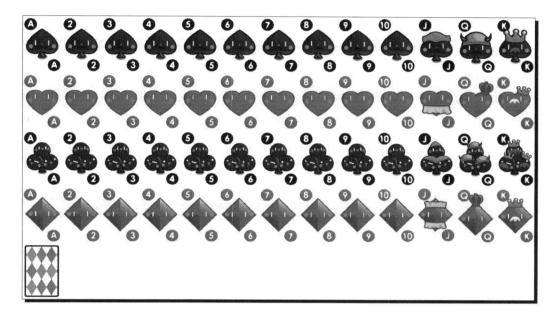

Setting up the game environment

The graphics are ready, we will then need to set up a static page with the game objects prepared and placed on the game area. It is easier for adding game logic and interaction later:

Time for action – Preparing the card matching game

Before adding the complicated game logic to our matching game, let's prepare the HTML game structure and prepare all the CSS styles:

1. Let's continue on our code. Replace the `index.html` file with the following HTML:

```
<!DOCTYPE html>
<html lang=en>
<head>
  <meta charset=utf-8>
  <title>CSS3 Matching Game</title>
  <link rel="stylesheet" href="css/matchgame.css" />
</head>
<body>
```

```
<header>
  <h1>CSS3 Matching Game</h1>
</header>
<section id="game">
  <div id="cards">
    <div class="card">
      <div class="face front"></div>
      <div class="face back"></div>
    </div> <!-- .card -->
  </div> <!-- #cards -->
</section> <!-- #game -->
<footer>
  <p>This is an example of creating a matching game with CSS3.</
p>
</footer>
<script src="js/jquery-1.6.min.js"></script>
<script src="js/html5games.matchgame.js"></script>
</body>
</html>
```

2. In order to make the game more appealing, I prepared background images for the game table and the page. These graphic assets can be found in the code example bundle. The background images are optional and they will not affect the gameplay and the logic of the matching game.

3. We will also place the deck sprite sheet graphics into the images folder. Download the deck.png file from http://gamedesign.cc/html5games/css3-matching-game/images/deck.png and save it into the images folder.

4. Let's add style to the matching game before writing any logic. Open matchgame.css and add the following body styles:

```
body {
  text-align: center;
  background: #a46740 url(../images/bg.jpg);
}
```

5. Continue to add the styles to the game element. It will be the main area of the game:

```
#game {
  border-radius: 10px;
  border: 1px solid #666;
  background: #232 url(../images/table.jpg);
  width: 500px;
```

```
  height: 460px;
  margin: 0 auto;
  display: box;
  box-pack: center;
  box-align: center;
}
```

6. We will put all card elements into a parent DOM named `cards`. By doing this, we can easily center all cards to the game area:

```
#cards {
  position: relative;
  width: 380px;
  height: 400px;
}
```

7. For each card, we define a `perspective` property to give it a visual depth effect:

```
.card {
  -webkit-perspective: 600;
  width: 80px;
  height: 120px;
  position: absolute;
  -moz-transition: all .3s;
  -webkit-transition: all .3s;
  transition: all .3s;
}
```

8. There are two faces on each card. The face will be rotated later and we will define the transition properties to animate the style changes. We also want to make sure the back face is hidden:

```
.face {
  border-radius: 10px;
  width: 100%;
  height: 100%;
  position: absolute;
  -webkit-transition-property: opacity, transform, box-shadow;
  -webkit-transition-duration: .3s;

  -webkit-backface-visibility: hidden;
}
```

9. Then we set the front and back face styles. They are almost the same as the flipping card example, except that we are now giving them background images and box shadows:

```
.front {
  background: #999 url(../images/deck.png) 0 -480px;
  z-index: 10;
}
.back {
  background: #efefef url(../images/deck.png);
  -webkit-transform: rotate3d(0,1,0,-180deg);
  z-index: 8;
}
.card:hover .face, .card-flipped .face {
  -webkit-box-shadow: 0 0 10px #aaa;
}
.card-flipped .front {
  -webkit-transform: rotate3d(0,1,0,180deg);
  z-index: 8;
}
.card-flipped .back {
  -webkit-transform: rotate3d(0,1,0,0deg);
  z-index: 10;
}
```

10. When any card is removed, we want to fade it out. Therefore, we declare a card-removed class with 0 opacity:

```
.card-removed {
  opacity: 0;
}
```

11. In order to show different playing card graphics from the sprite sheet of the card deck, we clip the background of the card into different background positions:

```
.cardAQ {background-position: -880px 0;}
.cardAK {background-position: -960px 0;}
.cardBQ {background-position: -880px -120px;}
.cardBK {background-position: -960px -120px;}
.cardCQ {background-position: -880px -240px;}
.cardCK {background-position: -960px -240px;}
.cardDQ {background-position: -880px -360px;}
.cardDK {background-position: -960px -360px;}
```

12. We have defined a lot of CSS styles. It is now time for the JavaScript logic. Open the `html5games.matchgame.js` file and put the following code inside:

```
$(function(){
  // clone 12 copies of the card
  for(var i=0;i<11;i++){
```

```
        $(".card:first-child").clone().appendTo("#cards");
    }
    // initialize each card's position
    $("#cards").children().each(function(index) {
        // align the cards to be 4x3 ourselves.
        $(this).css({
            "left" : ($(this).width()  + 20) * (index % 4),
            "top"  : ($(this).height() + 20) * Math.floor(index / 4)
        });
    });
});
```

13. Now save all files and preview the game in the browser. The game should be well styled and 12 cards should appear in the center. However, we cannot click on the cards yet because we have not set any interaction logic to the cards.

What just happened?

We created the game structure in HTML and applied styles to the HTML elements. We also used jQuery to create 12 cards on the game area once the web was loaded and ready. The styles of flipping and removing of the cards are also prepared and can be applied to the card by using the game logic later.

Since we are using absolute positioning for each card, we need to align the cards into 4x3 tiles ourselves. In the JavaScript logic, we loop through each card and align it by calculating the position with the looping index:

```
$("#cards").children().each(function(index) {
  // align the cards to be 4x3 ourselves.
  $(this).css({
    "left" : ($(this).width()  + 20) * (index % 4),
    "top"  : ($(this).height() + 20) * Math.floor(index / 4)
  });
});
```

The "%" in JavaScript is the **modulus operator** that returns the remainder left after division. The remainder is used to get the column count when looping the cards. The following diagram shows the row/column relationship with the index number:

0	1	2	3
4	5	6	7
8	9	10	11

The division, on the other hand, is used to get the row count so we can position the card on that corresponding row.

Take index 3 as an example, 3 % 4 is 3. So the card at index 3 is on the third column. And 3 / 4 is 0, so it is on the first row.

Let's pick another number to see how the formula works. Let's see index 8. 8 % 4 is 0 and it is on the first column. 8 / 4 is 2 so it is on the third row.

Cloning DOM elements with jQuery

In our HTML structure, we only have one card and in the result, we have 12 cards there. It is because we used the `clone` function in jQuery to clone the card element. After cloning the target element, we called the `appendTo` function to append the cloned card element as a child in the cards element:

```
$(".card:first-child").clone().appendTo("#cards");
```

Selecting the first child of an element in jQuery by using child filters

When we selected the card element and cloned it, we used the following selector:

```
$(".card:first-child")
```

The `:first-child` is a **child filter** that selects the first child of the given parent element.

Besides `:first-child`, we can also select the last child by using `:last-child`.

You can also check other child-related selectors on the jQuery document:
`http://api.jquery.com/category/selectors/child-filter-selectors/`

Vertically aligning a DOM element

We put the cards DIV in the center of the game element. **CSS3 flexible box layout module** introduces an easy method to achieve the **vertical center alignment**. As this module is still in progress, we need to apply a browser vendor prefix. We will use Webkit as an example here:

```
display: -webkit-box;
-webkit-box-pack: center;
-webkit-box-align: center;
```

The flexible box module defines the alignment of the element when there are extra spaces in their container. We can set the element to behaviors as a flexible box container by using the display, a CSS2 property, with the value `box`, a new CSS3 property value.

`box-pack` and `box-align` are two properties for defining how it aligns and uses the extra free space horizontally and vertically. We can center the element by setting both properties to `center`.

Vertical alignment is just a small part of the flexible box layout module. It is very powerful when making layout in web design. You may find further information on the W3C page of the module (`http://www.w3.org/TR/css3-flexbox/`) or the CSS3 Info website (`http://www.css3.info/introducing-the-flexible-box-layout-module/`).

Using CSS sprite with a background position

The **CSS sprite** sheet is a big image that contains many individual graphics. The big sprite sheet image is applied as background image for the elements. We can clip each graphic out by moving the background position on a fixed width and height element.

Our deck image contains a total of 53 graphics. In order to demonstrate the background position easily, let's assume we have an image that contains three card images, such as the following screenshot:

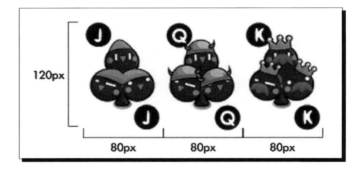

In the CSS style, we set the card element to 80px width and 120px height, with the background image set to the big deck image. If we want the top left graphic, we apply both the X and Y of the background position to 0. If we want the second graphic, we move the background image to left 80px. That means setting the X position to -80px and Y to 0. Since we have a fixed width and height, only the clipped 80x120 area shows the background image. The rectangle in the following screenshot shows the viewable area:

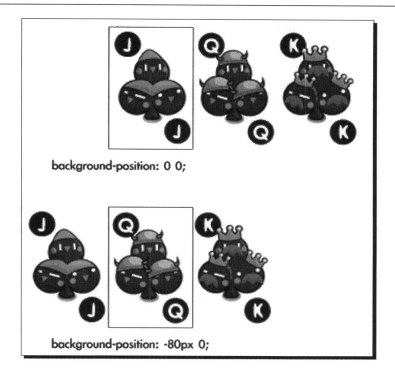

background-position: 0 0;

background-position: -80px 0;

Adding game logic to the matching game

Let's now imagine holding a real deck in our hand and setting up the matching game.

We first shuffle the cards in our hand and then we put each card on the table with the back facing up. For easier game play, we align the cards into a 4x3 array. Now the game is set up.

Now we are going to play the game. We pick up one card and flip it to make it face up. We pick another one and face it upwards. Afterwards, we have two possible actions. We take away those two cards if they are in the same pattern. Otherwise, we put it back facing down again, as if we have not touched them. The game continues until we pair all cards and take them all.

The code flow will be much more clear after we have the step-by-step scenario in our mind. Actually, the code in this example is exactly the same as the procedure we play with a real deck. We just need to replace the human language into the JavaScript code.

Time for action – Adding game logic to the matching game

We have prepared the game environment in the last example and decided the game logic to be the same as playing a real deck. It is time to code the JavaScript logic now:

1. Let's begin from our last matching game example. We have styled the CSS and now it is time to add the game logic in the `html5games.matchgame.js` file.

2. The game is to match pairs of playing cards. We have 12 cards now so we need six pairs of playing cards. The following global array declares six pairs of card patterns:

```
var matchingGame = {};
matchingGame.deck = [
  'cardAK', 'cardAK',
  'cardAQ', 'cardAQ',
  'cardAJ', 'cardAJ',
  'cardBK', 'cardBK',
  'cardBQ', 'cardBQ',
  'cardBJ', 'cardBJ',
];
```

3. We aligned the cards in the jQuery `ready` function in the previous chapter. Now we need to prepare and initialize more codes in the `ready` function. Change the `ready` function to the following code. The changed code is highlighted:

```
$(function(){
  matchingGame.deck.sort(shuffle);
  for(var i=0;i<11;i++){
    $(".card:first-child").clone().appendTo("#cards");
  }
  $("#cards").children().each(function(index) {
    $(this).css({
      "left" : ($(this).width()  + 20) * (index % 4),
      "top"  : ($(this).height() + 20) * Math.floor(index / 4)
    });
    // get a pattern from the shuffled deck
    var pattern = matchingGame.deck.pop();
    // visually apply the pattern on the card's back side.
    $(this).find(".back").addClass(pattern);
    // embed the pattern data into the DOM element.
    $(this).attr("data-pattern",pattern);
    // listen the click event on each card DIV element.
```

```
      $(this).click(selectCard);
    });
});
```

4. Similar to playing a real deck, the first thing we want to do is shuffle the deck. Add the following `shuffle` function to the JavaScript file:

```
function shuffle() {
  return 0.5 - Math.random();
}
```

5. When we click on the card, we flip it and schedule the checking function. Append the following codes to the JavaScript file:

```
function selectCard() {
  // we do nothing if there are already two card flipped.
  if ($(".card-flipped").size() > 1) {
    return;
  }
  $(this).addClass("card-flipped");
  // check the pattern of both flipped card 0.7s later.
  if ($(".card-flipped").size() == 2) {
    setTimeout(checkPattern,700);
  }
}
```

6. When two cards are opened, the following function executes. It controls whether we remove the card or flip the card back:

```
function checkPattern() {
  if (isMatchPattern()) {
    $(".card-flipped").removeClass("card-flipped").addClass
    ("card-removed");
    $(".card-removed").bind("webkitTransitionEnd",
    removeTookCards);
  } else {
    $(".card-flipped").removeClass("card-flipped");
  }
}
```

7. It is time for the pattern checking function. The following function accesses the custom pattern attribute of the opened cards and compares whether they are in the same pattern:

```
function isMatchPattern() {
  var cards = $(".card-flipped");
  var pattern = $(cards[0]).data("pattern");
  var anotherPattern = $(cards[1]).data("pattern");
```

```
      return (pattern == anotherPattern);
}
```

8. After the matched cards fade out, we execute the following function to remove the cards:

```
function removeTookCards() {
  $(".card-removed").remove();
}
```

9. The game logic is ready now. Let's open the game HTML in a browser and play. Remember to check the console window in Developer Tools if there is any error.

What just happened?

We coded the game logic of the CSS3 matching game. The logic adds the mouse click interaction to the playing cards and it controls the flow of the pattern checking.

Executing code after CSS transition ended

We remove the pair cards after playing the fade out transition. We can schedule a function to be executed after the transition is ended by using the `TransitionEnd` event. The following code snippet from our code example adds a `card-removed` class to the pair card to start the transition. Then, it binds the `TransitionEnd` event to remove the card complete in DOM afterwards. Also, please note the `webkit` vendor prefix for the event because it is not yet finalized:

```
$(".card-flipped").removeClass("card-flipped").addClass("card-
removed");
$(".card-removed").bind("webkitTransitionEnd", removeTookCards);
```

Delaying code execution on flipping cards

The game logic flow is designed in the same way as playing a real deck. One big difference is that we used several `setTimeout` functions to delay the execution of the code. When the second card is clicked, we schedule the `checkPattern` function to be executed 0.7 seconds later in the following code example snippet:

```
if ($(".card-flipped").size() == 2) {
  setTimeout(checkPattern,700);
}
```

The reason we delay the function call is to give time to the player to memorize the card pattern. That's why we delayed it by 0.7 seconds before checking the card patterns.

Randomizing an array in JavaScript

There is no built-in array randomize function in JavaScript. We have to write our own. Luckily, we can get help from the built-in array sorting function.

Here is the usage of the `sort` function:

```
sort(compare_function);
```

The `sort` function takes one optional argument.

Argument	Definition	Discussion
compare_function	A function that defines the sort order of the array. The compare_function requires two arguments	The sort function compares two elements in the array by using the compare function. Therefore, the compare function requires two arguments.
		When the compare function returns any value that is bigger than 0, it puts the first argument at the lower index than the second argument.
		When the return value is smaller than 0, it puts the second argument at a lower index than the first argument.

The trick here is that we used the compare function that returns a random number between -0.5 and 0.5:

```
anArray.sort(shuffle);
function shuffle(a, b) {
   return 0.5 - Math.random();
}
```

By returning a random number in the compare function, the sort function sorts the same array in an inconsistent way. In another words, we are shuffling the array.

The following link from the Mozilla Developer Network provides a detailed explanation on using the sort function with example:

```
https://developer.mozilla.org/en/JavaScript/Reference/
Global_Objects/Array/sort
```

Storing internal custom data with an HTML5 custom data attribute

We can store custom data inside the DOM element by using the **custom data attribute**. We can create a custom attribute name with data- prefix and assign a value to it.

For instance, we can embed custom data to the list elements in the following code:

```
<ul id="games">
  <li data-chapter="2" data-difficulty="easy">Ping-Pong</li>
  <li data-chapter="3" data-difficulty="medium">Matching Game</li>
</ul>
```

This is a new feature proposed in the HTML5 spec. According to the W3C, the custom data attributes are intended to store custom data private to the page or application, for which there are no more appropriate attributes or elements.

W3C also stated that this custom data attribute is "intended for use by the site's own script and not a generic extension mechanism for publicly-usable metadata."

We are coding our matching game and embedding our own data to the card elements, therefore, custom data attribute fits our usage.

We used the custom attribute to store the card pattern inside each card so we can check whether the two flipped cards match in JavaScript by comparing the pattern value. Also, the pattern is used to style the playing cards into corresponding graphics as well:

```
$(this).find(".back").addClass(pattern);
$(this).attr("data-pattern",pattern);
```

Pop quiz

1. According to W3C's guideline about the custom data attribute, which of the following statements is true?

    a. We may create a `data-href` attribute to store the link of the `a` tag.

    b. We may want to access the custom data attribute in a third party game portal website.

    c. We may want to store a `data-score` attribute in each player's DOM element to sort the ranking in our web page.

    d. We may create a `ranking` attribute in each player's DOM element to store the ranking data.

Accessing custom data attribute with jQuery

In the matching game example, we used the `attr` function from the jQuery library to access our custom data:

```
pattern = $(this).attr("data-pattern");
```

The `attr` function returns the value of the given attribute name. For example, we can get the links in all `a` tags by calling the following code:

```
$("a").attr("href");
```

For the HTML5 custom data attribute, jQuery provides us with another function to access the HTML5 custom data attribute. It is the `data` function.

`Data` function was designed to embed custom data into the jQuery object of the HTML elements. It was designed before the HTML5 custom data attribute.

Here is the usage of the `data` function:

```
.data(key)
.data(key,value)
```

The `data` function accepts two types of functions:

Function type	Arguments definition	Discussion
`.data(key)`	`key` is a string naming the entry of the data	When there is only the key given, the `data` function reads the data associated with the jQuery object and returns the corresponding value.
		In the recent jQuery update, this function is extended to support the HTML5 custom data attribute.
`.data(key, value)`	`key` is a a string naming the entry of the data `value` is the data to be associated to the jQuery object	When both key and value arguments are given, the `data` function sets a new data entry to the jQuery object.
		The value can be any JavaScript type, including array and object.

In order to support the HTML5 custom data attribute, jQuery extends the `data` function to let it access the custom data defined in the HTML code.

The following code explains how we use the `data` function.

Given the following HTML code:

```
<div id="target" data-custom-name="HTML5 Games"></div>
```

We can access the `data-custom-name` attribute by calling the `data` function in jQuery:

```
$("#target").data("customName")
```

It will return "HTML5 Games".

Pop quiz

1. Given the following HTML code:

   ```
   <div id="game" data-score="100"></div>
   ```

   which two of these jQuery statements reads the custom score data and returns 100?

   a. $("#game").attr("data-score");

   b. $("#game").attr("score");

   c. $("#game").data("data-score");

   d. $("#game").data("score");

Have a go hero

We have created the CSS3 matching game. What is missing here? The game logic does not check whether the game is over. Try adding a **You won** text when the game is over. You can also animate the text by using the techniques we discussed in this chapter.

Making other playing card games

This CSS3 playing card approach is suitable for creating card games. There are two sides in a card that fit the flipping. The transition is suitable for moving the cards. With both moving and flipping, we can just define the playing rule and make the most of the card games.

Have a go hero

Can you use the playing card graphics and flipping techniques to create another game? How about poker?

Embedding web fonts into our game

Over the years, we have been using limited fonts to design web pages. We could not use whatever fonts we wanted because the browser loaded the font from the visitor's local machine. We cannot control and ensure that visitors have our desired fonts.

Although we can embed **web fonts** back to Internet Explorer 5 with limited type format, we have to wait until browser vendors support embedding the most common TrueType font format.

Imagine that we can control the mood of the game by embedding different styles of web fonts. We can design the games with our desired fonts and have more control over the appeal of game. Let's try embedding a web font to our matching memory game.

Time for action – Embedding a font from Google Font Directory

Google Font Directory is a web font service that lists free-to-use web fonts. We will embed a web font chosen from the Google Font Directory:

1. Go to the Google Font Directory site: `http://code.google.com/webfonts`.

2. In the font directory, there is a list of web fonts that is under an open source license and can be used freely.

3. Choose one of them and click on the font name to proceed to the next step. In this example, I used **Droid Serif**.

4. After clicking on a font, the font directory displays detailed information about that font. There are several actions we can carry out there, such as preview the fonts, choose from variants, and most importantly get the font embedding code.

5. Click on the **Get the code** tab and you will see the following screenshot. It shows a guide on how to embed this font to our web page:

6. Copy the `link` tag provided by Google and paste it into the HTML code. It should be placed before any other style definition:

```
<link href='http://fonts.googleapis.com/css?family=Droid+Serif:
regular,bold&subset=latin' rel='stylesheet' type='text/css'>
```

7. Now we can use the font to style our text. Set the body's font family property to the following code:

```
body {
    font-family: 'Droid Serif', arial, serif;
}
```

8. Save all the files and open the `index.html` file. The browser will download the font from the Google server and embed it into the web page. Keep an eye on the fonts, they should be loaded and rendered as our selected Google font.

What just happened?

We have just styled our game with a non-common web font. The font is hosted and delivered through the Google Font Directory.

Besides using the font directory, we can embed our font file by using the @ font face. The following link provides a bulletproof approach to embed a font ourselves:

```
http://www.fontspring.com/blog/the-new-bulletproof-
font-face-syntax
```

Check the font license before embedding

Normally the font licenses do not cover the usage on web pages. Be sure to check the license before embedding the font. All the fonts listed in the Google Font Directory are licensed under open source license and can be used on any website.

Choosing different font delivery services

Google Font Directory is just one of those font delivery services. Typekit (`http://typekit.com`) and Fontdeck (`http://fontdeck.com`) are two other font services providing hundreds of high quality fonts via yearly subscription plans.

Summary

In this chapter we learned about using different CSS3 new properties to create games.

Specifically, we covered:

- ◆ Transforming and animating the game object by transition module
- ◆ Flipping a card back and forth with perspective depth illusion
- ◆ Creating a matching memory game based on CSS3 styles and animation and game logic by jQuery
- ◆ Choosing and embedding web fonts from an online font delivery service

Now that we've learned about creating DOM-based HTML5 games with the help of CSS3 features, we are going to explore another approach of creating HTML5 games in the next chapter, which is using the new Canvas tag and the drawing API.

4
Building the Untangle Game with Canvas and Drawing API

One new highlighted feature in HTML5 is the Canvas element. We can treat the canvas element as a dynamic area that we can draw graphics and shapes on with scripts.

Images in websites have been static for years. There is animation gif but it cannot interact with its visitors. Canvas is dynamic. We draw and modify the context in canvas dynamically through JavaScript drawing API. We can also add interaction to the canvas and thus make games.

In the past two chapters, we have discussed DOM-based game development with CSS3 and few HTML5 features. In the coming two chapters, we will focus on using new HTML5 features to create games. In this chapter, we will take a look at a core feature, canvas, and some basic drawing techniques.

In this chapter, we shall cover the following topics:

- ◆ Introducing the HTML5 canvas element
- ◆ Drawing a circle in canvas
- ◆ Drawing lines in the canvas element
- ◆ Interacting with drawn objects in canvas with mouse events
- ◆ Detecting line intersection
- ◆ Building the Untangle puzzle game with canvas

The Untangle puzzle game is a game where players are given circles with some lines connecting them. The lines may intersect the others and the players need to drag the circles so that no line intersects anymore.

The following screenshot previews the game that we are going to achieve through this chapter:

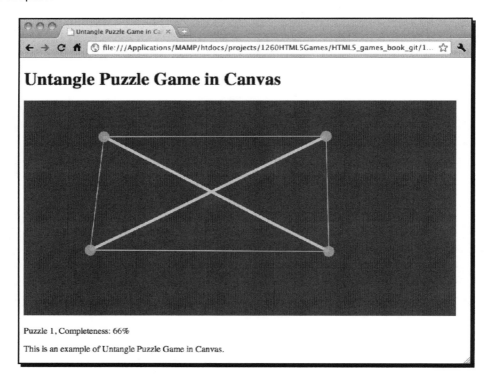

So let's start making our canvas game from scratch.

Introducing the HTML5 Canvas Element

W3C community states that the canvas element and the drawing functions are:

> *A resolution-dependent bitmap canvas, which can be used for rendering graphs, game graphics, or other visual images on the fly.*

The canvas element contains context for drawing and the actual graphics and shapes are drawn by the JavaScript drawing API.

Drawing a circle in canvas

Let's start our drawing on canvas from the basic shape—circle.

Time for action – Drawing color circles on canvas

1. First, let's set up the new environment for the example. That is an HTML file that will contain the canvas element, a jQuery library to help us on JavaScript, a JavaScript file containing the actually drawing logic, and a style sheet.

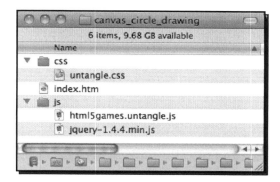

2. Put the following HTML code into the `index.html`. It is a basic HTML document containing the canvas element:

```
<!DOCTYPE html>
<html lang="en">
<head>
  <meta charset="utf-8">
  <title>Drawing Circles in Canvas</title>
  <link rel="stylesheet" href="css/untangle.css" />
</head>
<body>
  <header>
    <h1>Drawing in Canvas</h1>
  </header>

  <canvas id="game" width="768" height="400">
    Sorry, your web browser does not support Canvas content.
  </canvas>

<script src="js/jquery-1.6.min.js"></script>
<script src="js/html5games.untangle.js"></script>
</body>
</html>
```

3. Use CSS to set the background color of the canvas inside `untangle.css`:

```css
canvas {
  background: #333;
}
```

4. In the `html5games.untangle.js` JavaScript file, we put a jQuery `ready` function and draw a color circle inside it:

```javascript
$(function(){
  var canvas = document.getElementById("game");
  var ctx = canvas.getContext("2d");
  ctx.fillStyle = "rgba(200, 200, 100, .6)";
  ctx.beginPath();
  ctx.arc(100, 100, 50 , 0, Math.PI*2, true);
  ctx.closePath();
  ctx.fill();
});
```

5. Open the `index.html` file in a web browser and we will get the following screenshot:

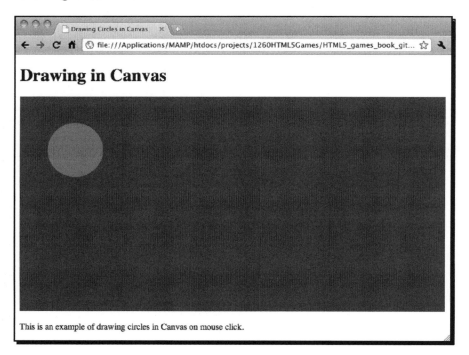

What just happened?

We have just created a simple canvas **context** with circles on it.

There are not many settings for the canvas element itself. We set the width and height of the canvas, same as we have a fixed the dimensions of a real drawing paper. Also, we assign an ID attribute to the canvas for easier reference again in JavaScript:

```
<canvas id="game" width="768" height="400">
  Sorry, your web browser does not support Canvas content.
</canvas>
```

Putting fallback content when the web browser does not support canvas

Not every web browser supports the canvas element. Especially, those aged old version ones. The Canvas element provides an easy way to provide **fallback content** if the canvas element is not supported. Anything inside the canvas open and close tag is the fallback content. This content is hidden if the web browser supports the element. Browsers that don't support canvas will instead display that fallback content. It is good practice to provide useful information in the fallback content. For instance, if the canvas purpose is a dynamic picture, we may consider placing a `<img>` alternative there. Or we may also provide some links to modern web browsers for the visitor to upgrade their browser easily.

In this example, we provided a sentence inside the canvas element. This sentence is hidden from any browsers that support the canvas element. It will show to the visitor if their browsers do not support the new HTML5 canvas feature. The following screenshot shows the old version of Internet Explorer displaying the fallback content instead of drawing the canvas element:

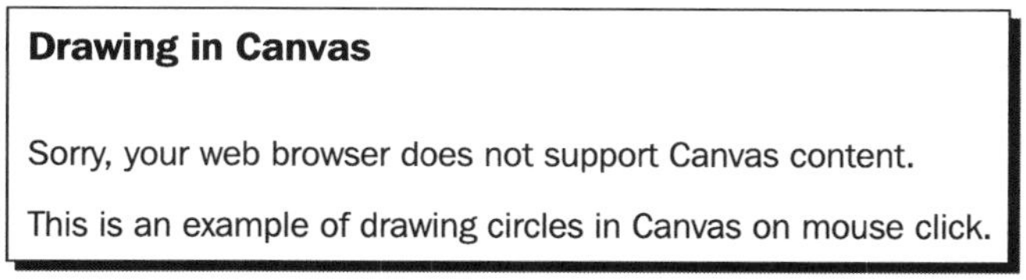

Drawing in Canvas

Sorry, your web browser does not support Canvas content.

This is an example of drawing circles in Canvas on mouse click.

Drawing circles and shapes with canvas arc function

There is no circle function to draw a circle. Canvas drawing API provides a function to draw different arcs, including the circle. The Arc function accepts following arguments

Arguments	Discussion
X	The center point of the arc in x axis.
Y	The center point of the arc in y axis.
radius	The radius is the distance between the center point and the arc perimeter. When drawing a circle, a larger radius means a larger circle.
startAngle	The starting point is an angle in radian. It defines where to start drawing the arc on the perimeter.
endAngle	The ending point is an angle in radian. The arc is drawn from the position of the starting angle to this end angle.
counter-clockwise	This is a Boolean indicating the arc from `startingAngle` to `endingAngle` drawn in a clockwise or counter-clockwise direction.
	This is an optional argument with the default value false.

Converting degree to radians

The angle arguments used in the arc function are in **radian** instead of **degree**. If you are familiar with the degrees angle, you may need to convert the degree into radians before putting the value into the arc function. We can convert the angle unit by using the following formula:

```
radians = п/180 x degrees
```

The following graph contains some common angle values in both degree and radian units. The graph also indicates the position of the angle value for us to easily pick the starting angle and ending angle argument when drawing arc in canvas.

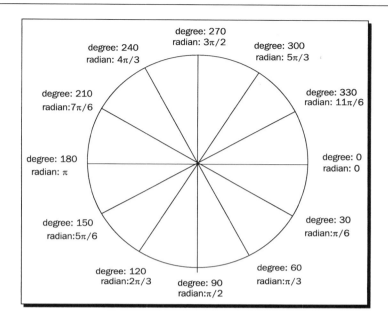

In order to be clearer on drawing different arcs with the starting angle and ending angle, let's draw some arcs.

Time for action – Drawing different arcs with arc function

Let's do some experiments on using the `arc` function by giving different starting and ending angles:

1. Open the `html5games.untangle.js` file we just used to draw the circle.

2. Replace the circle drawing code by using the following arcs drawing codes:
```
$(function(){
  var canvas = document.getElementById('game');
  var ctx = canvas.getContext('2d');
  ctx.fillStyle = "rgba(200, 200, 100, .6)";

  // draw bottom half circle
  ctx.beginPath();
  ctx.arc(100, 110, 50 , 0, Math.PI);
  ctx.closePath();
  ctx.fill();

  // draw top half circle
  ctx.beginPath();
```

```
      ctx.arc(100, 90, 50 , 0, Math.PI, true);
      ctx.closePath();
      ctx.fill();

      // draw left half circle
      ctx.beginPath();
      ctx.arc(230, 100, 50 , Math.PI/2, Math.PI*3/2);
      ctx.closePath();
      ctx.fill();

      // draw right half circle
      ctx.beginPath();
      ctx.arc(250, 100, 50 , Math.PI*3/2, Math.PI/2);
      ctx.closePath();
      ctx.fill();

      // draw a shape that is almost a circle
      ctx.beginPath();
      ctx.arc(180, 240, 50 , Math.PI*7/6, Math.PI*2/3);
      ctx.closePath();
      ctx.fill();

      // draw a small arc
      ctx.beginPath();
      ctx.arc(150, 250, 50 , Math.PI*7/6, Math.PI*2/3, true);
      ctx.closePath();
      ctx.fill();
});
```

3. It is time to test it in a web browser. There should be six different half circles and arcs on the canvas as shown in the following screenshot:

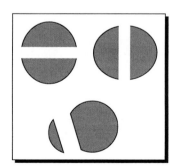

What just happened?

We have used different `startAngle` and `endAngle` arguments in the arc function to draw six different arc shapes. These arc shapes demonstrate how the arc function works.

Let's recall the degrees and radians relationship circle and take a look at the top half circle. The top half circle begins at angle 0 and ends at angle π, and the arc is drawn in an counter-clockwise direction. If we take a look at the circle, it looks like the following graph:

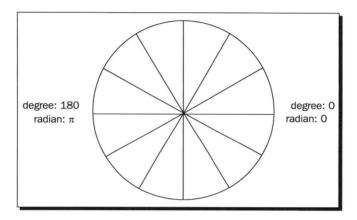

And if we start at angle 210 degrees and end at angle 120 degrees, in a clockwise direction, we will get the following arc:

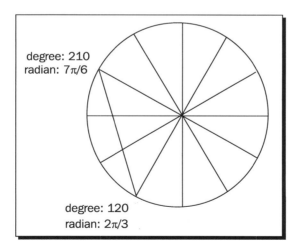

1. Which arc command we can use to draw the following arc?

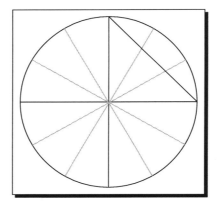

a. ctx.arc(300, 250, 50 , Math.PI*3/2, Math.PI/2, true);

b. ctx.arc(300, 250, 50 , Math.PI*3/2, Math.PI/2);

c. ctx.arc(300, 250, 50 , Math.PI*3/2, 0, true);

d. ctx.arc(300, 250, 50 , Math.PI*3/2, 0);

Executing the path drawing in canvas

When we are calling the arc function or other path drawing functions, we are not drawing the path immediately on the canvas. Instead, we are adding it into a list of the paths. These paths will not be drawn until we execute the drawing command.

There are two drawing executing commands. One command for filling the paths and the other for drawing the stroke.

We fill the paths by calling the `fill` function and draw the stroke of the paths by calling the `stroke` function, which we will use later when drawing lines:

```
ctx.fill();
```

Beginning a path for each style

The `fill` and `stroke` function fills and draws the paths on canvas but it does not clear the list of paths. Take the following code snippet as an example. After filling our circle with red color, we add other circles and fill it with green. What happens to the code is both the circles are filled with green color, instead of only the new circle being filled by green color:

```
var canvas = document.getElementById('game');
var ctx = canvas.getContext('2d');
ctx.fillStyle = "red";
ctx.arc(100, 100, 50 , 0, Math.PI*2, true);
ctx.fill();

ctx.arc(210, 100, 50, 0, Math.PI*2, true);
ctx.fillStyle = "green";
ctx.fill();
```

It is because when calling the second `fill` command, the list of paths in the canvas contain both circles. Therefore, the `fill` command fills both circles with green and overrides the red color circle.

In order to fix this issue, we want to ensure we call `beginPath` before drawing a new shape every time.

`beginPath` empties the list of paths so next time we call the `fill` and `stroke` command, it will only apply to all paths after the last `beginPath`.

Have a go hero

We have just discussed a code snippet where we intend to draw two circles with one in red color and the other in green. The code turns out drawing both circles in green color. How can we add a `beginPath` command to the code so that it draws one red circle and one green circle correctly?

Closing a path

The `closePath` function will draw a straight line from the last point of the latest path to the first point of the path. That is closing the path. If we are only going to fill the path and not going to draw the stroke outline, the `closePath` function does not affect the result. The following screenshot compares the result on a half circle with one calling `closePath` and the other not calling `closePath`:

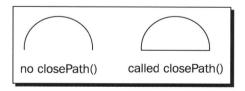

1. Do we need to use the `closePath` function on the shape we are drawing if we just want to fill the color and not draw the outline stroke?

   a. Yes, we need the `closePath` function.

   b. No, it does not care if we have the `closePath` function.

Wrapping the circle drawing in function

Drawing a circle is a common function that we will use a lot. It is better to create a function for drawing a circle instead of entering several code lines now.

Time for action – Putting the circle drawing code into a function

Let's make a function for the circle drawing and draw some circles on the canvas:

1. Open the `html5games.untangle.js` file.

2. Replace the original code in the JavaScript file with the following code. It basically puts the circle drawing code we just used into a function and uses a for-loop to randomly place five circles on the canvas:

```
var untangleGame = {};

function drawCircle(ctx, x, y, radius) {
  ctx.fillStyle = "rgba(200, 200, 100, .9)";
  ctx.beginPath();
  ctx.arc(x, y, radius, 0, Math.PI*2, true);
  ctx.closePath();
  ctx.fill();
}
$(function(){
  var canvas = document.getElementById('game');
  var ctx = canvas.getContext('2d');

  var circleRadius = 10;

  var width = canvas.width;
  var height = canvas.height;

  // random 5 circles
  var circlesCount = 5;
  for (var i=0;i<circlesCount;i++) {
    var x = Math.random()*width;
```

```
    var y = Math.random()*height;
    drawCircle(ctx, x, y, circleRadius);
  }
});
```

3. Open the HTML file in the web browser to see the result.

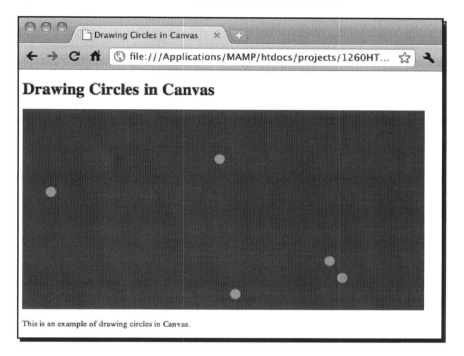

What just happened?

The code of drawing circles is executed after the page is loaded and ready. We used a loop to draw several circles in random places on the canvas.

Generating random numbers in JavaScript

In game development, we often use `random` functions. We may want to randomly summon a monster for the player to fight, we may want to randomly drop a reward price when the player makes progress, and we may want a random number to be the result of rolling a dice. In this code, we place the circles randomly in the canvas.

To generate a random number in JavaScript, we use the `Math.random()` function.

There is no argument in the `random` function. It always returns a floating number between 0 and 1. The number is equal or bigger than 0 and smaller than 1.

There are two common ways to use the `random` function. One way is to generate random numbers within a given range. The other way is generating a true or false value

Usage	Code	Discussion
Getting a random integer between A and B	Math.floor(Math.random()*B)+A	`Math.floor()` function cuts the decimal point of the given number.
		Take `Math.floor(Math.random()*10)+5` as an example.
		`Math.random()` returns a decimal number between 0 to 0.9999....
		`Math.random()*10` is a decimal number between 0 to 9.9999....
		`Math.floor(Math.random()*10)` is an integer between 0 to 9.
		Finally, `Math.floor(Math.random()*10) + 5` is an integer between 5 to 14.
Getting a random Boolean	(Math.random() > 0.495)	`(Math.random() > 0.495)` means there is 50 percent false and 50 percent true.
		We can further adjust the true/false ratio.
		`(Math.random() > 0.7)` means there is almost 70 percent false and 30 percent true.

Saving the circle position

When we are developing a DOM-based game, such as the games we built in previous chapters, we often put the game objects into DIV elements and access them later in code logic. It is a different story in canvas-based game development.

In order to access our game objects after they are drawn on the canvas, we need to remember their states ourselves. Lets say now we want to know how many circles are drawn and where they are, and we will need an array to store their position.

Time for action – Saving the circle position

1. Open the `html5games.untangle.js` file in the text editor.

2. Add the following `circle` object definition code at the top of the JavaScript file:

```
function Circle(x,y,radius){
  this.x = x;
  this.y = y;
  this.radius = radius;
}
```

3. Now we need an array to store the circles position. Add a new array to the `untangleGame` object:

```
var untangleGame = {
  circles: []
};
```

4. After drawing every circle on the canvas, we save the position of the circle into the `circles` array. Add the highlighted line after calling the `drawCircle` function:

```
$(function(){
  var canvas = document.getElementById('game');
  var ctx = canvas.getContext('2d');
  var circleRadius = 10;

  var width = canvas.width;
  var height = canvas.height;

  // random 5 circles
  var circlesCount = 5;
  for (var i=0;i<circlesCount;i++) {
    var x = Math.random()*width;
    var y = Math.random()*height;
    drawCircle(ctx, x, y, circleRadius);
    untangleGame.circles.push(new Circle(x,y,circleRadius));
  }
});
```

5. Now we can test the code in the web browser. There is no visual difference between this code and the last example when drawing random circles on canvas. It is because we are saving the circles but have not changed any code that affects the appearance.

What just happened?

We saved the position and color of each circle. This is because we cannot directly access the drawn object in canvas. All lines and shapes are drawn on the canvas and we cannot access the lines or shapes as individual objects. The drawn items are drawn on a canvas. We cannot just move a house in an oil painting, the same way we cannot directly manipulate any drawn items in the canvas element.

Defining a basic class definition in JavaScript

JavaScript is **object-oriented programming** language. We can define some object structure for our use. The `Circle` object provides a data structure for us to easily store a collection of x and y positions and the radii.

After defining the `Circle` object, we can create a new `Circle` instance with an x, y, and radius value by the following code:

```
var circle1 = new Circle(100, 200, 10);
```

 For more detail usage on object-oriented programming JavaScript, please read the Mozilla Developer Center in the following link:
```
https://developer.mozilla.org/en/Introduction_to_
Object-Oriented_JavaScript
```

Have a go hero

We have drawn several circles randomly on the canvas. They are in the same style and same size. How about we randomly draw the size of the circles? And fill the circles with different colors? Try modifying the code and play with the drawing API.

Drawing lines in canvas

Now we have several circles here, how about connecting them with lines? Let's draw a straight line between each circle.

Time for action – Drawing straight lines between each circle

1. Open the `index.html` we have just used in the circle drawing example.

2. Change the wordings **drawing circles in Canvas** to **drawing lines in Canvas**.

3. Open the `html5games.untangle.js` JavaScript file.

4. We are going to add the line drawing code on top of our existing circles drawing code. Replace the original code with the following. The modified code is highlighted:

```
function Circle(x,y,radius){
  this.x = x;
  this.y = y;
  this.radius = radius;
}

function Line(startPoint,endpoint, thickness) {
  this.startPoint = startPoint;
  this.endPoint = endPoint;
  this.thickness = thickness;
}

var untangleGame = {
  circles: [],
  thinLineThickness: 1,
  lines: []
};


function drawLine(ctx, x1, y1, x2, y2, thickness) {
  ctx.beginPath();
  ctx.moveTo(x1,y1);
  ctx.lineTo(x2,y2);
  ctx.lineWidth = thickness;
  ctx.strokeStyle = "#cfc";
  ctx.stroke();
}

function drawCircle(ctx, x, y, radius) {
  ctx.fillStyle = "rgba(200, 200, 100, .9)";
  ctx.beginPath();
  ctx.arc(x, y, radius, 0, Math.PI*2, true);
  ctx.closePath();
```

```
    ctx.fill();
}

$(function(){
  var canvas = document.getElementById('game');
  var ctx = canvas.getContext('2d');

  var circleRadius = 10;

  var width = canvas.width;
  var height = canvas.height;

  // random 5 circles
  var circlesCount = 5;
  for (var i=0;i<circlesCount;i++) {
    var x = Math.random()*width;
    var y = Math.random()*height;
    drawCircle(ctx, x, y, circleRadius);
    untangleGame.circles.push(new Circle(x,y,radius));
  }

  for (var i=0;i< untangleGame.circles.length;i++) {
    var startPoint = untangleGame.circles[i];
    for(var j=0;j<i;j++) {
      var endPoint = untangleGame.circles[j];
      drawLine(ctx, startPoint.x, startPoint.y, endPoint.x,
      endPoint.y, 1);
      untangleGame.lines.push(new Line(startPoint, endpoint,
      untangleGame.thinLineThickness));
    }
  }

});
```

5. Test the code in the web browser. We should see there are lines connected with each randomly placed circle.

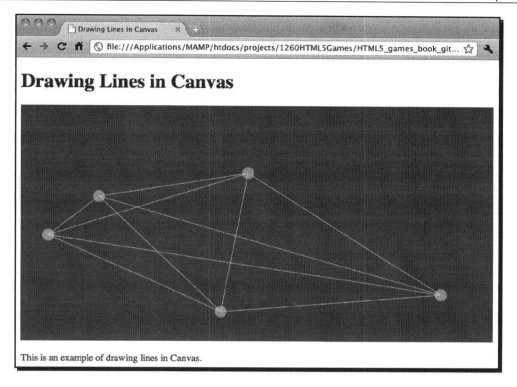

Drawing Lines in Canvas

This is an example of drawing lines in Canvas.

What just happened?

Similar to the way we saved the circles position, we have an array to save every line segment we draw. We declare a line class definition to store some essential information of a line segment. That is, we save the start and end point and the thickness of the line.

Introducing the line drawing API

There are some drawing APIs for us to draw and style the line stroke

Line drawing functions	Discussion
MoveTo	The `Moveto` function is like holding the pen in our hand and moving it on top of the paper without touching it with the pen.
LineTo	This function is like putting the pen down on the paper and drawing a straight line to the destination point.
lineWidth	`LineWidth` sets the thickness of the strokes we draw afterwards.
Stroke	`stroke` is the function to execute the drawing. We set up a collection of `moveTo`, `lineTo`, or styling functions and finally call the `stroke` function to execute it on canvas.

We usually draw lines by using the moveTo and lineTo pairs. Just like in the real world, we move our pen on top of the paper to the starting point of a line and put down the pen to draw a line. Then, keep on drawing another line or move to the other position before drawing. This is exactly the flow in which we draw lines on canvas.

 We just demonstrated drawing a simple line. We can set different line styles to lines in canvas. For more line styling detail, please read the styling guide in W3C (http://dev.w3.org/html5/2dcontext/#line-styles) and Mozilla Developer Center (https://developer.mozilla.org/En/Canvas_tutorial/Applying_styles_and_colors).

Interacting with drawn objects in canvas with mouse events

So far, we have shown that we can draw shapes in canvas dynamically based on our logic. There is one part missing in the game development that is, input.

Imagine now we can drag the circles around on the canvas, the connected lines will follow the circles. In this section, we will add mouse events to the canvas to make our circles **draggable**.

Time for action – Dragging the circles in canvas

1. Let's continue with our previous code. Open the html5games.untangle.js file.

2. We will need a function to clear all the drawing in the canvas. Add the following function to the end of the JavaScript file:

```
function clear(ctx) {
  ctx.clearRect(0,0,ctx.canvas.width,ctx.canvas.height);
}
```

3. Remove the line drawing code in the jQuery ready function. We are going to separate it into two parts, the line data and the drawing.

4. Add the following function that assigns lines to connect each circle. These lines will be drawn later:

```
function connectCircles()
{
  // connect the circles to each other with lines
  untangleGame.lines.length = 0;
  for (var i=0;i< untangleGame.circles.length;i++) {
    var startPoint = untangleGame.circles[i];
```

```
    for(var j=0;j<i;j++) {
      var endPoint = untangleGame.circles[j];
      untangleGame.lines.push(new Line(startPoint, endPoint,
      untangleGame.thinLineThickness));
    }
  }
}
```

5. Add the mouse event listener code to the jQuery `ready` function. The following code is how the function looks now. The highlighted code is the mouse event handlers:

```
$(function(){
  // get the reference of canvas element.
    var canvas = document.getElementById("game");
    var ctx = canvas.getContext("2d");

    var circleRadius = 10;

  var width = canvas.width;
  var height = canvas.height;

  // random 5 circles
  var circlesCount = 5;
  for (var i=0;i<circlesCount;i++) {
    var x = Math.random()*width;
    var y = Math.random()*height;
    drawCircle(ctx, x, y, circleRadius);
    untangleGame.circles.push(new Circle(x,y,circleRadius));
  }
  connectCircles();

  // Add Mouse Event Listener to canvas
  // we find if the mouse down position is on any circle
  // and set that circle as target dragging circle.
  $("#game").mousedown(function(e) {
    var canvasPosition = $(this).offset();
    var mouseX = e.layerX || 0;
    var mouseY = e.layerY || 0;

  for(var i=0;i<untangleGame.circles.length;i++)
  {
    var circleX = untangleGame.circles[i].x;
    var circleY = untangleGame.circles[i].y;
    var radius = untangleGame.circles[i].radius;
```

```
    if (Math.pow(mouseX-circleX,2) + Math.pow(mouseY-circleY,2) <
    Math.pow(radius,2))
    {
      untangleGame.targetCircle = i;
      break;
    }
  }
});


// we move the target dragging circle when the mouse is moving
$("#game").mousemove(function(e) {
  if (untangleGame.targetCircle != undefined)
  {
  var canvasPosition = $(this).offset();
  var mouseX = e.layerX || 0;
  var mouseY = e.layerY || 0;
  var radius = untangleGame.circles[untangleGame.targetCircle].
  radius;
  untangleGame.circles[untangleGame.targetCircle] = new
  Circle(mouseX, mouseY,radius);
  }
connectCircles();
});


// We clear the dragging circle data when mouse is up
$("#game").mouseup(function(e) {
  untangleGame.targetCircle = undefined;
});


// setup an interval to loop the game loop
setInterval(gameloop, 30);


});
```

6. Then we add the `gameloop` function that is responded to draw the updated circles and lines:

```
function gameloop() {
  // get the reference of the canvas element and the drawing
     context.
  var canvas = document.getElementById('game');
  var ctx = canvas.getContext('2d');
```

```
    // clear the canvas before re-drawing.
       clear(ctx);

    // draw all remembered line
    for(var i=0;i<untangleGame.lines.length;i++) {
      var line = untangleGame.lines[i];
      var startPoint = line.startPoint;
      var endPoint = line.endPoint;
      var thickness = line.thickness;
      drawLine(ctx, startPoint.x, startPoint.y, endPoint.x,
      endPoint.y, thickness);
    }

    // draw all remembered circles
    for(var i=0;i<untangleGame.circles.length;i++) {
      var circle = untangleGame.circles[i];
      drawCircle(ctx, point.x, point.y, circle.radius);
    }
  }
```

7. Open `index.html` in a web browser. There should be five circles with lines connecting them. Try dragging the circles. The dragged circle will follow the mouse cursor and the connected lines will follow too.

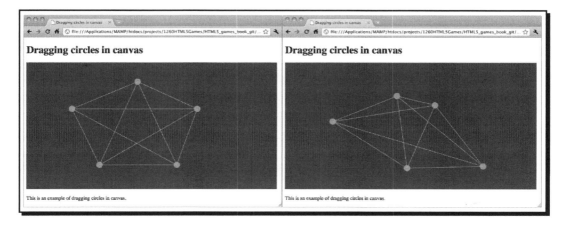

What just happened?

We have set up three mouse event listeners in the jQuery `ready` function. They are the mouse down, move, and up events.

Getting the mouse position in the canvas element

We can get the mouse cursor position relative to the element in the mouse event from the `layerX` and `layerY` property. The following shows the code snippet we used in our code example. The `|| 0` is to make the result 0 when the `layerX` or `layerY` is undefined:

```
var mouseX = e.layerX || 0;
var mouseY = e.layerY || 0;
```

Please note that we need to explicitly set the position property of the element in order to get the correct `layerX` and `layerY` property.

Detecting mouse events on circles in canvas

After discussing the difference between DOM-based development and Canvas-based development, we cannot directly listen to the mouse events of any drawn shapes in the canvas. There is no such thing. We cannot monitor the event on any drawn shapes in the canvas. We can only get the mouse event of the canvas element and calculate the relative position of the canvas. Then we change the states of the game objects according to the mouse position and finally redraw it on canvas.

How do we know we are clicking on a circle?

We can use the **point-in-circle** formula. That is to check the distance between the center point of the circle and the mouse position. The mouse clicks on the circle when the distance is less than the circle radius.

We use the following formula to get the distance between two points:

```
Distance = (x2-x1)2 + (y2-y1)2
```

The following graph shows that when the distance between the center point and the mouse cursor is smaller than the radius, the cursor is in the circle:

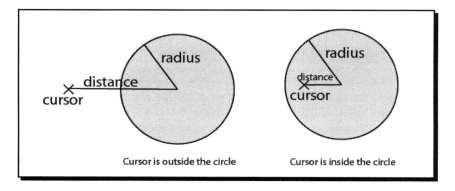

Cursor is outside the circle   Cursor is inside the circle

The following code we used explains how we can apply the distance checking to know whether the mouse cursor is inside the circle in the mouse down event handler:

```
if (Math.pow(mouseX-circleX,2) + Math.pow(mouseY-circleY,2) < Math.
pow(untangleGame.circleRadius,2))
{
  untangleGame.targetCircle = i;
  break;
}
```

When we know that the mouse cursor is pressing the circle in canvas, we mark it as the targeted circle to be dragged on the mouse move event. During the mouse move event handler, we update the target dragged circle's position to the latest cursor position. When the mouse is up, we clear the target circle's reference.

Pop quiz

1.   Can we directly access an already drawn shape in the canvas?

   a.   Yes

   b.   No

2.   Which method can we use to check whether a point is inside a circle?

   a.   The coordinate of the point is smaller than the coordinate of the center of the circle.

   b.   The distance between the point and the center of the circle is smaller than the circle radius.

   c.   The x coordinate of the point is smaller than the circle radius.

   d.   The distance between the point and the center of the circle is bigger than the circle radius.

Game loop

In Chapter 2, *Getting Started with DOM-based Game Development*, we discussed the game loop approach. In the Ping Pong game in Chapter 2, the **game loop** manipulates the keyboard input and updates the position of the DOM-based game objects.

Here, the game loop is used to redraw the canvas to present the later game states. If we do not redraw the canvas after changing the states, say the position of the circles, we will not see it.

It is like refreshing the image on television. The TV refreshes the screen 12 times per second. We also redraw the canvas scene several times a second. In each redraw, we draw the game state on canvas based on the current circle position.

Clearing the canvas

When we drag the circle, we redraw the canvas. The problem is the already drawn shapes on canvas won't disappear automatically. We will keep adding new paths to the canvas and finally mess up everything on the canvas. The following screenshot is what will happen if we keep dragging the circles without clearing the canvas on every redraw:

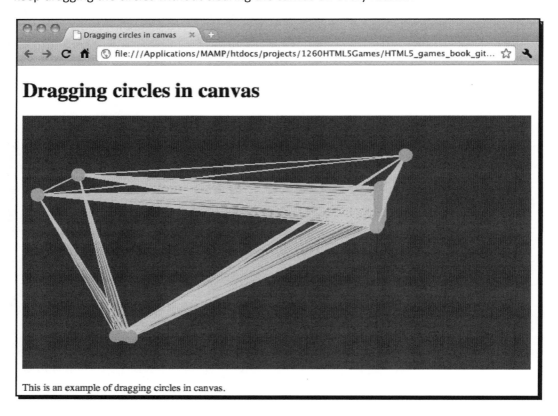

Since we have saved all game statuses in the JavaScript, we can safely clear the entire canvas and draw the updated lines and circles with the latest game status. To clear the canvas, we use the `clearRect` function provided by canvas drawing API. The `clearRect` function clears a rectangle area by providing a rectangle clipping region. It accepts the following arguments as the clipping region:

ctx.clearRect(x,context.clearRect(x, y, width, height)

Argument	Definition
x	The top left point of the rectangle clipping region, in x-axis.
y	The top left point of the rectangle clipping region, in y-axis.
width	The width of the rectangle region.
height	The height of the rectangle region.

The x and y set the top left position of the region to be cleared. The width and height defines how much area is to be cleared. To clear the entire canvas, we can provide (0,0) as the top left position and the width and height of the canvas to the clearRect function. The following code clears all drawn things on the entire canvas:

```
ctx.clearRect(0, 0, ctx.canvas.width, ctx.canvas.height);
```

Pop quiz

1. Can we clear a portion of the canvas by using the clearRect function?

   a. Yes

   b. No

2. Does the following code clear things on the drawn canvas?

   ```
   ctx.clearRect(0, 0, ctx.canvas.width, 0);
   ```

   a. Yes

   b. No

Detecting line intersection in canvas

We have draggable circles and connected lines on the canvas. Some lines intersect others and some do not. Imagine now we want to distinguish the intersected lines. We need some mathematics formula to check them and bold those intersected lines.

Time for action – Distinguishing the intersected lines

Let's increase the thickness of those intersected lines so we can distinguish them in the canvas:

1. Open the html5games.untangle.js file in the text editor.

2. We have the `thinLineThickness` setting as the default line thickness. We add the following code to define a thickness for bold lines:

```
var untangleGame = {
  circles: [],
  thinLineThickness: 1,
  boldLineThickness: 5,
  lines: []
};
```

3. In order to make the code more reusable and readable, we want to isolate the line intersection logic from the game logic. We create a function to check whether the given two lines intersect. Add the following functions to the end of the JavaScript file:

```
function isIntersect(line1, line2)
{
  // convert line1 to general form of line: Ax+By = C
  var a1 = line1.endPoint.y - line1.point1.y;
  var b1 = line1.point1.x - line1.endPoint.x;
  var c1 = a1 * line1.point1.x + b1 * line1.point1.y;

  // convert line2 to general form of line: Ax+By = C
  var a2 = line2.endPoint.y - line2.point1.y;
  var b2 = line2.point1.x - line2.endPoint.x;
  var c2 = a2 * line2.startPoint.x + b2 * line2.startPoint.y;

  // calculate the intersection point
  var d = a1*b2 - a2*b1;

  // parallel when d is 0
  if (d == 0) {
    return false;
  }else {
    var x = (b2*c1 - b1*c2) / d;
    var y = (a1*c2 - a2*c1) / d;

    // check if the interception point is on both line segments
    if ((isInBetween(line1.startPoint.x, x, line1.endPoint.x) ||
      isInBetween(line1.startPoint.y, y, line1.endPoint.y)) &&
      (isInBetween(line2.startPoint.x, x, line2.endPoint.x) ||
        isInBetween(line2.startPoint.y, y, line2.endPoint.y)))
    {
      return true;
    }
```

```
    }

    return false;
}

// return true if b is between a and c,
// we exclude the result when a==b or b==c
function isInBetween(a, b, c) {
  // return false if b is almost equal to a or c.
  // this is to eliminate some floating point when
  // two value is equal to each other but different with
0.00000...0001
  if (Math.abs(a-b) < 0.000001 || Math.abs(b-c) < 0.000001) {
    return false;
  }

  // true when b is in between a and c
  return (a < b && b < c) || (c < b && b < a);
}
```

4. Next, we have a function to check whether our lines intersect and mark that line in bold. Add the following new function to the code:

```
function updateLineIntersection()
{
  // checking lines intersection and bold those lines.
  for (var i=0;i<untangleGame.lines.length;i++) {
    for(var j=0;j<i;j++) {
      var line1 = untangleGame.lines[i];
      var line2 = untangleGame.lines[j];

      // we check if two lines are intersected,
      // and bold the line if they are.
      if (isIntersect(line1, line2)) {
        line1.thickness = untangleGame.boldLineThickness;
        line2.thickness = untangleGame.boldLineThickness;
      }
    }
  }
}
```

5. Finally we update the line intersection by adding the following function call in two places. One after connecting our circles and the other in the mouse move event handler:

```
updateLineIntersection();
```

6. It is time to test the intersection in the web browser. When viewing the circles and lines in canvas the lines with intersection should be thicker than those without intersection. Try dragging the circles to change the intersection relationship and the lines will become thin or thick.

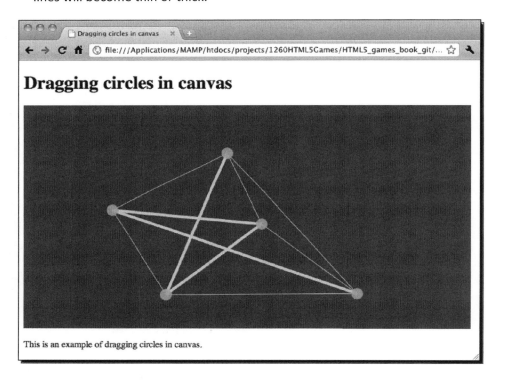

This is an example of dragging circles in canvas.

What just happened?

We have just added **line intersection** checking code to our existing circle dragging example. The line intersection code involves some mathematical formula to get the **intersection point** of two lines and checks whether the point is inside the line segment we provide. Let's look at the mathematics part and see how it works.

Determining whether two line segments intersect

According to the intersection equation we learnt from geometry, with two given lines in general form, we can get the intersection point.

What is **general form**? In our code, we have the starting point and ending point of a line in x and y coordinates. This is a **line segment** because it is just a segment part of the line in mathematics. A general form of a line is represented by $Ax + By = C$.

The following graph explains the line segment on a line in general form:

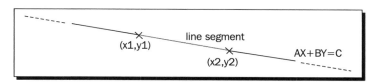

We can transform the line segment with point 1 in x1, y1 and point 2 in x2, y2 into general form by the following equation:

```
A = y2-y1
B = x1-x2
C = A * x1 + B * y2
```

Now we have a line equation $AX+BY = C$ where A, B, C are known and X and Y are unknown.

We are checking two lines intersecting. We can transform both lines into general form and get two line equations:

```
Line 1: A1X+B1Y = C1
Line 2: A2X+B2Y = C2
```

By putting the two general form equations together, X and Y are two variables that are unknown. We can then solve these two equations and get the intersection point of X and Y.

If $A1 * B2 - A2 * B1$ is zero, then two lines are parallel and there is no intersection point. Otherwise we get the interception point by using the following equation:

```
X = (B2 * C1 - B1 * C2) / (A1 * B2 - A2 * B1)
Y = (A1 * C2 - A2 * C1) / (A1 * B2 - A2 * B1)
```

The intersection point of the general forms only provides that the two lines are not parallel to each other and will intersect each other at some point. It does not guarantee the intersection point is on both line segments.

The following graphs show two possible results of the intersection point and the given line segments. The intersection point is not in between both line segments in the left graph, in this case, the two line segments are not intersected to each other. In the right-hand side graph, the point is in between both line segments so these two line segments intersect to each other:

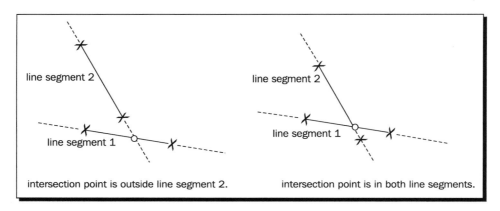

Therefore, we need another function named `isInBetween` to determine if a provided value is in between the beginning and ending value. Then we use this function to check whether the intersection point from the equation is in between both line segments that we are checking.

After getting the result of the lines intersection, we draw the thick line to indicate those intersected lines.

Making the untangle puzzle game

Now that we have created an interaction canvas we can drag the circles and the lines connecting the circles intersecting with other lines. How about we make it a game? There are some pre-defined circles and lines and our aim is to drag the circles so that there are no lines intersecting with others. This is called an **untangle puzzle game**.

Time for action – Making the untangle puzzle game in canvas

Let's add the game logic to our line intersection code:

1. Open the `index.html` file in text editor.

2. First, let's set the title as the following:

```
<header>
  <h1>Untangle Puzzle Game in Canvas</h1>
</header>
```

3. We also need to display the current level and the progress to the player. Add the following code after the canvas element:

```
<p>Puzzle <span id="level">0</span>, Completeness:
<span id="progress">0</span>%</p>
```

4. Open the `html5games.untangle.js` JavaScript file to add the game logic.

5. Add the variable info, the `untangleGame`. It stores the current level of the game:

```
var untangleGame = {
  circles: [],
  thinLineThickness: 1,
  boldLineThickness: 5,
  lines: [],
  currentLevel: 0
};
```

6. We need some pre-defined level data for the players to play. It is a collection of data defining where the circles are placed and how they connect to each other initially. Add the following level data code to the `untangleGame` object:

```
untangleGame.levels =
[
  {
    "level" : 0,
    "circles" : [{"x" : 400, "y" : 156},
          {"x" : 381, "y" : 241},
          {"x" : 84, "y" : 233},
          {"x" : 88, "y" : 73}],
    "relationship" : {
            "0" : {"connectedPoints" : [1,2]},
            "1" : {"connectedPoints" : [0,3]},
            "2" : {"connectedPoints" : [0,3]},
            "3" : {"connectedPoints" : [1,2]}
```

```
            }
    },
    {
      "level" : 1,
      "circles" : [{"x" : 401, "y" : 73},
            {"x" : 400, "y" : 240},
            {"x" : 88, "y" : 241},
            {"x" : 84, "y" : 72}],
      "relationship" : {
                "0" : {"connectedPoints" : [1,2,3]},
                "1" : {"connectedPoints" : [0,2,3]},
                "2" : {"connectedPoints" : [0,1,3]},
                "3" : {"connectedPoints" : [0,1,2]}
                }
    },
    {
      "level" : 2,
      "circles" : [{"x" : 92, "y" : 85},
            {"x" : 253, "y" : 13},
            {"x" : 393, "y" : 86},
            {"x" : 390, "y" : 214},
            {"x" : 248, "y" : 275},
            {"x" : 95, "y" : 216}],
      "relationship" : {
                "0" : {"connectedPoints" : [2,3,4]},
                "1" : {"connectedPoints" : [3,5]},
                "2" : {"connectedPoints" : [0,4,5]},
                "3" : {"connectedPoints" : [0,1,5]},
                "4" : {"connectedPoints" : [0,2]},
                "5" : {"connectedPoints" : [1,2,3]}
                }
    }
];
```

7. When starting on each level, we need to set up the initial level data. To help make the code more readable, we create a function. Add the following code to the end of the JavaScript file:

```
function setupCurrentLevel() {
  untangleGame.circles = [];
  var level = untangleGame.levels[untangleGame.currentLevel];
  for (var i=0; i<level.circles.length; i++) {
    untangleGame.circles.push(new Point(level.circles[i].x, level.
    circles[i].y, 10));
  }
```

```
   // setup line data after setup the circles.
   connectCircles();
   updateLineIntersection();
}
```

8. This is a game with several levels. We need to check whether the player solves the puzzle in the current level and jumps to the next puzzle. Add the following function to the end of the file:

```
function checkLevelCompleteness() {
   if ($("#progress").html() == "100") {
     if (untangleGame.currentLevel+1 < untangleGame.levels.length)
       untangleGame.currentLevel++;
     setupCurrentLevel();
   }
}
```

9. We update the original mouse up event handler to check whether the player completes the level:

```
$("#game").mouseup(function(e) {
     untangleGame.targetCircle = undefined;

   // on every mouse up, check if the untangle puzzle is solved.
   checkLevelCompleteness();
});
```

10. We are going to draw the circles based on the level data instead of drawing them randomly. Therefore, we delete the circle drawing code in the jQuery `ready` function.

11. On the place we deleted the circle drawing code in the jQuery `ready` function, we add the following code to set up the circles level data for game loop to use:

```
setupCurrentLevel();
```

12. Next, we update the `connectCircles` function to connect circles based on the level data:

```
function connectCircles()
{
// setup all lines based on the circles relationship
var level = untangleGame.levels[untangleGame.currentLevel];
untangleGame.lines.length = 0;
for (var i in level.relationship) {
  var connectedPoints = level.relationship[i].connectedPoints;
```

```
      var startPoint = untangleGame.circles[i];
      for (var j in connectedPoints) {
        var endPoint = untangleGame.circles[connectedPoints[j]];
        untangleGame.lines.push(new Line(startPoint, endPoint));
      }
    }
  }
  }
```

13. We need another function to update the game progress. Add the following function to the code:

```
function updateLevelProgress()
{
  // check the untangle progress of the level
  var progress = 0;
  for (var i=0;i<untangleGame.lines.length;i++) {
    if (untangleGame.lines[i].thickness == untangleGame.
    thinLineThickness) {
      progress++;
    }
  }
  var progressPercentage = Math.floor(progress/untangleGame.lines.
  length*100);
  $("#progress").html(progressPercentage);

  // display the current level
  $("#level").html(untangleGame.currentLevel);
}
```

14. Finally, we need to update the level progress in the following mouse move event handler.

```
$("#game").mousemove(function(e) {
  …

    connectCircles();
    updateLineIntersection();
    updateLevelProgress();

  …
});
```

15. Save all files and test the game in the browser. We can drag the circles and the line thickness will indicate if it is intersected with other lines. During the mouse dragging, the level completeness percentage should change when more or less line intersections are detected. If we solve the puzzle, that is no lines are intersected, the game will jump to the next level. When the game reaches the last level, it will keep showing the last level again. It is because we have not yet added the game over screen.

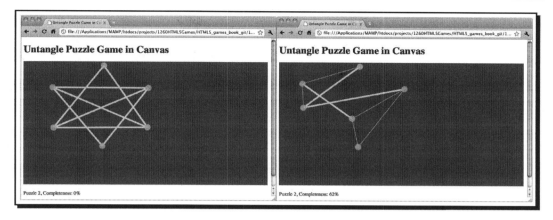

What just happened?

We have added the game logic to our canvas so that we can play our circle dragging code that was created throughout the chapter.

Let's recall the variables we added to the untangleGame object. The following table lists the description and usage of these:

Variable	Description
circleRadius	The radius setting of all drawing circles.
thinLineThickness	The line thickness when drawing thin lines.
boldLineThickness	The line thickness when drawing bold lines.
circles	An array to store all drawn circles in the canvas.
lines	An array to store all drawn lines in the canvas.
targetCircle	Keeping track of the circle that we are dragging.
levels	Stores all initial data of each level in the JSON format.
currentLevel	A number to remember the current level.

Defining the leveling data

In each level, we have an initial position of the circles for the untangle puzzle. The level data is designed as an array of objects. Each object contains every level data. Inside every level data, there are three properties: level number, circles, and lines connecting the circles. The following table shows the properties in each level data:

Level property	Definition	Discussion
level	The level number of the object.	This is a number in each level object to let us easily know which level we are in.
circles	An array of circles' position in the level.	This defines how the circles are placed initially when the level is set up.
relationships	An array of relationships defining which circles connect to each other.	There are some lines connecting the circles in each level. We design the line connections so that there is a solution in each level. The line relationship defines which circle connects to which circle. For example, the following code means circle 1 is connected to circle 2: `{"connectedPoints" : [1,2]}`

After every level data is defined well with our custom structure

Determining level-up

The level is complete when there are no lines intersecting with each other. We loop through each line and see how many lines are thin. Thin lines mean they are not intersected with others. We can use the thin lines to all line ratios to get the percentage of the level of completeness:

```
var progress = 0;
for (var i in untangleGame.lines) {
  if (untangleGame.lines[i].thickness == untangleGame.
  thinLineThickness) {
    progress++;
  }
}
var progressPercentage =   Math.floor(progress/untangleGame.lines.
length * 100);
```

We can then simply determine the level has been completed when the progress is 100 percent:

```
if ($("#progress").html() == "100") {
  // level complete, level up code
}
```

Displaying current level and completeness progress

We have a sentence below the canvas game describing the current level status and progress. It is used for displaying the game status to the players so they know that they are making progress in the game:

```
<p>Puzzle <span id="level">0</span>, Completeness:
<span id="progress">0</span>%</p>
```

We use the jQuery HTML function that we discussed in Chapter 2, *Getting Started with DOM-based Game development*, to update the completeness progress:

```
$("#progress").html(progressPercentage);
```

Have a go hero

We have only defined three levels in the example untangle puzzle game. It is not fun enough to play with three levels. How about adding more levels to the game? If you cannot come up a level, try searching similar untangle games on the Internet and get some inspiration on the leveling.

Summary

We learned a lot in this chapter about drawing shapes and creating interaction with the new HTML5 canvas element and the drawing API.

Specifically, we covered:

◆ Drawing different paths and shapes in canvas, including circles, arcs, and lines.

◆ Adding mouse events and interaction with the drawn paths in the canvas.

◆ Dragging drawn paths in the canvas.

◆ Checking line intersection with the help of mathematics formulas.

◆ Creating an untangle puzzle game in which players need to drag the circles so the connecting lines are not intersected by each other.

Now that we've learned about basic drawing functions in the canvas and drawing API, use them to create a puzzle solving game in canvas. We're ready to learn some advanced drawing techniques in canvas. In the next chapter, we will enhance our untangle puzzle game with more canvas drawing APIs, such as drawing text, drawing images, and drawing gradients.

5

Building a Canvas Games Masterclass

In the previous chapter, we explored some basic canvas context drawing APIs and created a game named Untangle. In this chapter, we are going to enhance the game by using some other context drawing APIs.

In this chapter we shall:

◆ Fill our game objects with gradient color
◆ Fill text in the canvas with custom webfont
◆ Draw images in Canvas
◆ Animate a sprite sheet image
◆ And build multiple canvas layers

The following screenshot is a preview to the final result that we are going to build through this chapter. It is a canvas-based Untangle game with an animated game guideline and several subtle details:

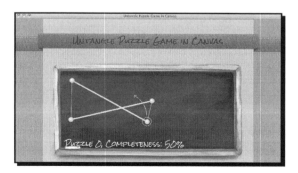

So let's get on with it...

Filling shapes with gradient color

We covered filling solid color in the last chapter. Canvas can do far more when filling shapes. We can fill the shape with both linear and radial gradient.

Time for action – Drawing a gradient color background to the Untangle game

Let's improve the black solid background we have now. How about drawing a gradient from top to bottom?

1. We will use the Untangle game we created in the last chapter as a starting point. Open the `html5games.untangle.js` JavaScript file in the text editor.

2. Add the following code in the `gameloop` function after clearing the canvas to draw the **gradient** background:

```
var bg_gradient = ctx.createLinearGradient(0,0,0,ctx.canvas.
height);
bg_gradient.addColorStop(0, "#000000");
bg_gradient.addColorStop(1, "#555555");
ctx.fillStyle = bg_gradient;
ctx.fillRect(0,0,ctx.canvas.width,ctx.canvas.height);
```

3. Save the files and preview the `index.html` in the browser. The background should be a linear gradient with black on top which gradually becomes grey at the bottom.

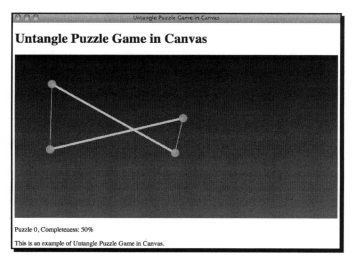

What just happened?

We just filled a rectangle with a **linear gradient** color. To fill linear gradient color, all we need to do is set the starting point and ending point of the gradient. Then we add several color stops between them.

Here is how we use the linear gradient function:

```
createLinearGradient(x1, y1, x2, y2);
```

Argument	Definition
x1	The starting point of the gradient.
y1	
x2	The ending point of the gradient.
y2	

Adding color stops in the gradient color

It is not enough to just have the starting and ending point. We also need to define what color we use and how it is applied to the gradient. It is called a **color stop** in gradient. We can add a color stop to the gradient by using the following `gradient` function:

```
addColorStop(position, color);
```

Argument	Definition	Discussion
position	A floating number between 0 and 1.	Position 0 means the color stops at the starting point and 1 means it stops at the ending point. Any number between 0 and 1 means it stops in between the starting and ending point.
		For example, 0.5 means a half and 0.33 means 30 percent away from the starting point.
color	The color style of that color stop.	The color style shares the same syntax from the CSS color styling. We may use the HEX expression, such as #FFDDAA. Or other color styles such as RGBA color name.

The follow screenshot shows a side-by-side comparison between a linear gradient setting and the result drawing. The starting point and ending point defines the scope and the angle of the gradient. The color stops define how the color mixes between the gradient scopes:

starting point (108, 180)
gradient.addColorStop(0, "#000");

gradient.addColorStop(0.5. "#bbb");

cyx.fillRect(150,150,200,200);

ending point (350,350)
gradient.addColorStop(1, "#333");

Adding color stop with opacity

We can set an opacity value to the color stop by using the RGBA function. The following code tells the gradient to start by using red color with half opacity:

```
gradient.addColorStop(0, "rgba(255, 0, 0, 0.5)");
```

Filling radial gradient color

There are two types of gradients in the Canvas drawing API. The one we just used is called linear gradient. The other one is **radial gradient**. The radial gradient fills the gradient from one circle to another circle.

Time for action – Filling the circles with radial gradient color

Imagine that we now fill our dragging circles to radial gradient. We will change the solid yellow circles to white-yellow gradient:

1. Open the `html5game.untangle.js` JavaScript file. We are going to modify the code we used to draw the circle in the game.

2. After we draw the circle path with the `arc` function and before we fill it we replace the original solid color style setting to the following radial gradient color:

```
function drawCircle(ctx, x, y) {
      // prepare the radial gradients fill style
      var circle_gradient = ctx.createRadialGradient(x-3,y-
      3,1,x,y,untangleGame.circleRadius);
      circle_gradient.addColorStop(0, "#fff");
      circle_gradient.addColorStop(1, "#cc0");
      ctx.fillStyle = circle_gradient;

   // draw the path
   ctx.beginPath();
   ctx.arc(x, y, untangleGame.circleRadius, 0, Math.PI*2, true);
   ctx.closePath();

   // actually fill the circle path
   ctx.fill();
}
```

3. Save the modified file and preview the `index.html` in a web browser. The circles are now filled with radial gradient color.

In the following screenshot I've scaled up the drawing to 200 percent to better demonstrate the radial gradient in the circle:

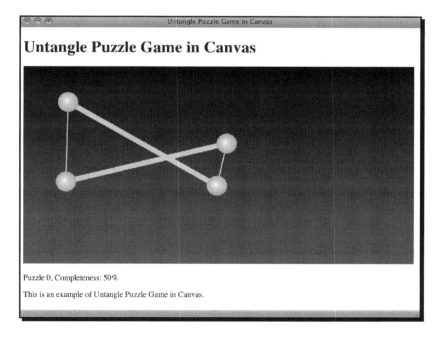

What just happened?

We just made the dragging circles look more realistic by filling a radial gradient.

Here is how we create a radial gradient:

```
createRadialGradient(x1, y1, r1, x2, y2, r2);
```

Argument	Definition
x1, y1	The center of the starting circle in x and y in the canvas coordinate.
r1	The radius of the starting circle.
x2, y2	The center of the ending circle in x and y in the canvas coordinate.
r2	The radius of the ending circle.

The following screenshot shows a side-by-side comparison between a radial gradient setting and the final result drawing in canvas:

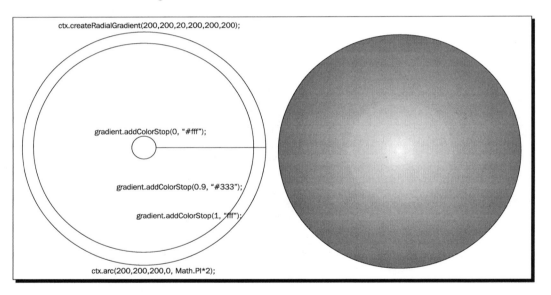

The radial gradient blends the color from the starting circle to the ending circle. In this gradient circle, the starting circle is a small circle in the center and the ending circle is the outermost circle. There are three color stops. A white color stops at both the starting and ending circle; another dark color stops 90 percent away from the starting circle.

Have a go hero – Filling gradients

We add color stops to the gradients to define how the colors blend. What happens if we forget to add any color stops to the gradient and fill a rectangle? What if we only define one color stop? Try experimenting with the color stop settings.

In the radial gradient example, the small starting circle is inside the bigger ending circle. What happens if the starting circle is bigger than the ending one? How about if the starting circle is not inside the ending circle? That is, what happens if the two circles do not overlap?

Drawing text in canvas

Imagine now we want to show the progress level directly inside the canvas. Canvas provides us with methods to draw text inside canvas.

Time for action – Displaying the progress level text inside the canvas element

1. We will continue using our Untangle game. Open the `html5games.untangle.js` JavaScript file in text editor.

2. First, let's make the level progress percentage a global variable so we can use it in different places:

```
var untangleGame = {
  circles: [],
  thinLineThickness: 1,
  boldLineThickness: 5,
  lines: [],
  currentLevel: 0,
    progressPercentage: 0
};
```

3. Add the following code after the canvas drawing code in the `gameloop` function:

```
// draw the title text
ctx.font = "26px Arial";
ctx.textAlign = "center";
ctx.fillStyle = "#ffffff";
ctx.fillText("Untangle Game",ctx.canvas.width/2,50);

// draw the level progress text
ctx.textAlign = "left";
ctx.textBaseline = "bottom";
```

```
ctx.fillText("Puzzle "+untangleGame.currentLevel+", Completeness:
" + untangleGame.progressPercentage + "%", 20,ctx.canvas.height-
5);
```

4. Save the file and preview the `index.html` in a web browser. We will see that the text is now drawn inside the canvas.

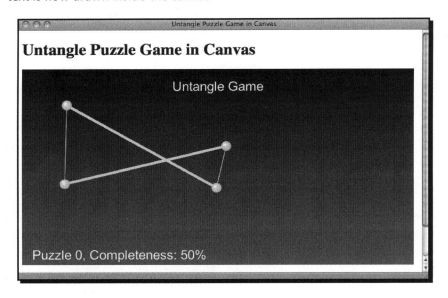

What just happened?

We have just drawn the title and the level progress text in our canvas-based game. We draw text in canvas by using the *fillText* function. The following table shows how we use the function:

```
fillText(string, x, y);
```

Argument	Definition
string	The text that we are going to draw.
x	The x coordinate that the text draws.
y	The y coordinate that the text draws.

This is the basic setting to draw a text. There are several more drawing context properties to set up the text drawing.

Context properties	Definition	Discussion
`context.font`	The font style of the text.	It shares the same syntax we used to declare font style in CSS. For example, the following code sets the font style to 20 pixels bold with Arial typeface: ```\nctx.font = "bold 20px\nArial";\n```
`context.textAlign`	The text alignment.	The **alignment** defines how the text aligns. It can be one of the following values: ◆ start ◆ end ◆ left ◆ right ◆ center For instance, if we are going to place a text on the right edge of the canvas. Using `left` alignment means we need to calculate text width in order to know the x coordinate of the text. When using right alignment in this case, all we need to do is set the x position directly to the canvas width. The text will then automatically be placed on the right edge of the canvas.
`context.textBaseline`	The text baseline.	The following lists the common value of a **textBaseline**: ◆ top ◆ middle ◆ bottom ◆ alphabet Similar to the text alignment, the `bottom` **baseline** is useful when we want to place our text at the bottom of the canvas. The y position of the `fillText` function is based on the bottom baseline of the text instead of the top. The `alphabet` baseline aligns the y position based on the lower case alphabet. The following screenshot shows our text drawing with **alphabet** baseline.

PUZZLE 0, COMPLETENESS: 50%

 Please beware that the text drawing in canvas is treated as bitmap image data. That means visitors cannot select the text; search engines cannot index the text; we cannot search them. For this reason, we should think carefully whether we want to draw the text inside a canvas or just place them directly in the DOM.

Pop quiz – Drawing text in canvas

1. If we are going to draw a text close to the bottom rightcorner of the canvas which alignment and baseline setting is better?

    a. Left alignment, bottom baseline.

    b. Center alignment, alphabet baseline.

    c. Right alignment, bottom baseline.

    d. Center alignment, middle baseline.

2. We are going to make a realistic book with a flipping effect with the latest open web standard. Which of the following settings is better?

    a. Draw the realistic book in canvas, including all the text and the flipping effect.

    b. Put all text and content in DOM and draw the realistic page-flipping effect in canvas.

Using embedded web font inside canvas

We used custom font in our memory matching game in the previous chapter. The custom font embedding also worked in the canvas. Let's conduct an experiment on drawing a custom font in our Untangle game in canvas.

Time for action – Embedding Google Web Font into the canvas element

Let's draw the canvas texts with a handwriting style font:

1. First, go to the Google Font Directory and choose a handwriting style font. I used the font **Rock Salt** and you can get it from the following URL:

   ```
   http://code.google.com/webfonts/family?family=Rock+Salt&subset=
   latin#code.
   ```

2. The Google font directory provides a CSS link code that we can add to our game in order to embed the font. Add the following CSS link to the head of index.html:

   ```
   <link href='http://fonts.googleapis.com/css?family=Rock+Salt'
   rel='stylesheet' type='text/css'>
   ```

3. The next thing is to use the font. We open the html5games.untangle.js JavaScript file and modify the context font property to the following:

   ```
   ctx.font = "26px 'Rock Salt'";
   ```

4. It is time to open our game in the web browser to test the result. The text drawn in the canvas now is using the font we choose in the Google font directory.

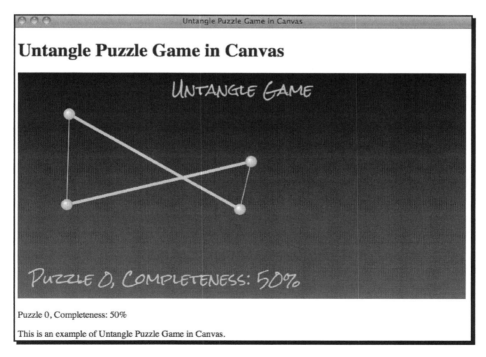

What just happened?

We just chose a web font and embedded it into the canvas when drawing text. It shows that we can style the font family of the filled text in canvas just like other DOM elements.

> Sometimes the width of the text varies in different font families although they have the same word count. In this case, we can use the measureText function to get the width of the text we draw. The following link to the Mozilla Developer Network explains how we can use the function:
>
> https://developer.mozilla.org/en/Drawing_text_using_a_canvas#measureText()

Drawing images in canvas

We have drawn some text inside canvas. What about drawing an image? Yes. Drawing images and image manipulation is one big feature that canvas has.

Time for action – Adding graphics to the game

We are going to draw a blackboard background to the game:

1. Download the graphic files from the code example bundle or the following URL. The graphics files include all graphics that we need in this chapter:

    http://gamedesign.cc/html5games/1260_05_example_graphics.zip

2. Put the newly downloaded graphics files into a folder named images.

3. We will load an image and loading means it may take a while until the image is loaded. Ideally, we should not start the game until all game assets are loaded. In this case, we can prepare a splash screen with loading words to let the player know the game is going to start later. Add the following code in the jQuery ready function after clearing the canvas context:

```
// draw a splash screen when loading the game background
// draw gradients background
var bg_gradient = ctx.createLinearGradient(0,0,0,ctx.canvas.
height);
bg_gradient.addColorStop(0, "#cccccc");
bg_gradient.addColorStop(1, "#efefef");
ctx.fillStyle = bg_gradient;
ctx.fillRect(0, 0, ctx.canvas.width, ctx.canvas.height);
```

```
// draw the loading text
ctx.font = "34px 'Rock Salt'";
ctx.textAlign = "center";
ctx.fillStyle = "#333333";
ctx.fillText("loading...",ctx.canvas.width/2,canvas.height/2);
```

4. Then it is time to really load the image. There is a `board.png` in the graphics file we just downloaded. It is a blackboard graphics we will draw to the canvas as background. Add the following code after the code we just added in the previous step:

```
// load the background image
untangleGame.background = new Image();
untangleGame.background.onload = function() {
  // setup an interval to loop the game loop
    setInterval(gameloop, 30);
}
untangleGame.background.onerror = function() {
  console.log("Error loading the image.");
}
untangleGame.background.src = "images/board.png";
```

5. In the `gameloop` function, we draw the image into the canvas after clearing the context and before drawing anything else. Since the image loading takes time, we also need to ensure it is loaded before drawing it:

```
// draw the image background
ctx.drawImage(untangleGame.background, 0, 0);
```

6. We had set up a `levels` array to store the level data including the initial circles position. Some circles are now overlapped with the border of the background image so we may want to alter the circles position. Update the circles array of level 2 with the following new values:

```
"circles" : [{"x" : 192, "y" : 155},
{"x" : 353, "y" : 109},
{"x" : 493, "y" : 156},
{"x" : 490, "y" : 236},
{"x" : 348, "y" : 276},
{"x" : 195, "y" : 228}],
```

7. Also we need to adjust the position of the level progress text. Modify the `fill text` function calling as the following code with a different position value:

```
ctx.fillText("Puzzle "+untangleGame.currentLevel+", Completeness:
" + untangleGame.progressPercentage + "%", 60, ctx.canvas.height-
80);
```

8. Next, we do not want a background color set to the canvas now because we have a PNG background with a transparent border. Open the `untangle.css` file and remove the background property in canvas.

9. Now save all files and open the `index.html` in the web browser. The background should be there and the handwritten fonts should match our blackboard theme.

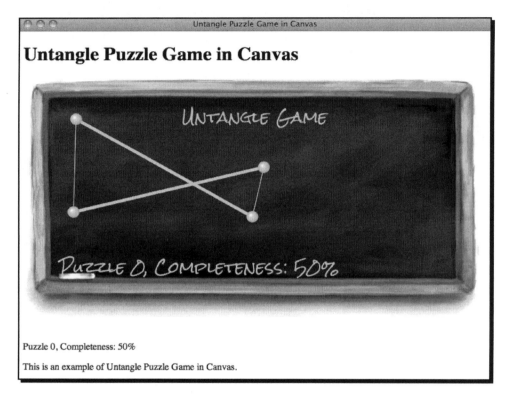

What just happened?

We just drew an image inside the canvas element.

There are two common ways to draw an image on canvas. We can either reference an existing `img` tag or load the image on the fly in JavaScript.

Here is how we reference the existing image tag in canvas.

Assuming that we have the following `img` tag in HTML:

```
<img id="board" src="img/board.png">
```

We can draw the image in canvas by using the following JavaScript code:

```
var img = document.getElementById('board');
context.drawImage(img, x, y);
```

Here is another code snippet to load the image without attaching the `img` tag into DOM. If we load the image inside JavaScript, we need to make sure the image is loaded before drawing it on canvas. Therefore, we draw the image after the `onload` event of the image:

```
var board = new Image();
board.onload = function() {
  context.drawImage(board, x, y);
}
board.src = "images/board.png";
```

The order meters when setting the onload event handler and assigning the image src

When we assign the `src` property to the image and if the image is cached by the browser, some browsers fire the `onload` event immediately. If we place the `onload` event handler after assigning the `src` property, we may miss it because it is fired before we set the event handler.

In our example, we used the latter approach. We create an Image object and load the background. When the image is loaded, we start the game loop and thus start the game.

Another event that we should handle when loading the image is the `onerror` event. It is especially useful when we are accessing extra network data. We have the following code snippet to check the error in our example:

```
untangleGame.background.onerror = function() {
  console.log("Error loading the image.");
}
```

Have a go hero

The error loading now only displays a message in the console. The console is normally not viewed by players. How about designing an alert dialog or some other approaches to tell players that the game failed to load the game assets?

Using the drawImage function

There are three behaviors to draw an image in the canvas. We can draw the image without any modification on a given coordinate, we can also draw the image with a scaling factor on a given coordinate, or we can even crop the image and draw only the clipping region.

The `drawImage` function accepts several arguments:

```
drawImage(image, x, y);
```

Argument	Definition	Discussion
image	The image reference that we are going to draw.	We either get the image reference by getting an existing `img` element or creating a JavaScript `Image` object.
x	The x position to place the image in canvas coordinate.	The x and y coordinate is where we place the image with respect to its top-left corner.
y	The y position to place the image in canvas coordinate.	

```
drawImage(image, x, y, width, height);
```

Argument	Definition	Discussion
image	The image reference that we are going to draw.	We either get the image reference by getting an existing `img` element or creating a JavaScript `Image` object.
x	The x position to place the image in canvas coordinate.	The x and y coordinate is where we place the image with respect to its top-left corner.
y	The y position to place the image in canvas coordinate.	
width	The width of the final drawn image.	We are applying scale to the image if the width and height is not the same as the original image.
height	The height of the final drawn image.	

```
drawImage(image, sx, sy, sWidth, sHeight, dx, dy, width, height);
```

Argument	Definition	Discussion
image	The image reference that we are going to draw.	We either get the image reference by getting an existing `img` element or creating a JavaScript `Image` object.
sx	The x coordinate of the top-left corner of the clipping region.	The clipping x, y, width, height together defines a rectangular clipping area. The given image is clipped by this rectangle.
sy	The y coordinate of the top-left corner of the clipping region.	
sWidth	The width of the clipping region.	
sHeight	The height of the clipping region.	

Argument	Definition	Discussion
dx	The x position to place the image in canvas coordinate.	The x and y coordinate is where we place the image with respect to its top-left corner.
dy	The y position to place the image in canvas coordinate.	
width	The width of the final drawn image.	We are applying scale to the clipped image if the width and height is not the same as the clipping dimension.
height	The height of the final drawn image.	

Have a go hero – Optimizing the background image

In the example, we draw the blackboard image as background in every call of the `gameloop` function. Since our background is static and does not change along the time, clearing it and redrawing it again and again is wasting CPU resources. How can we optimize this performance issue?

Decorating the canvas-based game

We have enhanced the canvas game with gradients and images. Before moving forward, let's decorate the web page of our canvas game.

Time for action – Adding CSS styles and images decoration to the game

We are going to build a center-aligned layout with a game title:

1. We embed another font from the Google font directory to style the normal body text. Add the following CSS link within the `head` in `index.html`:

   ```
   <link href='http://fonts.googleapis.com/css?family=Josefin+Sans:60
   0' rel='stylesheet' type='text/css'>
   ```

2. It is easier for us to style the layout with one grouping DOM element. We put all the elements inside the body into a section with `id` page:

   ```
   <section id="page">
     ...
   </section>
   ```

3. Let's apply CSS to the page layout. Replace existing content in the `untangle.css` file with the following code:

   ```
   html, body {
   ```

```
  background: url(../images/title_bg.png) 50% 0 no-repeat, url(../
  images/bg_repeat.png) 50% 0 repeat-y #889ba7;
  margin: 0;
  font-family: 'Josefin Sans', arial, serif;
  color: #111;
}

#game{
  position:relative;
}

#page {
  width: 821px;
  min-height: 800px;
  margin: 0 auto;
  padding: 0;
  text-align: center;
  text-shadow: 0 1px 5px rgba(60,60,60,.6);
}

header {
  height: 88px;
  padding-top: 36px;
  margin-bottom: 50px;
  font-family: "Rock Salt", Arial, sans-serif;
  font-size: 14px;
  text-shadow: 0 1px 0 rgba(200,200,200,.5);
  color: #121;
}
```

4. Now we have the header text in the ribbon. Showing the title again in canvas seems redundant. Let's remove the following line of code which draws the title:

   ```
   ctx.fillText("Untangle Game",ctx.canvas.width/2,50);
   ```

5. It is time to save all the files and preview it in the web browser. We should see a title ribbon and a well-styled layout that is center-aligned. The following screenshot shows the result:

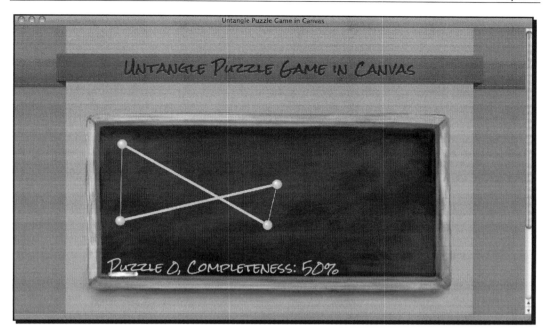

What just happened?

We just decorated the web page that contains our canvas-based game. Although our game is based on canvas drawing, it does not restrict us from decorating the whole web page with graphics and CSS styles.

Default background of the canvas element

The default background of the canvas element is transparent. If we do not set any background CSS style of the canvas, it will be transparent. It is useful when our drawing is not a rectangle. In this example, the textured layout background shows within the canvas region.

Pop quiz – Styling a canvas background

1. How can we set the canvas background to be transparent?

   a. Set the background color to #ffffff.

   b. Do nothing. It is transparent by default.

Animating a sprite sheet in canvas

We first used **sprite sheet** images in Chapter 3, *Building a Memory Matching Game in CSS3*, when displaying a deck of playing cards.

Time for action – Making a game guide animation

There is a graphics file named `guide_sprite.png` in the images folder. It is a game guideline graphic that contains each step of the animation.

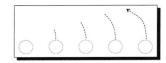

Let's draw this guide into our game with **animations**:

1. Open the `html5games.untangle.js` JavaScript file in the text editor.

2. In the jQuery `ready` function add the following code:

    ```
    // load the guide sprite image
    untangleGame.guide = new Image();
    untangleGame.guide.onload = function() {
      untangleGame.guideReady = true;

      // setup timer to switch the display frame of the guide sprite
      untangleGame.guideFrame = 0;
      setInterval(guideNextFrame, 500);
    }
    untangleGame.guide.src = "images/guide_sprite.png";
    ```

3. We add the following function to move the current frame to the next frame every 500 meters:

    ```
    function guideNextFrame()
    {
      untangleGame.guideFrame++;
      // there are only 6 frames (0-5) in the guide animation.
      // we loop back the frame number to frame 0 after frame 5.
      if (untangleGame.guideFrame > 5)
      {
        untangleGame.guideFrame = 0;
      }
    }
    ```

4. In the `gameloop` function, we draw the guide animation according to the current frame.

```
// draw the guide animation
if (untangleGame.currentLevel == 0 && untangleGame.guideReady)
{
  // the dimension of each frame is 80x130.
  var nextFrameX = untangleGame.guideFrame * 80;
  ctx.drawImage(untangleGame.guide, nextFrameX, 0, 80, 130, 325,
  130, 80, 130);
}
```

5. Let's watch the animation in the web browser by opening the index.html. The following screenshot demonstrates the animation of the game guideline. The guideline animation will play and loop until the player levels up:

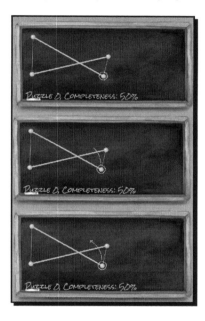

What just happened?

We can draw only a region of an image when using the drawImage context function.

The following screenshot demonstrates the process of the animation step by step. The rectangle is the clipping region. We used a variable named guideFrame to control which frame to show. The width of each frame is 80. Therefore, we get the x position of the clipping region by multiplying the width and the current frame number:

```
var nextFrameX = untangleGame.guideFrame * 80;
ctx.drawImage(untangleGame.guide, nextFrameX, 0, 80, 130, 325, 130,
80, 130);
```

The `guideFrame` variable is updated every 500 meters by the following `guideNextFrame` function:

```
function guideNextFrame()
{
  untangleGame.guideFrame++;
  // there are only 6 frames (0-5) in the guide animation.
  // we loop back the frame number to frame 0 after frame 5.
  if (untangleGame.guideFrame > 5)
  {
    untangleGame.guideFrame = 0;
  }
}
```

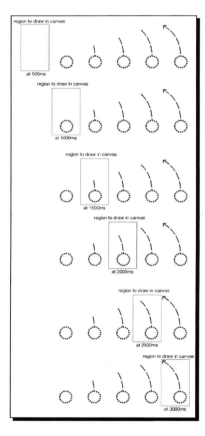

Animating a sprite is a commonly used technique when developing games. There are some benefits of using sprite animation when developing games in traditional video games. The reasons may not apply to the web game development but we have other benefits of using sprite sheet animation:

◆ All frames are loaded as one file so the whole animation is ready once the sprite file is loaded.

◆ Putting all frames into one file means we can reduce the HTTP request from the web browser to the server. If each frame is a file, the browser requests the file many times while now it just requests one file and uses one HTTP request.

◆ Putting different images into one file also helps reduce the duplicate file's header, footer, and meta data.

◆ Putting all frames into one image means we can easily clip the image to display any frame without the complex code to change the image source.

It is usually used in character animation. The following screenshot is a **sprite animation** of an angry cat that I used in an HTML5 game named Neighbours (`http://gamedesign.cc/html5games/neighbours/`):

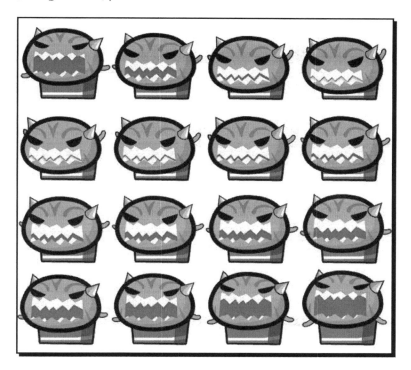

We built the sprite sheet animation by clipping the frame and setting up the timer ourselves in this example. When working with a lot of animations, we may want to use some third party sprite animation plugin or create our own canvas sprite animation to better reuse and manage the logic code.

Sprite animation is an important topic in HTML5 games development and there are many online resources discussing this topic. The following links are some of them:

The sprite animation tutorial (`http://codeutopia.net/blog/2009/08/21/using-canvas-to-do-bitmap-sprite-animation-in-javascript/`) from CodeUtopia discusses how we can make a sprite object from scratch and use it to animate a sprite.

The sprite animation demo (`http://www.johnegraham2.com/web-technology/html-5-canvas-tag-sprite-animation-demo/`) by John Graham provides another sprite object to animate a sprite in canvas.

The Spritely (`http://www.spritely.net/`), on the other hand, provides sprite animation over the DOM element with CSS. It is useful when we want to animate a sprite without using canvas.

Creating a multi-layers canvas game

Now all things are drawn into the context and it has no other state to distinguish the drawn items. We may split the canvas game into different layers and code the logic to control and draw each layer at a time.

Time for action – Dividing the game into four layers

We are going to separate our Untangle game into four layers:

1. In `index.htm`, we changed the canvas HTML to the following code. It contains several canvases within a section:

```
<section id="layers">
  <canvas id="bg" width="768" height="440">
    Sorry, your web browser does not support canvas content.
  </canvas>
  <canvas id="guide" width="768" height="440"></canvas>
  <canvas id="game" width="768" height="440"></canvas>
  <canvas id="ui" width="768" height="440"></canvas>
</section>
```

2. We also need to apply some styles to the canvas so they overlap with each other to create the multiple layers effect. Also we have to prepare a `fadeout` class and `dim` class to make the target transparent. Add the following code into the `untangle.css` file:

```
#layers {
```

```
    height: 440px;
    position: relative;
    margin: 0 auto;
    width:768px;
    height: 440px;
}
#layers canvas{
    left: 50%;
    margin-left: -384px;
    position: absolute;
}
#guide {
    opacity: .7;
}
#guide.fadeout {
    opacity: 0;
    -webkit-transition: opacity .5s linear;
    transition: opacity .5s linear;
}
#ui {
    -webkit-transition: opacity .3s linear;
    transition: opacity .3s linear;
}
#ui.dim {
    opacity: .3;
}
```

3. In the `html5games.untangle.js` JavaScript file, we modify the code to support the layers feature. First, we add an array to store the context reference of each canvas:

```
untangleGame.layers = new Array();
```

4. Then, we get the context reference and store them in the array:

```
// prepare layer 0 (bg)
var canvas_bg = document.getElementById("bg");
untangleGame.layers[0] = canvas_bg.getContext("2d");

// prepare layer 1 (guide)
var canvas_guide = document.getElementById("guide");
untangleGame.layers[1] = canvas_guide.getContext("2d");

// prepare layer 2 (game)
var canvas = document.getElementById("game");
var ctx = canvas.getContext("2d");
```

```
untangleGame.layers[2] = ctx;

// prepare layer 3 (ui)
var canvas_ui = document.getElementById("ui");
untangleGame.layers[3] = canvas_ui.getContext("2d");
```

5. Since now the game canvas are overlapped together, the mouse event listener we had in the `game` canvas does not fire anymore. We can listen to the event from the parent `layers` DIV which has the same position and dimension of the canvas:

```
$("#layers").mousedown(function(e)
$("#layers").mousemove(function(e)
$("#layers").mouseup(function(e)
```

6. We are going to separate the drawing part into different functions for different layers. In the following `drawLayerBG` function, it is only in charge of drawing the background:

```
function drawLayerBG()
{
  var ctx = untangleGame.layers[0];

  clear(ctx);
  // draw the image background
  ctx.drawImage(untangleGame.background, 0, 0);
}
```

7. We draw the background layer when the background image is loaded. Add the following highlighted code into the `onload` event of the background:

```
untangleGame.background.onload = function() {
  drawLayerBG();

  // setup an interval to loop the game loop
  setInterval(gameloop, 30);
}
```

8. We divide the game loop into three different functions for the specified layer:

```
function gameloop() {
  drawLayerGuide();
  drawLayerGame();
  drawLayerUI();
}
```

9. We put the guideline animation into a dedicated canvas now so we can easily apply CSS style to fade out the guideline later:

```
function drawLayerGuide()
{
  var ctx = untangleGame.layers[1];

  clear(ctx);

  // draw the guide animation
  if (untangleGame.guideReady)
  {
    // the dimension of each frame is 80x130.
    var nextFrameX = untangleGame.guideFrame * 80;
    ctx.drawImage(untangleGame.guide, nextFrameX, 0, 80, 130, 325,
    130, 80, 130);
  }

  // fade out the guideline after level 0
  if (untangleGame.currentLevel == 1)
  {
    $("#guide").addClass('fadeout');
  }
}
```

10. The following `drawLayerGame` keeps all the drawing code we used in the gameplay. Most of the code is from the original `gameloop` function:

```
function drawLayerGame()
{
  // get the reference of the canvas element and the drawing
  context.
  var ctx = untangleGame.layers[2];

  // draw the game state visually
  // clear the canvas before drawing.
  clear(ctx);

  // draw all remembered line
  for(var i=0;i<untangleGame.lines.length;i++) {
    var line = untangleGame.lines[i];
    var startPoint = line.startPoint;
    var endPoint = line.endPoint;
    var thickness = line.thickness;
    drawLine(ctx, startPoint.x, startPoint.y, endPoint.x,
    endPoint.y, thickness);
```

```
  }

  // draw all remembered circles
  for(var i=0;i<untangleGame.circles.length;i++) {
    var circle = untangleGame.circles[i];
    drawCircle(ctx, circle.x, circle.y, circle.radius);
  }

}
```

11. The level progress text is now placed in the UI layer and drawn by the `drawLayerUI` function. It uses a dedicated layer so we can easily dim the opacity when the text is overlapped with the game objects, such as circles:

```
function drawLayerUI()
{
  var ctx = untangleGame.layers[3];

  clear(ctx);

  // draw the level progress text
  ctx.font = "26px 'Rock Salt'";
  ctx.fillStyle = "#dddddd";
  ctx.textAlign = "left";
  ctx.textBaseline = "bottom";
  ctx.fillText("Puzzle "+untangleGame.currentLevel+",
  Completeness: ", 60,ctx.canvas.height-80);
  ctx.fillText(untangleGame.progressPercentage+"%",450,
  ctx.canvas.height-80);

  // get all circles, check if the ui overlap with the game
  objects
  var isOverlappedWithCircle = false;
  for(var i in untangleGame.circles) {
    var point = untangleGame.circles[i];
    if (point.y > 310)
    {
      isOverlappedWithCircle = true;
    }
  }
  if (isOverlappedWithCircle)
  {
    $("#ui").addClass('dim');
  }
  else
```

```
  {
    $("#ui").removeClass('dim');
  }
}
```

12. Save all the files and check our big code changes in the web browser. The game
should be displayed as if we haven't changed anything. Try dragging the circle down
close to the bottom edge of the blackboard. The level progress text should dim to
a low opacity. When you finish the first level, the guideline animation will fade out
gracefully. The following screenshot shows the level progress in half opacity:

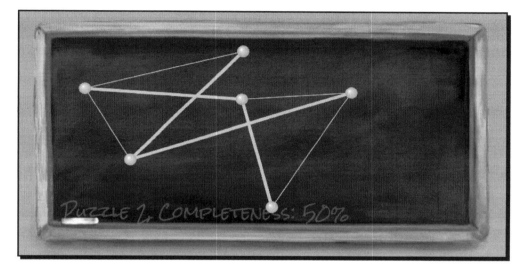

What just happened?

There are four canvases in total now. Each canvas is in charge of one layer. The layers are
divided into background, game guideline, game itself, and the user interface showing the
level progress.

By default, the canvases, like other elements, are placed one after the other. In order
to overlap all canvases to construct the layer effect, we applied the `absolute` position
to them.

The following screenshots show the four layers setting now in our game. By default, the later added DOM is on top of the one added before. Therefore, `bg` canvas is at the bottom and `ui` is on the top:

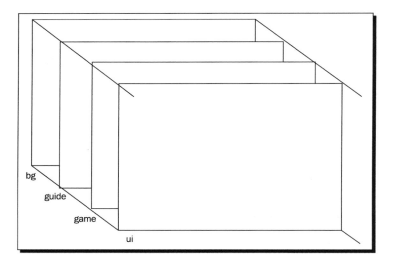

Mixing CSS technique with Canvas drawing

We are creating a canvas-based game but we are not restricted to use only a canvas drawing API. The level progress information is now in another canvas with ID `ui`. In this example, we mixed the CSS technique we discussed in Chapter 3, *Building a Memory Matching Game in CSS3*.

When we drag the circles around the canvas, they may overlap the level information. When drawing the UI canvas layer, we check whether any circle's coordinate is too low and is overlapping the text. We then fade the UI canvas CSS opacity so it does not distract the player from the circles.

We also fade out the guideline animation after the player levels up. This is done by fading out the whole `guide` canvas with CSS transition easing to 0 opacity. Since the `guide` canvas is only in charge of that animation, hiding that canvas does not affect other elements:

```
if (untangleGame.currentLevel == 1)
{
  $("#guide").addClass('fadeout');
}
```

Clearing only the changed region to boost canvas performance

We can use the `clear` function to only clear part of the canvas context. This will give the performance some boost because it avoids redrawing the entire canvas context every time. This is achieved by marking the 'dirty' region of the context which has changed state since last drawn.

In the guide canvas layer in our example, we may consider clearing only the region of the sprite sheet image drawing instead of the whole canvas.

We may not see significant differences in simple canvas examples but it helps boost the performance when we have a complex canvas game that includes many sprite images animations and complex shape drawings.

Have a go hero

We fade out the guide when the players advance to level 2. How about we fade out the guide animation once the player drags any circles? How can we do that?

Summary

We learned a lot in this chapter about drawing gradients, text, and images in canvas.

Specifically, we covered:

- Filling shapes with either linear or radial gradient
- Filling text in canvas with font-face embedding and other text styles
- Drawing images into canvas
- Animating a sprite sheet by the `clipping` function when drawing images
- Dividing the game into several layers by stacking several canvas elements
- Mixing the CSS transition animation in a canvas-based game

One thing we haven't mentioned in this book is the bitmap manipulation in canvas. Canvas context is a bitmap data where we can apply an operation on each pixel. For instance, we may draw an image in the canvas and apply Photoshop-like filters to the image. We will not cover that in the book because image manipulation is an advanced topic and the application may not relate to game development.

There are some good canvas games examples on the Internet. The Canvas Demo (`http://www.canvasdemos.com/type/games/`) links the latest canvas games from other websites. The Game On 2010 gallery (`https://gaming.mozillalabs.com/games/`) from Mozilla lists a bundle of game entries for their gaming development competition. Some of them are made in canvas.

Now that we've learned about building games in canvas and making animation for game objects, such as game character, we are ready to add audio components and sound effects to our games in the next chapter.

We will get back to canvas-based games in *Chapter 9, Building a Physics Car Game with Box2D and Canvas*.

6
Adding Sound Effects to your Games

We have discussed several techniques of drawing game objects visually. In this chapter, we will focus on using the `audio` *tag that is introduced in the HTML5 specification. We can add sound effects, background music, and control the audio through the JavaScript API. In addition, we will build a music game in this chapter. It is a game that requires players to hit the correct string at the right time to produce the music.*

In this chapter, we will learn the following topics:

◆ Adding a sound effect to the play button

◆ Building a mini piano musical game

◆ Linking the music game and the play button

◆ Adding keyboard-driven to the game

◆ Creating a keyboard-driven music game

◆ Completing the musical game with level data recording and the game over event

The following screenshot shows the final result we will create through this chapter:

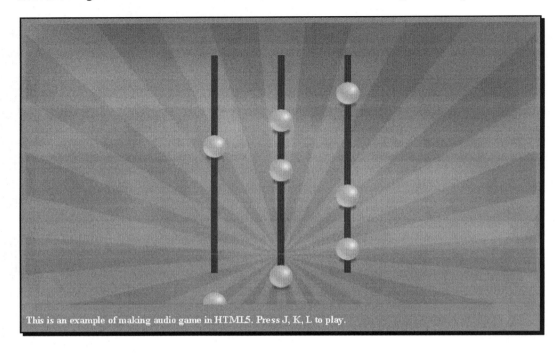

So, let's get on with it.

Adding a sound effect to the play button

We had several mouse interactions in the Untangle game examples in previous chapters. Now imagine that we want to have sound effects with the mouse interaction. This requires us to instruct the game about the audio file to be used. We will use the audio tag to create a sound effect on a button.

Time for action – Adding sound effects to the play button

We will start with the code example available in the code bundle. We will have the folder structure similar to the one shown in the following screenshot:

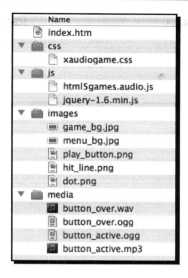

1. The `index.htm` file contains the basic structure of the HTML. Now let's add the following code to the body section of the `index.htm` file:

```
<div id="game">
    <section id="menu-scene" class="scene">
        <a href="#game"><span>Play</span></a>
    </section>
</div>
<audio id="buttonover">
    <source src="media/button_over.wav" />
    <source src="media/button_over.ogg" />
</audio>
<audio id="buttonactive">
    <source src="media/button_active.mp3" />
    <source src="media/button_active.ogg" />
</audio>
```

2. The HTML file accomplishes with a stylesheet. The file can be found in the code bundle named `audiogame.css`.

3. Next, we will add a sound effect to the button in the JavaScript file. Add the following JavaScript in the `html5games.audio.js` file:

```
//a global object variable to store all game scope variable.
var audiogame = {};

// init function when the DOM is ready
$(function(){
```

```
// get the references of the audio element.
audiogame.buttonOverSound =
    document.getElementById("buttonover");
audiogame.buttonOverSound.volume = 0.3;
audiogame.buttonActiveSound =
    document.getElementById("buttonactive");
audiogame.buttonActiveSound.volume = 0.3;

// listen the button event that links to #game
$("a[href='#game']")
.hover(function(){
    audiogame.buttonOverSound.currentTime = 0;
    audiogame.buttonOverSound.play();
}, function(){
    audiogame.buttonOverSound.pause();
});
.click(function(){
    audiogame.buttonActiveSound.currentTime = 0;
    audiogame.buttonActiveSound.play();

    return false;
});
});
```

4. Open the `index.htm` file in a browser. There, you should see a **PLAY** button on a yellow background, as shown in the following screenshot. Try to move the mouse on the button and click on it. You should be able to hear a sound when you hover over the button and another sound when you click on it:

What just happened?

We just created a basic HTML5 game layout with a play button placed in the middle of the page. The JavaScript file handles the mouse hover and clicks of the button and plays corresponding sound effects.

Defining an audio element

The easiest way to use the `audio` tag is by providing a source file. The following code snippet shows how we can define an audio element:

```
<audio>
    <source src="media/button_active.mp3" />
    <source src="media/button_active.ogg" />
    <!-- Any code for browser that does not support audio tag -->
</audio>
```

Showing the fallback content in the audio tag

The `audio` tag is newly introduced in the HTML5 specification. We can put the fallback content inside the `audio` tag, such as Flash movie to play the audio. The following link from HTML5 Rocks shows a quick guide on using the `audio` tag with Flash fallback:

`http://www.html5rocks.com/tutorials/audio/quick/`

Besides setting the source file of the `audio` tag, we can have additional controls by using several attributes. The following table shows the attributes we can set to the audio element:

Arguments	Definition	Explanation

src	Defines the source file of the audio element	When we use the `src` attribute in the `audio` tag, it specifies one source file of the audio file. For example, we load a sound effect `Ogg` file in the following code:
		
		`<audio src='sound.ogg'>`
		
		If we want to specify multiple files with different formats, then we use the `source` tag inside the audio element. The following code specifies the `audio` tag with different formats to support different web browsers:
		
		`<audio>`
		`    <source src='sound.ogg'>`
		`    <source src='sound.mp3'>`
		`    <source src='sound.wav'>`
		`</audio>`

Arguments	Definition	Explanation

autoplay	Specifies that the audio plays automatically once it is loaded	Autoplay is used as a standalone attribute. This means that there is no difference in the following two lines of code:
		
		``
		<audio src='file.ogg'
		    autoplay>
		<audio src='file.ogg
		    autoplay="autoplay">
		``

loop	Specifies that the audio plays from beginning again after playback finishes	This is also used as a standalone attribute.
preload	Specifies that the audio source is loaded once the page is loaded	The preload attribute takes either of the following values: ◆ preload="auto" ◆ preload="metadata" ◆ preload="none" When the preload is used as a standalone attribute, it acts as setting it to auto and the browser will preload the audio. When it is set as metadata, the browser will not preload the content of the audio. However, it will load the meta data of the audio such as the duration and size. When it is set to none, the browser will not preload the audio at all. The content and metadata is loaded once it is played.
controls	Shows the playback control of the audio	The controls attribute is a standalone attribute. It instructs the browser to show a playback control in the audio position.

The following screenshot shows the Chrome displaying controls:

Playing a sound

We can get the reference of the audio element by calling the `getElementById` function. Then, we play it by calling the `play` function. The following code plays the `buttonactive` audio:

```
<audio id="buttonactive">
   <source src="media/button_active.mp3" />
   <source src="media/button_active.ogg" />
</audio>
<script>
   document.getElementById("buttonactive").play();
</script>
```

The `play` function plays the audio from the elapsed time, which is stored in the `currentTime` property. The default value of `currentTime` is zero. The following code plays the audio from 3.5 seconds:

```
<script>
   document.getElementById("buttonactive").currentTime = 3.5;
   document.getElementById("buttonactive").play();
</script>
```

Pausing a sound

Similar to the play button, we can also pause the playback of an audio element by using the `pause` function. The following code pauses the `buttonactive` audio element:

```
<script>
   document.getElementById("buttonactive").pause();
</script>
```

> There is no `stop` function to stop the audio element. Instead, we can pause the audio and reset the `currentTime` property of the element to zero. The following code shows how we can stop an audio element:
>
> ```
> <script>
> document.getElementById("buttonactive").pause();
> document.getElementById("buttonactive").currentTime =
> 0;
> </script>
> ```

Adjusting the sound volume

We can also set the volume of the audio element. The volume must range between 0 and 1. We can set the volume to 0 to mute it, and set it to 1 for the maximum volume. The following code snippet sets the volume of the `buttonactive` audio to 30%:

```
<script>
  document.getElementById("buttonactive").volume = 0.3;
</script>
```

Using the jQuery hover event

jQuery provides a `hover` function to define the behavior when we mouse over and mouse out a DOM element. Here is how we use the `hover` function:

```
.hover(function1, function2);
```

Arguments	Discussion
function1	The function is executed when the mouse moves in.
function2	This is optional. The function is executed when the mouse moves out. When this function is not provided, the move out behavior is the same as function1.

In the following code, we play the mouse over sound effect when moving the mouse in and pause the sound during mouse out:

```
$("a[href='#game']").hover(function(){
   audiogame.buttonOverSound.currentTime = 0;
   audiogame.buttonOverSound.play();
},function(){
   audiogame.buttonOverSound.pause();
});
```

Creating the Ogg format audio to support Mozilla Firefox

We use an MP3 format and the **Ogg** format file when we define the source of the audio element. The Ogg is a free and open source media container format which is supported in Mozilla Firefox. We will use a free audio convertor to convert our MP3 files into an Ogg file.

 Wikipedia contains a detailed explanation on the Ogg format at the following URL:
`http://en.wikipedia.org/wiki/Ogg`

Time for action – Converting an MP3 sound to Ogg format with Audacity

Ogg is an open source standard that is free to use. There are many music players and convertors supporting it. We will use free software named **Audacity** to convert our MP3 files to the Ogg format:

1. Go to the following URL to download Audacity:

   `http://audacity.sourceforge.net/download/`

2. Install Audacity by following the instructions of the installer.

3. Open `button_over.mp3` in Audacity. The following screenshot shows Audacity with the MP3 file opened, waiting for us to start the conversion:

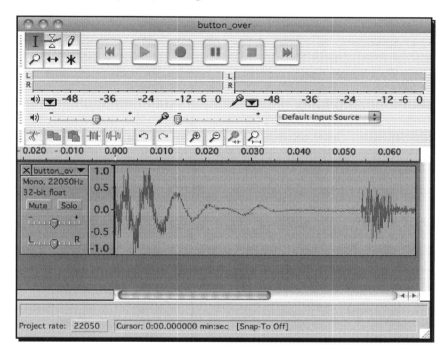

4. Click on **File | Export As Ogg Vorbis** to open the export dialog.

 At the time of writing this book, Audacity 1.3 beta was released and the export layout changed. Click on **File | Export ...** and choose the Ogg format in the export dialog.

5. Save the Ogg format file in the working directory.

What just happened?

We just converted an MP3 format sound effect into the Ogg format in order to make the audio work in browsers that do not support an MP3 format.

Supporting different web browsers with different audio formats

The following table shows the audio formats supported by the latest popular web browsers at the time of writing this book:

Browser	Ogg	MP3	WAV
Firefox 3.6+	Yes	-	Yes
Safari 5+	-	Yes	Yes
Chrome	Yes	Yes	-
Opera 10.5+	Yes	-	Yes
Internet Explorer 9	-	Yes	Yes

Pop quiz – Using the audio tag

1. How can we stop an audio element playing?

   a. Use the `stop` function

   b. Use the `pause` function and reset the `currentTime` to 0

   c. Reset the `currentTime` to 0

2. How can we put fallback content to display in browsers that do not support `audio` tags?

Building a mini piano musical game

Imagine now we are not only playing a sound effect, but also playing a full song with the `audio` tag. Along with the song playing, there are some music dots moving downwards as a visualization of the music.

Time for action – Creating a basic background to the music game

First, we will draw a few paths in canvas as the background of the music playback.

1. We will continue working with our example and draw the background. Open the
`index.htm` file in a text editor and add the following highlighted code that defines
the game scene with two canvases set up:

```
<div id="game">
  <section id="menu-scene" class="scene">
    <a href="#game"><span>Play</span></a>
  </section>

  <section id="game-scene" class="scene">
    <canvas id="game-background-canvas" width="768" height="440">
      Sorry, your web browser does not support canvas content.
    </canvas>
    <canvas id="game-canvas" width="768" height="440"></canvas>
  </section>
</div>
```

2. We added a game scene in the HTML file. We want to make it on top of the menu
scene, so we style the game scene to have `absolute` position by adding the
following to `audiogame.css`:

```
#game-scene {
    background: #efefef   url(../images/game_bg.jpg);
}
#game-canvas, #game-background-canvas {
    position: absolute;
}
```

3. It is time for the background drawing code. Open the `html5games.audio.js`
JavaScript file.

4. In the jQuery `ready` function, we call a `drawBackground` function to draw the
background as follows:

```
drawBackground();
```

5. Add the following `drawBackground` function to the end of the JavaScript file. The
code draws three black lines and one grey line in the `game-background-canvas`
canvas:

```
function drawBackground()
{
    // get the reference of the canvas and the context.
    var game = document.getElementById("game-background-canvas");
    var ctx = game.getContext('2d');

    // set the line style of the three vertical lines.
```

```
      ctx.lineWidth = 10;
      ctx.strokeStyle = "#000";

      var center = game.width/2;

      // draw the three lines
      // the left line is placed 100 pixels on the left of center.
      ctx.beginPath();
      ctx.moveTo(center-100, 50);
      ctx.lineTo(center-100, ctx.canvas.height - 50);
      ctx.stroke();

      // the middle line is placed at the center
      ctx.beginPath();
      ctx.moveTo(center, 50);
      ctx.lineTo(center, ctx.canvas.height - 50);
      ctx.stroke();

      // the right line is placed 100 pixels on the right of center.
      ctx.beginPath();
      ctx.moveTo(center+100, 50);
      ctx.lineTo(center+100, ctx.canvas.height - 50);
      ctx.stroke();

      // draw the horizontal line
      ctx.beginPath();
      ctx.moveTo(center-150, ctx.canvas.height - 80);
      ctx.lineTo(center+150, ctx.canvas.height - 80);
      // reset the line style to 1px width and grey before actually
         drawing the horizontal line.
      ctx.lineWidth = 1;
      ctx.strokeStyle = "rgba(50,50,50,.8)";
      ctx.stroke();
  }
```

6. When we open the index.htm file in a browser, we will see four lines with a background, as shown in the following screenshot. Do not worry that the play button is hidden for now, we will show it again later:

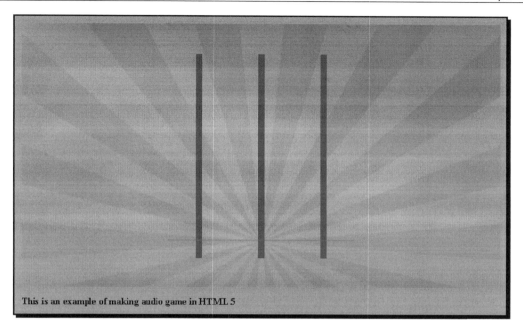

This is an example of making audio game in HTML 5

What just happened?

We have created a canvas where we draw the music game background. In this music game example, we introduced the basic scene management in HTML5 games.

Creating scenes in HTML5 games

Creating **scenes** in HTML5 is similar to creating **layers** like we did in the last chapter. It is a DOM element that contains several children. All the children elements are positioned in absolute. We have two scenes in our example now. The following code snippet shows a possible scene structure in an entire game with a game over scene, credit scene, and leaderboard scene included:

```
<div id="game">
   <section id="menu-scene" class="scene"></section>
   <section id="game-scene" class="scene"></section>
<section id="gameover-scene" class="scene"></section>
<section id="credit-scene" class="scene"></section>
<section id="leaderboard-scene" class="scene"></section>
</div>
```

The following screenshot shows that the scenes are placed at the same place in a web page. It is very similar to the layers structure. The difference is that we will control the scene by showing and hiding each scene:

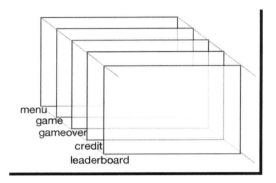

menu
game
gameover
credit
leaderboard

Visualizing the music play back

If you have ever played the Dance Dance Revolution, Guitar Hero, or the Tap Tap Revenge game, then you may be familiar with the music dots moving downwards or upwards and the player hitting the music dots when it moves to the right place. The following screenshot demonstrates the Tap Tap Revenge game:

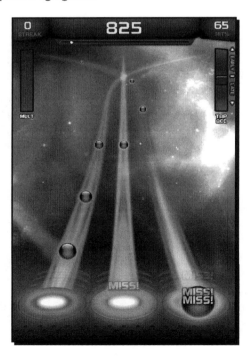

We will play a song in the audio tag with similar music visualization in the canvas.

Time for action – Creating the playback visualization in the music game

Carry out the following steps:

1. We need a song with both a melody part and a base part. Copy the minuet_in_ g.ogg, minuet_in_g.mp3, minuet_in_g_melody.ogg, and minuet_in_g_ melody.mp3 files from the downloaded files or from the code bundle in the media folder.

2. Then, add the audio tag with the song as a source file. Open the index.htm file and add the following code:

```
<audio id="melody">
   <source src="media/minuet_in_g_melody.mp3" />
   <source src="media/minuet_in_g_melody.ogg" />
</audio>

<audio id="base">
   <source src="media/minuet_in_g.mp3" />
   <source src="media/minuet_in_g.ogg" />
</audio>
```

3. The music visualization is mainly done in JavaScript. Open the html5games. audio.js JavaScript file in a text editor.

4. Add a MusicNote object type to represent the music data and a Dot object type to represent the visual dot of the music note in the canvas as follows:

```
function MusicNote(time,line){
   this.time = time;
   this.line = line;
}
function Dot(distance, line) {
   this.distance = distance;
   this.line = line;
   this.missed = false;
}
```

5. Then, we need several game variables to store the MusicNote instances, the Dot instance, and other information. The level data is a sequence of time and the appearing line that is separated by a semi-colon. The level data represents the time and line at which the music note should appear:

```
// an array to store all music notes data.
```

```
audiogame.musicNotes = [];
audiogame.leveldata = "1.592,3;1.984,2;2.466,1;2.949,2;4.022,3;";
// the visual dots drawn on the canvas.
audiogame.dots = [];
// for storing the starting time
audiogame.startingTime = 0;
// reference of the dot image
audiogame.dotImage = new Image();
```

6. The level data is stored in a string format. We have the following function to extract the string in the `MusicNote` object instances and store in an array:

```
function setupLevelData()
{
    var notes = audiogame.leveldata.split(";");
    for(var i in notes)
    {
        var note = notes[i].split(",");
        var time = parseFloat(note[0]);
        var line = parseInt(note[1]);
        var musicNote = new MusicNote(time,line);
        audiogame.musicNotes.push(musicNote);
    }
}
```

7. Add the following code in the starting of the jQuery `ready` function. It references the `melody` and `base` audio tags and loads the dot image for later use:

```
audiogame.melody = document.getElementById("melody");
audiogame.base = document.getElementById("base");
// load the dot image
audiogame.dotImage.src = "images/dot.png";
```

8. Then, add the following code in the end of the jQuery `ready` function:

```
setupLevelData();
setInterval(gameloop, 30);
startGame();
```

9. Add the following two functions in the JavaScript file. The `startGame` function sets the starting time and executes the `playMusic` function with a delay. The latter function plays both the melody and base audios:

```
function startGame()
{
    // starting game
    var date = new Date();
```

```
    audiogame.startingTime = date.getTime();
    setTimeout(playMusic, 3550);
}
function playMusic()
{
    // play both the melody and base
    audiogame.melody.play();
    audiogame.base.play();
}
```

10. Add the following `gameloop` function to JavaScript. The `gameloop` function creates new dots at the top of the game and moves the existing notes down:

```
// logic that run every 30ms.
function gameloop()
{
  var game = document.getElementById("game-canvas");
  var ctx = game.getContext('2d');

  // show new dots
  // if the game is started
  if (audiogame.startingTime != 0)
  {
    for(var i in audiogame.musicNotes)
    {
      // get the elapsed time from beginning of the melody
      var date = new Date();
      var elapsedTime = (date.getTime() -
        audiogame.startingTime)/1000;
      var note = audiogame.musicNotes[i];

      // check if the dot appear time is as same as
        the elapsed time
      var timeDiff = note.time - elapsedTime;
      if (timeDiff >= 0 && timeDiff <= .03)
      {
        // create the dot when the appear time is within
          one frame of the elapsed time
        var dot = new Dot(ctx.canvas.height-150, note.line);
        audiogame.dots.push(dot);
      }
    }
  }

  // move the dots
```

```
for(var i in audiogame.dots)
{
  audiogame.dots[i].distance -= 2.5;
}

// only clear the dirty area, that is the middle area
ctx.clearRect(ctx.canvas.width/2-200, 0, 400,
  ctx.canvas.height);

// draw the music note dots
for(var i in audiogame.dots)
{
  // prepare the radial gradients fill style
  var circle_gradient = ctx.createRadialGradient
    (-3,-3,1,0,0,20);
  circle_gradient.addColorStop(0, "#fff");
  circle_gradient.addColorStop(1, "#cc0");
  ctx.fillStyle = circle_gradient;

  // prepare the dot position to draw
  ctx.save();
  var center = game.width/2;
  var dot = audiogame.dots[i];
  var x = center-100
  if (dot.line == 2)
  {
    x = center;
  }
  else if (dot.line == 3)
  {
    x = center+100;
  }

  // draw the dot at position according to the line and distance
  ctx.translate(x, ctx.canvas.height-80-
    audiogame.dots[i].distance);
  ctx.drawImage(audiogame.dotImage, -audiogame.dotImage.width/2,
   -audiogame.dotImage.height/2);
  ctx.restore();
}
}
```

11. Save all files and open the `index.htm` file in web a browser. The following screenshot shows the music playing with the music dots appearing on the top and moving downwards:

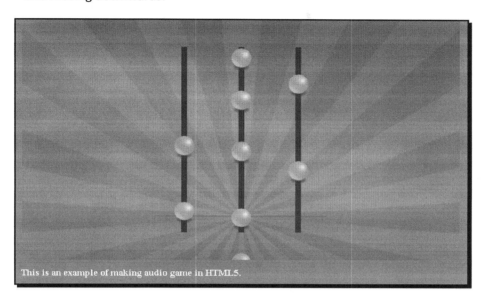

What just happened?

We just built a fully functional music game and this is the basic playback function. It plays the song with both the melody and the base part with some music dots moving downwards.

Choosing the right song for the music game

We have to be careful of the copyright issue when choosing a song for the music game. It usually requires paying a usage fee or making an agreement with the song copyright owner to use a song with copyright. It is fine if you are building a commercial music game that is going to be a hit in the game industry and the earnings can overcome the copyright usage expense. However, as a book example here, we are going to use a copyright-free song. That is why we use the classical song Minute in G which is free public domain.

Storing and extracting the song level data

The level data shown in the *Time for action* section is just a portion of the entire level data. It is a very long string storing music note information, including the time and the line. It is stored in the following format:

```
music_current_time, line; music_current_time, line; …
```

Each music dot data contains the time to show up and which line it shows. This data is separated by a comma. Every piece of music dot data is separated by a semi-colon. The following code extracts the level string into a `MusicNote` object by splitting the semi-colon and the comma:

```
audiogame.musicNotes = [];
audiogame.leveldata = "1.592,3;1.984,2;2.466,1;2.949,2;4.022,3;";
function setupLevelData()
{
    var notes = audiogame.leveldata.split(";");
    for(var i in notes)
    {
        var note = notes[i].split(",");
        var time = parseFloat(note[0]);
        var line = parseInt(note[1]);
        var musicNote = new MusicNote(time,line);
        audiogame.musicNotes.push(musicNote);
    }
}
```

The level data string is recorded by the keyboard and we are going to discuss the recording later in this chapter.

The level data contains only several music notes here. In the code bundle, there is the whole level data of the complete song.

There is an optional second parameter for the JavaScript `parseInt` function. It defines the radix of the number to parse. By default, it uses decimal but `parseInt` will parse the string as octal when the string begins with zero. For example, `parseInt("010")` return result 8 instead of 10. If we want the decimal number, then we can use `parseInt("010",10)` to specify the radix.

Getting the elapsed time of the game

Although we know the elapsed time of an audio element by accessing the `currentTime` property, we want to get the time from the starting of the game.

We can get the elapsed time by storing the current computer time when starting the game and subtracting the current time value to get the elapsed time.

We get the current computer time by using the `Date` object. The following code snippet shows how we use `startingTime` to get the elapsed time:

```
// starting game
var date = new Date();
audiogame.startingTime = date.getTime();

// some time later
var date = new Date();
var elapsedTime = (date.getTime() - audiogame.startingTime)/1000;
```

The following screenshot shows the preceding code snippet running in console:

```
> var audiogame = {};
  undefined
> var date = new Date();
  undefined
> audiogame.startingTime = date.getTime();
  1306138121829
> // some time later
  undefined
> var date = new Date();
  undefined
> var elapsedTime = (date.getTime() - audiogame.startingTime) / 1000;
  undefined
> elapsedTime + "seconds"
  "39.608seconds"
> |
```

Creating music dots

In the `gameloop` function, we check all the `MusicNote` instances and see whether it is time to create the visual dot of that music note. The following code shows the logic we used to create the visual music dot. Basically, we get the elapsed time of the game and compare it with the current time of each music note. If the time difference between the note's current time and elapsed time is within 30 ms, then we create the visual dot instance and let the `gameloop` function draw it:

```
if (audiogame.startingTime != 0)
{
  for(var i in audiogame.musicNotes)
  {
    // get the elapsed time from beginning of the melody
    var date = new Date();
    var elapsedTime = (date.getTime() -
      audiogame.startingTime)/1000;
    var note = audiogame.musicNotes[i];
```

```
    // check if the dot appear time is as same as the elapsed time
    var timeDiff = note.time - elapsedTime;
    if (timeDiff >= 0 && timeDiff <= .03)
    {
      // create the dot when the appear time is within one frame
        of the elapsed time
      var dot = new Dot(ctx.canvas.height-150, note.line);
      audiogame.dots.push(dot);
    }
  }
}
```

Moving the music dots

There is a time difference between the game start and music start. The game starts several seconds before the song starts playing. It is because we need to show the music dots and move it down before the music starts.

The music dots should match the song when the dots are in the grey line. The music dots appear from the top of the game and move down towards the grey line. We delay the music play to wait as the dots move from top to bottom. It is around 3.55 seconds in this example, so we delay the music playing by 3.55 seconds.

When the dot is created, it is placed at a given distance. We decrease all dots' distance by 2.5 every time the gameloop function executes. The distance is stored in each dot object representing how far away it is from the grey line:

```
for(var i in audiogame.dots)
{
    audiogame.dots[i].distance -= 2.5;
}
```

The y position of the dot is calculated by the grey line subtracting the distance as follows:

```
// draw the dot
ctx.save();
var x = ctx.canvas.width/2-100
if (audiogame.dots[i].line == 2)
{
    x = ctx.canvas.width/2;
}
else if (audiogame.dots[i].line == 3)
{
    x = ctx.canvas.width/2+100;
}
ctx.translate(x, ctx.canvas.height-80-audiogame.dots[i].distance);
```

```
ctx.drawImage(audiogame.dotImage, -audiogame.dotImage.width/2, -
   audiogame.dotImage.height/2);
```

The following screenshot shows the distance between the grey line and each dot. When the distance is zero, it is exactly on the grey line:

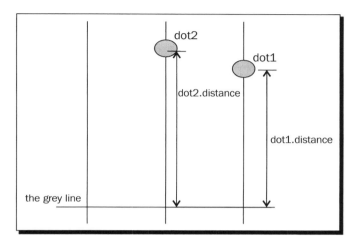

Linking the play button to the music game scene

We have a game scene now playing our song. However, it covers the menu scene we made with a play button inside. Imagine now we open the game with the play button being displayed, then we click on the button and the game scene slides in and starts playing the music.

Time for action – Animating the scene transition

We will hide the game scene by default and show it after the play button is clicked:

1. First, we have to modify the stylesheet. Open the `audiogame.css` file.

2. Add the following highlighted overflow property to #game. It helps to clip the game into a 768x440px mask:

    ```
    #game {
        position: relative;
        width: 768px;
        height: 440px;
        overflow: hidden;
    }
    ```

3. Next, we add the following highlighted code to style the game scene:

```
#game-scene {
    background: #efefef url(../images/game_bg.jpg);
    top: -440px;
}

#game-scene.show-scene {
    top: 0;
    -webkit-transition: top .3s linear;
    -moz-transition: top .3s linear;
    transition: top .3s linear;
}
```

4. Then, we will move on to the JavaScript part. Open the `html5games.audio.js` JavaScript file.

5. Delete the `startGame` function calling in the jQuery ready function. We will call it when the play button is clicked.

6. In the play button click handler, we add the following highlighted code:

```
$("a[href='#game']").click(function(){
    audiogame.buttonActiveSound.currentTime = 0;
    audiogame.buttonActiveSound.play();

    $("#game-scene").addClass('show-scene');
    startGame();

    return false;
});
```

Save all files and open the `index.htm` in a browser. There should be a slide-in animation to show the music playback scene when we click on the play button. The following screenshot sequence shows the slide-in animation:

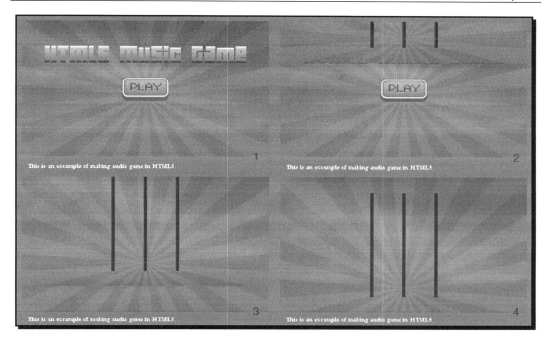

What just happened?

We just created a transition between the menu scene and the game scene.

Creating a slide-in effect in CSS3

The game scene slides in from the top when the play button is clicked. This scene transition effect is done by moving the game scene by CSS3 transition. The game scene position is initially placed with a negative top value. We then change the top position from negative value to zero with a transition, so it animates from the top to the correct position.

Another important thing to make the sliding effect work is to set the overflow of the parent DIV of the scenes to hidden. Without the hidden overflow, the game scene is visible even with a negative top position. Therefore, it is important to set the parent DIV of the scenes to the hidden overflow.

The following screenshot illustrates the slide-in transition of the game scene. The #game DIV is the parent of both menu scene and game scene. The game scene moves from the top when we add the .show-scene class which sets the top value to 0 with transition:

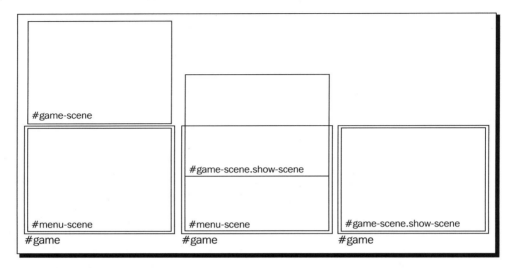

Have a go hero – Creating different scene transition effects

We made a slide-in effect to the scene transition when showing the game. By using JavaScript and CSS3, we can make many different scene transition effects creatively. Try making your own transition effect to the game, such as fading in, pushing in from the right, or even flipping with a 3D rotation.

Creating a keyboard-driven mini piano musical game

Now we can click on the **play** button. The music game slides in and plays the song with music notes dropping down. Our next step is adding interaction to the music notes. Therefore, we will add keyboard events to control the three lines to hit the music notes.

Time for action – Creating a mini piano musical game

Carry out the following steps:

1. We want to show an indication when pressing the keyboard. Open the index.htm file and add the following highlighted HTML:

```
<section id="game-scene" class="scene">
    <canvas id="game-background-canvas" width="768" height="440">
        Sorry, your web browser does not support canvas content.
```

```
    </canvas>
    <canvas id="game-canvas" width="768" height="440">
        Sorry, your web browser does not support canvas content.
    </canvas>
    <div id="hit-line-1" class="hit-line hide"></div>
    <div id="hit-line-2" class="hit-line hide"></div>
    <div id="hit-line-3" class="hit-line hide"></div>
</section>
```

2. Then, we may want to inform visitors that they can play the game by pressing the *J*, *K*, and *L* keys. Modify the footer content as follows:

```
<footer>
    <p>This is an example of making audio game in HTML5.
        Press J, K, L to play.
    </p>
</footer>
```

3. Now, we will move on to the stylesheet. The stylesheet is included in the code bundle with a folder named audio_game_scene_transition.

4. Next, we will add the keyboard event in the JavaScript part. Open the html5games. audio.js JavaScript file and add the following code inside the jQuery ready function:

```
// keydown
$(document).keydown(function(e){
    var line = e.which-73;
    $('#hit-line-'+line).removeClass('hide');
    $('#hit-line-'+line).addClass('show');

     // our target is J(74), K(75), L(76)
    var hitLine = e.which-73;

    // check if hit a music note dot
    for(var i in audiogame.dots)
    {
        if (hitLine == audiogame.dots[i].line &&
          Math.abs(audiogame.dots[i].distance) < 20)
        {
            // remove the hit dot from the dots array
            audiogame.dots.splice(i, 1);
        }
    }
});
$(document).keyup(function(e){
```

```
        var line = e.which-73;
        $('#hit-line-'+line).removeClass('show');
        $('#hit-line-'+line).addClass('hide');
});
```

5. Now save all files and open the game in a browser. Try pressing the *J*, *K*, and *L* keys. The three hit line indicator should appear and fade out when the key is pressed. If the music dot passes by the grey line when hitting the right key, then it disappears:

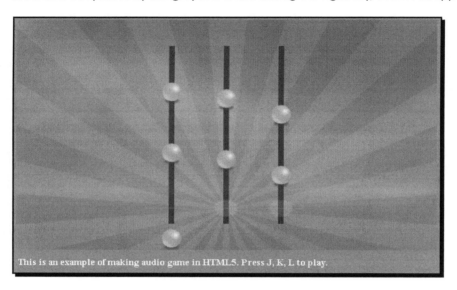

This is an example of making audio game in HTML5. Press J, K, L to play.

What just happened?

We just added keyboard interaction to our music game. There is a glow animation when hitting the keys. The music dot will disappear when the right key is pressed at the right moment.

Hitting the three music lines by key down

We use the *J*, *K*, and *L* keys to hit the three music lines in the game. The *J* key controls the left line, the *K* key controls the middle line, and the *L* key controls the right one.

There is also an indication showing that we just hit the music line. This is done by placing the following image at the intersection of the grey line and music lines:

Then, we can control the showing and hiding of the hit indication graphics with the following jQuery code:

```
$(document).keydown(function(e){
    var line = e.which-73;
    $('#hit-line-'+line).removeClass('hide');
    $('#hit-line-'+line).addClass('show');
});
$(document).keyup(function(e){
    var line = e.which-73;
    $('#hit-line-'+line).removeClass('show');
    $('#hit-line-'+line).addClass('hide');
});
```

J, *K*, and *L* keys control the music line 1 to 3. As J, K, and L have the key code 74, 75, and 76 respectively, we know which line number it is by subtracting the key code by 73.

Determining music dot hits on key down

The distance is close to zero if the dot is almost on the grey horizontal line. This helps us in determining if the dots hit the grey line. By checking both the key down event and the dot distance, we can determine if we successfully hit a music dot. The following code snippet shows that we consider the dot is hit when the distance is within 20 pixels:

```
$(document).keydown(function(e){
    var line = e.which-73;
    $('#hit-line-'+line).removeClass('hide');
    $('#hit-line-'+line).addClass('show');

     // our target is J(74), K(75), L(76)
    var hitLine = e.which-73;

    // check if hit a music note dot
    for(var i in audiogame.dots)
    {
       if (hitLine == audiogame.dots[i].line &&
         Math.abs(audiogame.dots[i].distance) < 20)
       {
          // remove the hit dot from the dots array
          audiogame.dots.splice(i, 1);
       }
    }
});
```

With determination, we remove the music dots when we hit them. The missed dots will still pass through the grey line and move towards the bottom. This creates a basic game play where the player has to eliminate all the music dots by hitting them correctly at the right moment when the song is playing.

Removing an element in an array with the given index

We remove the music dot data from an array when it is hit (and thus it will not be drawn anymore). To remove an element in an array, we use the `splice` function. The following line of code removes one element from an array at the given index:

```
array.splice(index, 1);
```

The `splice` function is a little tricky to use. This is because it allows us to add or remove elements in an array. Then, it returns removed elements as another array. It sounds complicated. Therefore, we will perform some experiments.

Time for action – Removing music dots with the splice function

We will open the JavaScript console in a web browser to perform a few tests on the `splice` function:

1. Open the JavaScript console.

2. Input the following commands to the console line by line. That is, pressing *Enter* on each command line. These commands create an array and manipulate it with the `splice` function.

3. We should get a result similar to the one shown in the following screenshot:

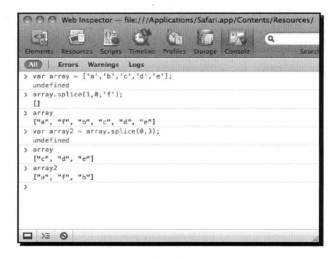

What just happened?

We just created an array and tried adding and removing elements by using the `splice` function. Please note that the splice array returns another array with the removed elements.

Here is how we use the `splice` function:

```
array.splice(index, length, element1, element2, …, elementN);
```

The following table shows how we use the arguments:

Argument	Definition	Discussion
`index`	Specifies the index of an element to be added or removed in the array	The index starts from 0. 0 means the first element, 1 means the second one, and so on. We can also use negative indexes, such as -1 which means the last element, -2 which means the second last element, and so on.
`length`	Specifies how many elements we want to remove	Putting 0 means we do not remove any element.
`element1, element2 … elementN`	The new elements to be added into the array; this is optional	This is optional. Putting a list of elements here means we add the elements at the given index.

 The following Mozilla Developer Network link discusses different usages of the `splice` function:

`https://developer.mozilla.org/en/JavaScript/Reference/Global_Objects/Array/splice`

Have a go hero

In similar commercial music games, there are some words showing when the player hits or misses a music dot. How can we add this feature to our game?

Adding additional features to the mini piano game

We have created basic interaction to the game. We can go further to make the game better, by adding melody volume feedback to make the performance playing realistic, and counting the success rate of the performance.

Adjusting the music volume according to the player

Imagine now we are in a performance playing the music. We hit the music dots to play the melody. If we miss any of them, then we fail to perform it well and the melody disappears.

Time for action – Removing missed melody notes

We will store some gameplay statistics and use it to adjust the melody volume. We will continue with our JavaScript file:

1. First, add the following variables in the variable declaration region:

```
audiogame.totalDotsCount = 0;
audiogame.totalSuccessCount = 0;

// storing the success count of last 5 results.
audiogame.successCount = 5;
```

2. In the setupLevelData function, we get the total amount of dots with the highlighted code:

```
function setupLevelData()
{
    var notes = audiogame.leveldata.split(";");

    // store the total number of dots
    audiogame.totalDotsCount = notes.length;

    for(var i in notes)
    {
        var note = notes[i].split(",");
        var time = parseFloat(note[0]);
        var line = parseInt(note[1]);
        var musicNote = new MusicNote(time,line);
        audiogame.musicNotes.push(musicNote);
    }
}
```

3. We want to not only remove a dot but also keep track of the result when we hit it by using a keyboard. Add the following code inside the keyboard handler in the jQuery ready function:

```
// check if hit a music note dot
for(var i in audiogame.dots)
{
    if (hitLine == audiogame.dots[i].line &&
```

```
            Math.abs(audiogame.dots[i].distance) < 20)
        {
            // remove the hit dot from the dots array
            audiogame.dots.splice(i, 1);

            // increase the success count
            audiogame.successCount++;

            // keep only 5 success count max.
            audiogame.successCount = Math.min
                (5, audiogame.successCount);

            // increase the total success count
            audiogame.totalSuccessCount ++;
        }
    }
```

4. In the `gameloop` function, we calculate all missed dots and store the result. Then, we can use these statistics to get the successful rate of the game. Add the following code to the `gameloop` function:

```
// check missed dots
for(var i in audiogame.dots)
{
    if (!audiogame.dots[i].missed &&
        audiogame.dots[i].distance < -10)
    {
        // mark the dot as missed if it is not mark before
        audiogame.dots[i].missed = true;

        // reduce the success count
        audiogame.successCount--;

        // reset the success count to 0 if it is lower than 0.
        audiogame.successCount = Math.max
            (0, audiogame.successCount);
    }

    // remove missed dots after moved to the bottom
    if (audiogame.dots[i].distance < -100)
    {
        audiogame.dots.splice(i, 1);
    }
}
```

```
// calculate the percentage of the success in last 5 music dots
var successPercent = audiogame.successCount / 5;

// prevent the successPercent to exceed range(fail safe)
successPercent = Math.max(0, Math.min(1, successPercent));
```

5. At last, we adjust the melody volume by using the successful rate. Put the following code after the code we just added in the `gameloop` function:

```
audiogame.melody.volume = successPercent;
```

6. Save all files and test our game in a browser. When the player continues to play the game well, the melody keeps playing. When the player misses several music dots, the melody disappears and only the base plays.

What just happened?

We just used the player performance as a feedback on the melody volume. It gives a feeling that we are really performing the music. When we perform poorly, the melody volume is low and the song sounds poor too.

Removing dots from the game

We want to remove the dots either after it drops under the bottom bound or when they are being hit by the player. The game loop displays all the dots in the dot list on the game canvas. We can remove the dot graphic by removing its data from the array of dots.

We use the following `splice` function to remove an entry in the array at the target index:

```
audiogame.dots.splice(index, 1);
```

Storing the success count in the last five results

In our game, we need to store the success count in the last five results to calculate the success rate. We can do this by using a counter representing this. When a dot is successfully hit, the counter increases by one, but when the player fails on hitting a dot, the counter decreases by 1.

The counter is then representing the successful counts within the last several results if we limit the counter to have a range, such as 0 to 5 in our example.

Have a go hero

We discussed how to display the game progress in the Untangle game in the last chapter. Can we apply a similar technique in the music game? We have the player's success percentage during game play. How about displaying it as a percentage bar on the top of the game?

Recording music notes as level data

The game relies on the level data to play. The playback visualization will not work if there is no level data. We also cannot play it if the playback visualization is not working. So how can we record that level data?

Imagine now the music is playing without any music dots appearing in the game. We listen to the music carefully and press the *J, K, L* keys when the music plays. After the music ends, we print out all the keys and time we pressed. This data will then be used back in the playback visualization of the music.

Time for action – Adding functionality to record the music level data

Carry out the following steps:

1. First, we create a variable to toggle between the recording mode and normal playing mode. Open the `html5games.audio.js` file and add the code as follows:

```
audiogame.isRecordMode = true;
```

2. Next, we add the following highlighted code in the `keydown` event handler. This code stores all our pressed keys in an array and prints them out to the console when the semi-colon key is pressed:

```
$(document).keydown(function(e){
  var line = e.which-73;
  $('#hit-line-'+line).removeClass('hide');
  $('#hit-line-'+line).addClass('show');

  if (audiogame.isRecordMode)
  {
    // print the stored music notes data when press ";" (186)
    if (e.which == 186)
    {
      var musicNotesString = "";
      for(var i in audiogame.musicNotes)
      {
        musicNotesString += audiogame.musicNotes[i].time+",
```

```
          "+audiogame.musicNotes[i].line+";";
        }
        console.log(musicNotesString);
      }

    var currentTime = parseInt
      (audiogame.melody.currentTime * 1000)/1000;
    var note = new MusicNote(currentTime, e.which-73);
    audiogame.musicNotes.push(note);
  }
  else
  {
    // our target is J(74), K(75), L(76)
    var hitLine = e.which-73;

    // check if hit a music note dot
    ...
  }
});
```

3. Finally, we want to make sure that the `setupLevelData` and the `gameloop` functions are not executed during the recording mode. These functions are for playing mode only:

```
if (!audiogame.isRecordMode) {
  setupLevelData();
  setInterval(gameloop, 30);
}
```

4. Now open the `index.htm` in a browser. After clicking on the **play** button, the game starts and the music plays without the music notes. Try pressing the *J*, *K*, and *L* keys following the music beat. After finishing the music, press the semi-colon to print the level data in the console. The following screenshot shows the console displaying the level data string:

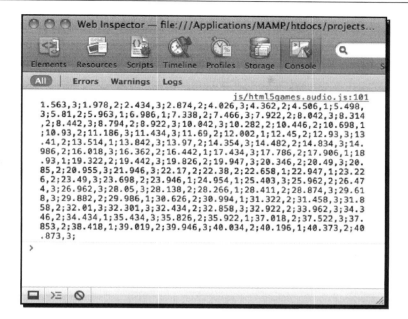

What just happened?

We just added a recording feature to our game. We can now record our music notes. We can toggle the record mode and playing mode by setting the `audiogame.isRecordMode` variable to true and false.

On every key press, we get the elapsed time of the melody and create a `MusicNote` instance with the time and line number. The following code shows how we record the pressed keys. The `currentTime` is cut to two decimal digits before saving:

```
var currentTime = audiogame.melody.currentTime.toFixed(3);
var note = new MusicNote(currentTime, e.which-73);
audiogame.musicNotes.push(note);
```

We also capture the semi-colon key to print out all the recorded `MusicNote` data into a string. The string follows the `time,line;time,line;` format, so we can directly copy the printed string and paste it as level data to play.

The `toFixed` function formats the number with the given number of trailing decimals. In our example, we used it to get the current time with 3 trailing decimals.

Handling the audio event on playback completes

We can play the game now, but there is no indication on game over. Imagine now, we want to know how well we played when the game completes. We will capture the melody-ending signal and display the successful rate of the game.

Time for action – Indicating a game over event in the console

Carry out the following steps:

1. Open the `html5games.audio.js` JavaScript file.

2. Add the following code in the jQuery ready function:

   ```
   $(audiogame.melody).bind('ended', onMelodyEnded);
   ```

3. Add the following event handler function to the end of the file:

   ```
   // show game over scene on melody ended.
   function onMelodyEnded()
   {
     console.log('song ended');
     console.log('success percent: ',audiogame.totalSuccessCount /
       audiogame.totalDotsCount * 100 + '%');
   }
   ```

4. It is time to save all files and play the game in a web browser. When the game is over, we should see that the successful rate is printed in the console as shown in the following screenshot:

What just happened?

We just listened to the `ended` event of the audio element and handled it with a handler function.

Handling audio events

There are many other events in the audio element. The following table lists a few commonly used audio events:

Event	Discussion
ended	Sent when the audio element finishes a playback
play	Sent when the audio element plays or resumes
pause	Sent when the audio element pauses
progress	Sent periodically when the audio element is downloading
timeupdate	Sent when the `currentTime` property changes

Here we just listed a few commonly used events; you can reference the complete audio event list in the Mozilla Developer Center at the following URL:

```
https://developer.mozilla.org/En/Using_audio_and_video_in_
Firefox#Media_events
```

Have a go hero

In our music game, we print out the successful rate in the console when the game is over. How about adding a game over scene to our game and showing it at the end of the game? It would be good to use animation transition when showing a game over scene too.

Summary

We learned a lot in this chapter about using the HTML5 audio element and built a music game.

Specifically, we covered the following topics:

◆ Adding the audio tag to the HTML. There are different attributes we can set to define how the audio tag behaves and loads different format sources.

◆ Controlling the audio playback and volume by using the JavaScript API.

◆ Adding sound effects on mouse hover and active with the help of jQuery.

◆ Creating a music game in canvas with keyboard inputs.

◆ Handling audio events; the audio element sends several events when its state changes.

We also discussed managing scenes and animating the transition.

We have learned about adding music and sound effects in our HTML5 games. Now we are ready to build a more complete game by adding a leaderboard to store game scores in the next chapter.

7
Using Local Storage to Store Game Data

Local storage is a new specification from HTML5. It allows a website to store information in the browser locally and access the stored data later. This is a useful feature in game development because we can use it as a memory slot to save any game data locally in a web browser.

We are going to add game data storing in the CSS3 memory matching game we built in *Chapter 3, Building* a *Memory Matching Game in CSS3*. Besides storing and loading the game data, we will also notify the player for breaking a record with a nice 3D ribbon with pure CSS3 styling.

In this chapter, we will cover the following topics:

◆ Storing data by using HTML5 local storage

◆ Saving the object in the local storage

◆ Notifying players for breaking a new record with a nice ribbon effect

◆ Saving the entire game progress

The following screenshot shows the final result we will create through this chapter. So, let's get on with it:

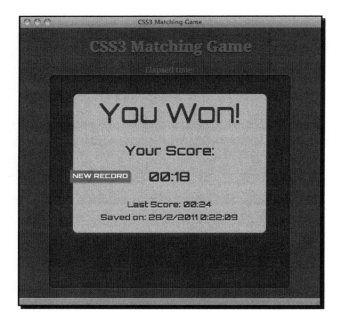

Storing data by using HTML5 local storage

Remember the CSS3 memory matching game we made in *Chapter 3*? Imagine now we have published our game and players are trying their best to perform well in the game.

We want to show the players whether they played better or worse than the last time. We will save the latest score and inform players whether they are better or not this time by comparing the scores.

They may feel proud when performing better. This may make them addicted and they may keep trying to get higher scores.

Creating a game over dialog

Before actually saving anything in the local storage, we need a game over screen. We have made a few games in previous chapters. We made a Ping Pong game, memory matching game, Untangle puzzle game, and a music game. In these games, we did not create any game over screen. Imagine now we are playing the CSS3 memory matching game that we built in *Chapter 3*. We successfully match and remove all cards. Once we finish, a game over screen pops up and shows the time we utilized to complete the game.

Time for action – Creating a game over dialog with the elapsed played time

We will continue with the code from the memory matching game we made in *Chapter 3*.
Carry out the following steps:

1. Open the CSS3 matching game folder as our working directory.

2. Download a background image from the following URL (we will use it as the background of the pop up):

   ```
   http://gamedesign.cc/html5games/popup_bg.jpg
   ```

3. Place the image in the `images` folder.

4. Open `index.html` into any text editor.

5. We will need a font for the game over pop up. Add the following font embedding CSS into the `head` section:

   ```
   <link href="http://fonts.googleapis.com/css?family=Orbitron:400,70
   0" rel="stylesheet" type="text/css" >
   ```

6. Before the `game` section, we add a `div` named `timer` to show the elapsed playing time. In addition, we add a new `popup` section containing the HTML markup of the pop-up dialog:

   ```
   <div id="timer">
       Elapsed time: <span id="elapsed-time">00:00</span>
   </div>
   <section id="game">
       <div id="cards">
           <div class="card">
               <div class="face front"></div>
               <div class="face back"></div>
           </div> <!-- .card -->
       </div> <!-- #cards -->
   </section> <!-- #game -->

   <section id="popup" class="hide">
       <div id="popup-bg">
       </div>
       <div id="popup-box">
           <div id="popup-box-content">
               <h1>You Won!</h1>
               <p>Your Score:</p>
               <p><span class='score'>13</span></p>
   ```

```
    </div>
  </div>
</section>
```

7. We will now move on to the style sheet. As it is just for styling and not related to our logic yet, we can simply copy the `matchgame.css` file from `matching_game_with_game_over` in the code example bundle.

8. It is time to edit the game logic part. Open the `html5games.matchgame.js` file in an editor.

9. In the jQuery ready function, we need a variable to store the elapsed time of the game. Then, we create a timer to count the game every second as follows:

```
$(function(){
    ...
// reset the elapsed time to 0.
matchingGame.elapsedTime = 0;

// start the timer
    matchingGame.timer = setInterval(countTimer, 1000);
}
```

10. Next, add a `countTimer` function which will be executed every second. It displays the elapsed seconds in the minute and second format:

```
function countTimer()
{
    matchingGame.elapsedTime++;

    // calculate the minutes and seconds from elapsed time
    var minute = Math.floor(matchingGame.elapsedTime / 60);
    var second = matchingGame.elapsedTime % 60;

    // add padding 0 if minute and second is less then 10
    if (minute < 10) minute = "0" + minute;
    if (second < 10) second = "0" + second;

    // display the elapsed time
    $("#elapsed-time").html(minute+":"+second);
}
```

11. In the `removeTookCards` function which we wrote earlier, add the following highlighted code that executes the game over logic after removing all cards:

```
function removeTookCards()
{
```

```
$(".card-removed").remove();

// check if all cards are removed and show game over
if ($(".card").length == 0)
{
    gameover();
}
}
```

12. At last, we create the following `gameover` function. It stops the counting timer, displays the elapsed time in the game over pop up, and finally shows the pop up:

```
function gameover()
{
    // stop the timer
    clearInterval(matchingGame.timer);

    // set the score in the game over popup
    $(".score").html($("#elapsed-time").html());

    // show the game over popup
    $("#popup").removeClass("hide");
}
```

13. Now, save all files and open the game in a browser. Try finishing the memory matching game and the game over screen will pop up, as shown in the following screenshot:

What just happened?

We have used the CSS3 transition animation to show the game over pop up. We benchmark the score by using the time a player utilized to finish the game.

Saving scores in the browser

Imagine now we are going to display how well the player played the last time. The game over screen includes the elapsed time as the last score alongside the current game score. Players can then see how well they do this time compared to last time.

Time for action – Saving the game score

1. First, we need to add a few markups in the popup section to display the last score. Add the following HTML in the popup section in index.html:

```
<p>
  <small>Last Score: <span class='last-score'>20</span>
  </small>
</p>
```

2. Then, we open the html5games.matchgame.js to modify some game logic in the gameover function.

3. Add the following highlighted code in the gameover function. It loads the saved score from local storage and displays it as the score last time. Then, save the current score in the local storage:

```
function gameover()
{
    // stop the timer
    clearInterval(matchingGame.timer);

    // display the elapsed time in the game over popup
    $(".score").html($("#elapsed-time"));

    // load the saved last score from local storage
    var lastElapsedTime = localStorage.getItem
        ("last-elapsed-time");

    // convert the elapsed seconds into minute:second format
    // calculate the minutes and seconds from elapsed time
    var minute = Math.floor(lastElapsedTime / 60);
    var second = lastElapsedTime % 60;
```

```
    // add padding 0 if minute and second is less then 10
    if (minute < 10) minute = "0" + minute;
    if (second < 10) second = "0" + second;

    // display the last elapsed time in game over popup
    $(".last-score").html(minute+":"+second);

    // save the score into local storage
    localStorage.setItem
        ("last-elapsed-time", matchingGame.elapsedTime);

    // show the game over popup
    $("#popup").removeClass("hide");
}
```

4. It is now time to save all files and test the game in the browser. When you finish the game for the first time, the last score should be 00:00. Then, try to finish the game for the second time. The game over pop up will show the elapsed time you played the last time. The following screenshot shows the game over screen with the current and last score:

What just happened?

We just built a basic scoring system that compares a player's score with his/her last score.

Storing and loading data with local storage

We can store data by using the setItem function from the localStorage object. The following table shows the usage of the function:

```
localStorage.setItem(key, value);
```

Argument	Definition	Description
key	The key is the name of the record that we used to identify an entry.	The key is a string and each record has a unique key. Writing a new value to an existing key overwrites the old value.
value	The value is any data which will be stored.	It can be any data, but the final storage is in a string. We will discuss this shortly.

In our example, we save the game elapsed time as the score with the following code by using the key last-elapsed-item:

```
localStorage.setItem("last-elapsed-time", matchingGame.elapsedTime);
```

Complementary to setItem, we get the stored data by using the getItem function in the following way:

```
localStorage.getItem(key);
```

The function returns the stored value of the given key. It returns null when trying to get a non-existent key. This can be used to check whether we have stored any data for a specific key.

The local storage saves the string value

The local storage stores data in a key-value pair. The key and value are both strings. If we save numbers, Boolean, or any type other than string, then it will convert the value into a string while saving.

Usually, problems occur when we load a saved value from the local storage. The loaded value is a string regardless of the type we are saving. We need to explicitly parse the value into the correct type before using it.

For example, if we save a floating number into the local storage, we need to use the parseFloat function when loading it. The following code snippet shows how we can use parseFloat to retrieve a stored floating number:

```
var score = 13.234;

localStorage.setItem("game-score",score);
// result: stored "13.234".

var gameScore = localStorage.getItem("game-score");
// result: get "13.234" into gameScore;

gameScore = parseFloat(gameScore);
// result: 13.234 floating value
```

In the preceding code snippet, the manipulation may be incorrect if we forget to convert the `gameScore` from string to float. For instance, if we add the `gameScore` by 1 without the `parseFloat` function, the result will be **13.2341** instead of **14.234**. So, be sure to convert the value from local storage to its correct type.

Size limitation of local storage

There is a size limitation on the data stored through `localStorage` for each domain. This size limitation may be slightly different in different browsers. Normally, the size limitation is 5 MB. If the limit is exceeded, then the browser throws a `QUOTA_EXCEEDED_ERR` exception when setting a key-value into `localStorage`.

Treating the local storage object as an associated array

Besides using the `setItem` and `getItem` functions, we can treat the `localStorage` object as an associated array and access the stored entries by using square brackets.

For instance, we can replace the following code with the latter version:

Using the `setItem` and `getItem`:

```
localStorage.setItem("last-elapsed-time", elapsedTime);
var lastElapsedTime = localStorage.getItem("last-elapsed-time");
```

Access `localStorage` as an array as follows:

```
localStorage["last-elapsed-time"] = elapsedTime;
var lastElapsedTime = localStorage["last-elapsed-time"];
```

Saving objects in the local storage

Now, imagine that we are saving not only the score, but also the date and time when the ranking is created. We can either save two separate keys for the score and date time of playing, or pack the two values into one object and store it in the local storage.

We will pack all the game data into one object and store it.

Time for action – Saving the time alongside the score

Carry out the following steps:

1. First, open the `index.html` file from our CSS3 memory matching game.

2. Replace the HTML markup with the last score by the following HTML (it shows both scores and the date time in the game over pop up):

```
<p>
   <small>Last Score: <span class='last-score'>20</span><br>
     Saved on: <span class='saved-time'>13/4/2011 3:14pm</span>
   </small>
</p>
```

3. The HTML markup is now ready. We will move on to the game logic. Open the `html5games.matchgame.js` file in a text editor.

4. We will modify the `gameover` function. Add the following highlighted code to the `gameover` function. It gets the current date time when the game ends and packs a formatted date time with elapsed time together into local storage:

```
function gameover()
{
   // stop the timer
   clearInterval(matchingGame.timer);

   // display the elapsed time in the game over popup
   $(".score").html($("#elapsed-time"));

   // load the saved last score and save time from local storage
   var lastScore = localStorage.getItem("last-score");

   // check if there is no any saved record
   lastScoreObj = JSON.parse(lastScore);
   if (lastScoreObj == null)
   {
      // create an empty record if there is no any saved record
      lastScoreObj = {"savedTime": "no record", "score": 0};
   }
   var lastElapsedTime = lastScoreObj.score;

   // convert the elapsed seconds into minute:second format
   // calculate the minutes and seconds from elapsed time
   var minute = Math.floor(lastElapsedTime / 60);
   var second = lastElapsedTime % 60;
```

```
// add padding 0 if minute and second is less then 10
if (minute < 10) minute = "0" + minute;
if (second < 10) second = "0" + second;

// display the last elapsed time in game over popup
$(".last-score").html(minute+":"+second);

// display the saved time of last score
var savedTime = lastScoreObj.savedTime;
$(".saved-time").html(savedTime);

// get the current datetime
var currentTime = new Date();
var month = currentTime.getMonth() + 1;
var day = currentTime.getDate();
var year = currentTime.getFullYear();
var hours = currentTime.getHours();
var minutes = currentTime.getMinutes();
// add padding 0 to minutes
if (minutes < 10) minutes = "0" + minutes;
var seconds = currentTime.getSeconds();
// add padding 0 to seconds
if (seconds < 10) seconds = "0" + seconds;

var now = day+"/"+month+"/"+year+"
  "+hours+":"+minutes+":"+seconds;

//construct the object of datetime and game score
var obj = { "savedTime": now, "score":
  matchingGame.elapsedTime};

// save the score into local storage
localStorage.setItem("last-score", JSON.stringify(obj));

// show the game over popup
$("#popup").removeClass("hide");
}
```

5. We will save the files and open the game in a web browser.

6. When we finish the game for the first time, we will get a screen similar to the following screenshot which will show our game score and state that there are no previous records:

7. Now try reloading the page and play the game again. When we finish the game for the second time, the game over dialog will show our saved record. The following screenshot shows how it should look:

What just happened?

We have just used a `Date` object in JavaScript to get the current date and time when the game is over. In addition, we packed the game over date and time and the game elapsed time in one object and saved it into the local storage. The saved object is encoded in a JSON string. It will also load the last saved date and time and the game elapsed time from the storage and parse it back to the JavaScript object from a string.

Getting the current date and time in JavaScript

The Date object in JavaScript is used to working with date and time. When we create an instance from the Date object, by default it stores the current date and time. Therefore, we can easily get the current date and time information by using the following code snippet:

```
var currentTime = new Date();
var month = currentTime.getMonth() + 1;
var day = currentTime.getDate();
var year = currentTime.getFullYear();
var hours = currentTime.getHours();
var minutes = currentTime.getMinutes();
var seconds = currentTime.getSeconds();
```

As we display the date and time in a human-friendly format, we also need to add zero padding to minutes and seconds when they are less than 10. We do this as follows:

```
if (minutes < 10) minutes = "0" + minutes;
if (seconds < 10) seconds = "0" + seconds;

var now = day+"/"+month+"/"+year+" "+hours+":"+minutes+":"+seconds;
```

The following table lists some useful functions in the Date object to get the date and time:

Function	Description
getFullYear	Returns the year in four digits
getMonth	Returns the month in integer, starting from 0 (Jan is 0 and Dec is 11)
getDate	Returns the day of the month, starting from 1
getDay	Returns the day of the week, starting from 0 (Sunday is 0 and Saturday is 6)
getHours	Returns the hour, starting from 0 to 23
getMinutes	Returns the minutes
getSeconds	Returns the seconds
getMilliseconds	Returns the milliseconds in 3 digits
getTime	Returns the number of milliseconds since 1 Jan, 1970 00:00

The Mozilla Developer Network provides a detailed reference for using the `Date` object at the following URL:

```
https://developer.mozilla.org/en/JavaScript/Reference/
Global_Objects/Date
```

Using the native JSON to encode an object into a string

We used JSON to represent the game level data in *Chapter 4, Building an Untangle Game with Canvas and Drawing API*.

JSON is an object notation format that is friendly for machines to parse and generate. In this example, we packed the final elapsed time and the date and time into an object. Then, we encoded the object into JSON. Modern web browsers come with a native JSON support. We can easily encode any JavaScript object into JSON by using the `stringify` function as follows:

```
JSON.stringify(anyObject);
```

Normally, we only use the first parameter for the `stringify` function. It is the object that we are going to encode as a string. The following code snippet demonstrates the result of an encoded JavaScript object:

```
var jsObj = {};
jsObj.testArray = [1,2,3,4,5];
jsObj.name = 'CSS3 Matching Game';
jsObj.date = '8 May, 2011';
JSON.stringify(jsObj);
// result: {"testArray":[1,2,3,4,5],"name":"CSS3 Matching
Game","date":"8 May, 2011"}
```

The `stringify` method can parse objects with data structure into a string well. However, it cannot convert anything from an object into a string. For instance, it will return an error if we try to pass a DOM element into it. It will return the string representing the date if we pass a Date object. Alternatively, it will drop all methods definition of the parsing object.

Loading a stored object from a JSON string

The complete form of **JSON** is **JavaScript Object Notation**. From the name, we know that it uses the syntax from JavaScript to represent an object. Therefore, it is very easy to parse a JSON formatted string back to a JavaScript object.

The following code snippet shows how we can use the parse function in the JSON object:

```
JSON.parse(jsonFormattedString);
```

We can open the console in the Web Inspector to test the JSON JavaScript functions. The following screenshot shows the running result of the code snippets we just discussed when encoding an object and parsing them:

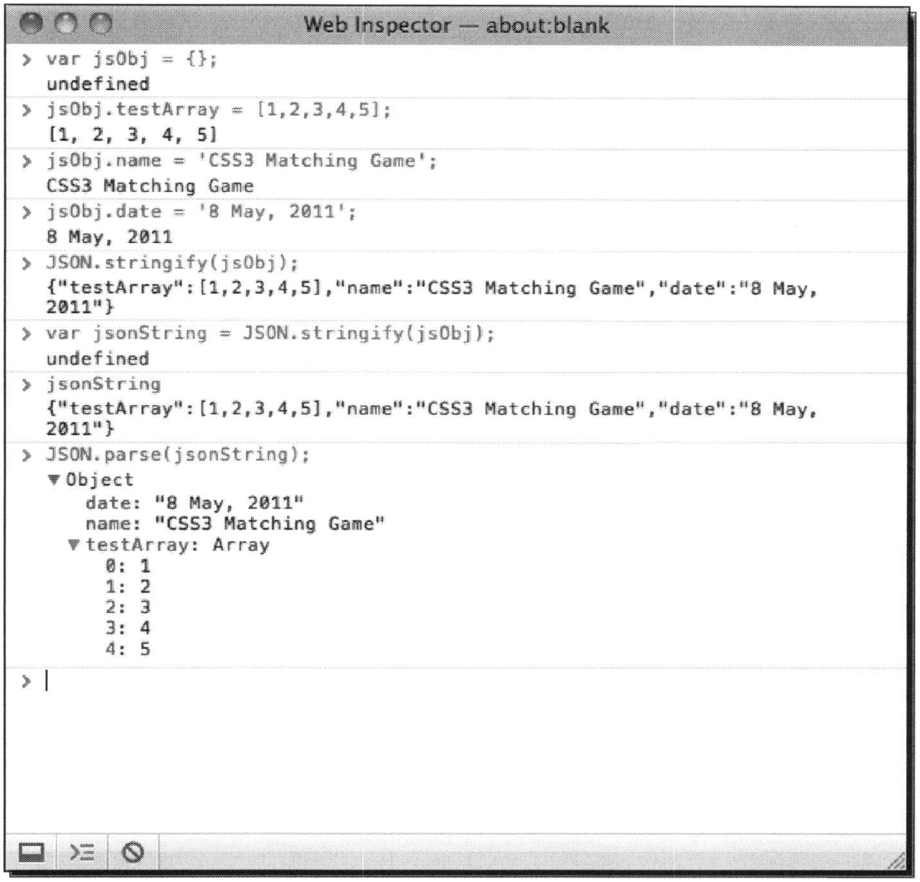

Inspecting the local storage in a console window

After we have saved something in the local storage, we may want to know what is exactly saved before we write the loading part. We can inspect what we have saved by using the storage panel in the Web Inspector. It lists all the saved key-value pairs under the same domain. The following screenshot shows that we have the **last-score** saved with value **{"savedTime":"23/2/2011 19:27:02","score":23}**.

The value is the result of the `JSON.stringify` function we used to encode the object into JSON. You may also try saving an object directly into local storage:

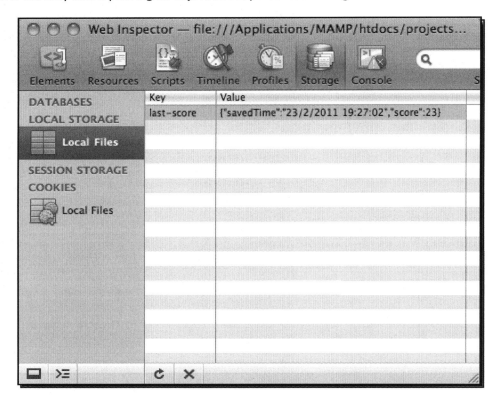

 Besides `localStorage`, there are other storage approaches that were not discussed. These approaches include the **Web SQL Database** (`http://www.w3.org/TR/webdatabase/`), which uses SQLite to store data, and **IndexedDB** (`https://developer.mozilla.org/en/IndexedDB`).

Notifying players of breaking a new record with a nice ribbon effect

Imagine that we want to encourage players by informing them that they broke a new record compared to the last score. We want to show a ribbon with `New Record` text on it. Thanks to the new CSS3 properties, we can create a ribbon effect completely in CSS.

Time for action – Creating a ribbon in CSS3

We will create a new record ribbon and display it when a player breaks his/her last score. So, carry out the following steps:

1. First, open `index.html` where we will add the ribbon HTML markup.

2. Add the following highlighted HTML right after `popup-box` and before `popup-box-content`:

```
<div id="popup-box">
    <div class="ribbon hide">
        <div class="ribbon-body">
            <span>New Record</span>
        </div>
        <div class="triangle"></div>
    </div>
    <div id="popup-box-content">
    ...
```

3. Next, we need to focus on the style sheet. The entire ribbon effect is done in CSS. Open the `matchgame.css` file in a text editor.

4. In the `popup-box` styling, we need to add a relative position to it. We do this as follows:

```
#popup-box {
    position: relative;
    ...
}
```

5. Then, we need to add the following styles that create the ribbon effect to the CSS file:

```
.ribbon.hide {
    display: none;
}
.ribbon {
    float: left;
    position: absolute;
    left: -7px;
    top: 165px;
    z-index: 0;

    font-size: .5em;
    text-transform: uppercase;
    text-align: right;
```

```
   }

   .ribbon-body {
      height: 14px;
      background: #ca3d33;
      padding: 6px;
      z-index: 100;
      -webkit-box-shadow: 2px 2px 0 rgba(150,120,70,.4);
      border-radius: 0 5px 5px 0;

      color: #fff;
      text-shadow: 0px 1px 1px rgba(0,0,0,.3);
   }

   .triangle{
      position: relative;
      height: 0px;
      width: 0;
      left: -5px;
      top: -32px;
      border-style: solid;
      border-width: 6px;
      border-color: transparent #882011 transparent transparent;
      z-index: -1;
   }
```

6. Lastly, we need to modify the game over logic a little bit. Open the `html5games.matchgame.js` file and locate the `gameover` function.

7. Add the following code to the `gameover` function which compares the current score with the last score to determine the new record:

```
if (lastElapsedTime == 0 || matchingGame.elapsedTime <
lastElapsedTime)
{
   $(".ribbon").removeClass("hide");
}
```

8. We will test the game in a web browser. Try finishing a game slowly and then finish another game fast. When you break the last score, the game over pop up shows a nice **NEW RECORD** ribbon, as shown in the following screenshot:

What just happened?

We have just created a ribbon effect in a pure CSS3 style with some help from JavaScript to show and hide it. The ribbon is composited by a little triangle overlaid by a rectangle, as shown in the following screenshot:

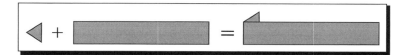

Now, how can we create a triangle in CSS? We can create a triangle by setting both width and height to 0 and drawing only one border. The size of the triangle is then decided by the border width. The following code is for the triangle CSS we used in our new record ribbon:

```
.triangle{
   position: relative;
   height: 0px;
   width: 0;
   left: -5px;
   top: -32px;
   border-style: solid;
   border-width: 6px;
   border-color: transparent #882011 transparent transparent;
   z-index: -1;
}
```

The following PVM Garage website provides a detailed explanation on pure CSS3 ribbon usage:

`http://www.pvmgarage.com/2010/01/how-to-create-depth-and-nice-3d-ribbons-only-using-css3/`

Have a go hero – Saving and comparing only to the fastest time

Each time the game finishes, it compares the last score with the current score. Then, it saves the current score.

How about changing the code to save the highest score and show the new record ribbon when breaking the highest score?

Saving the entire game progress

We have enhanced our CSS3 memory matching game by adding a game over screen and storing the game record. Imagine now that a player is in the mid game and accidentally closes the web browser. Once the player opens the game again, the game starts from the beginning and the game that the player was playing is lost. With the local storage, we can encode the entire game data into JSON and store them. In this way, players can resume their game later.

Saving the game progress

We are going to pack the game data into one object and save it into the local storage every second.

Time for action – Saving all essential game data in the local storage

We will continue work with our CSS3 memory matching game:

1. Open the `html5games.matchgame.js` JavaScript file.

2. Add the following code at the top of the JavaScript file after declaring the `matchingGame` variable. This code creates an object named `savingObject` to save the array of deck and removed cards and the current elapsed time:

```
matchingGame.savingObject = {};

matchingGame.savingObject.deck = [];
```

```
// an array to store which card is removed by storing their index.
matchingGame.savingObject.removedCards = [];

// store the counting elapsed time.
matchingGame.savingObject.currentElapsedTime = 0;
```

3. In the jQuery function, add the following highlighted code. It clones the order of the deck to the `savingObject`. In addition, it assigns an index to each card in the DOM data attribute:

```
$(function(){

    // shuffling the deck
    matchingGame.deck.sort(shuffle);

    // copying the deck into saving object.
    matchingGame.savingObject.deck = matchingGame.deck.slice();

    // clone 12 copies of the card DOM
    for(var i=0;i<11;i++){
        $(".card:first-child").clone().appendTo("#cards");
    }
    ...

// embed the pattern data into the DOM element.
$(this).attr("data-pattern",pattern);

// save the index into the DOM element, so we know which is the
next card.
$(this).attr("data-card-index",index);
...
```

4. We have a `countTimer` function that executes every second. We add the following highlighted code in the `countTimer` function. It saves the current elapsed time in the `savingObject` and also saves the object in the local storage:

```
function countTimer()
{
    matchingGame.elapsedTime++;

    // save the current elapsed time into savingObject.
    matchingGame.savingObject.currentElapsedTime =
      matchingGame.elapsedTime;
    ...
    // save the game progress
```

```
        saveSavingObject();
}
```

5. The game removes cards when the player finds a matching pair. We replace the original `$(".card-removed").remove();` code with the following highlighted code in the `removeTookCards` function. It remembers which cards are removed in the `savingObject`:

```
function removeTookCards()
{
    // add each removed card into the array which store which cards
       are removed
    $(".card-removed").each(function(){
        matchingGame.savingObject.removedCards.push
           ($(this).data("card-index"));
        $(this).remove();
    });

    // check if all cards are removed and show game over
    if ($(".card").length == 0)
    {
        gameover();
    }
}
```

6. We have to remove the saved game data in the local storage when the game is over. Add the following code in the `gameover` function:

```
function gameover()
{

    //at last, we clear the saved savingObject
    localStorage.removeItem("savingObject");
}
```

7. At last, we have a function to save the `savingObject` in the local storage:

```
function saveSavingObject()
{
    // save the encoded saving object into local storage
    localStorage["savingObject"] =
      JSON.stringify(matchingGame.savingObject);
}
```

8. We have modified the code a lot and it is now time to test the game in a web browser. After the game runs, try clearing several matching cards. Then, open the storage panel in the Web Inspector. The local storage should contain an entry similar to the one shown in the following screenshot. It is a record with a key `savingObject` and a value with a long string in a JSON format. The JSON string contains the shuffled deck, removed cards, and the current elapsed time:

What just happened?

We have just entered all essential game data into an object named `savingObject`. This `savingObject` contains all information that we need to recreate the game later. It includes the order of cards, removed cards, and the current elapsed time.

Lastly, we saved `savingObject` in `localStorage` on each second. The object is encoded into JSON using the `stringify` function we used earlier in this chapter. Then, we recreated the game by parsing the JSON string from the local storage.

Removing a record from the local storage

We need to remove the saved record when the game is over. Otherwise, the new game will not start. Local storage provides a `remoteItem` function to remove a specific record.

Here is how we use the function to remove the record with the given key:

```
localStorage.removeItem(key);
```

 If you want to remove all stored records, then you can use the `localStorage.clear()` function.

Cloning an array in JavaScript

We cloned the shuffled deck in `savingObject`, so that we could use the order of the deck to recreate the cards when we resumed the game. However, we cannot copy an array by assigning the array to another variable. The following code fails to copy an array A to array B:

```
var a = [1,2,3,4,5];
var b = a;
a.pop();
// result:
// a: [1,2,3,4]
// b: [1,2,3,4]
```

The `slice` function provides an easy way to clone an array with only primitive types of elements. We can clone an array with the `slice` function as long as it does not contain another array or object as an element. The following code successfully clones an array A to B:

```
var a = [1,2,3,4,5];
var b = a.slice();
a.pop();
// result:
// a: [1,2,3,4]
// b: [1,2,3,4,5]
```

The `slice` function is normally used to create a new array by selecting a range of elements from an existing array. When using the `slice` function without any arguments, it clones the entire array. The Mozilla Developer Network provides a detailed usage on the `slice` function at the following URL:

```
https://developer.mozilla.org/en/JavaScript/Reference/Global_Objects/
Array/slice
```

Resuming the game progress

We have saved the game progress, but have not yet written the logic for resuming the game. So, let's move on to the resuming part.

Time for action – Resuming a game from the local storage

Carry out the following steps:

1. Open the `html5games.matchgame.js` JavaScript file.

2. In the jQuery ready function, we used the saved order of deck in the previous game instead of shuffling a new deck. Add the following highlighted code into the `ready` function:

```
$(function(){

    // shuffling the deck
    matchingGame.deck.sort(shuffle);

    // re-create the saved deck
    var savedObject = savedSavingObject();
    if (savedObject != undefined)
    {
        matchingGame.deck = savedObject.deck;
    }
    ...
```

3. After initializing the cards in the ready function, we remove cards which were removed in the previous game. We also restore the saved elapsed time from the saved value. Add the following highlighted code in the jQuery ready function:

```
// removed cards that were removed in savedObject.
if (savedObject != undefined)
{
  matchingGame.savingObject.removedCards =
    savedObject.removedCards;
  // find those cards and remove them.
  for(var i in matchingGame.savingObject.removedCards)
  {
    $(".card[data-card-index="+matchingGame.savingObject.
      removedCards[i]+"]").remove();
  }
}

// reset the elapsed time to 0.
matchingGame.elapsedTime = 0;

// restore the saved elapsed time
if (savedObject != undefined)
{
    matchingGame.elapsedTime = savedObject.currentElapsedTime;
    matchingGame.savingObject.currentElapsedTime = savedObject.
    currentElapsedTime;
}
```

4. Finally, we create the following function to retrieve `savingObject` from the local storage:

```
// Returns the saved savingObject from the local storage.
function savedSavingObject()
{
    // returns the saved saving object from local storage
    var savingObject = localStorage["savingObject"];
    if (savingObject != undefined)
    {
        savingObject = JSON.parse(savingObject);
    }
    return savingObject;
}
```

5. Save all files and open the game in web a browser. Try playing the game by removing several matching cards. Then, close the browser window and open the game again. The game should resume from the state where we closed the window, as shown in the following screenshot:

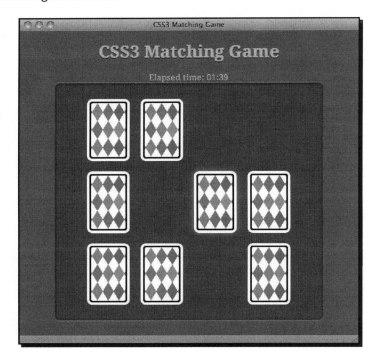

What just happened?

We just finished the game loading part by parsing the saved JSON string of the entire game status.

Then, we restored the elapsed time and order of deck from the loaded `savingObject`. Restoring these two properties is simply variable assigning. The tricky part is recreating the card removing. In the game saving section, we assigned an index to each card DOM by **custom data attribute** `data-card-index`. We stored the index of each removed card when saving the game, so we can know which cards are removed when loading the game. Then, we can remove those cards when the game sets up. The following code removes the cards in a jQuery game `ready` function:

```
if (savedObject != undefined)
{
    matchingGame.savingObject.removedCards = savedObject.removedCards;
    // find those cards and remove them.
```

```
for(var i in matchingGame.savingObject.removedCards)
{
    $(".card[data-card-index="+matchingGame.savingObject.
    removedCards[i]+"]").remove();
}
}
```

> **Tracking the storage changes with the storage event**
>
> Sometimes, we may want to listen to the changes of the `localStorage`.
> We can do that by listening to the `storage` event. It is fired when anything
> is changed in the `localStorage`. The following link from *Dive into HTML5*
> provides a detailed discussion on how we can use the event:
>
> `http://diveintohtml5.org/storage.html#storage-event`

Pop quiz – Using local storage

Consider whether each of the following statements is true or not:

1. We can save an integer or object directly in the local storage.
2. We can save the data of an object into the local storage by encoding them into a string.
3. We can use `localStorage["hello"] = "world"` to save the value "world" with key "hello" in the local storage.

Summary

We learned a lot in this chapter about using the local storage to save the game data in a web browser.

Specifically, we covered:

◆ Saving and retrieving basic data into the key-value pair local storage
◆ Encoding an object into the JSON formatted string and parsing the string back to a JavaScript object
◆ Saving the entire game progress, so the game can resume even if left mid way

We also created a nice 3D ribbon as a **new record** badge in pure CSS3 styling.

Now that we have learned about improving our previous games by using the local storage, we are ready to move on to an advanced feature named **WebSocket** which connects players together in a real time interaction.

8

Building a Multiplayer Draw-and-Guess Game with WebSockets

We built several local single player games in previous chapters. In this chapter, we will build a multiplayer game with the help of WebSockets. WebSockets enable us to create event-based server-client architecture. The messages passed between all connected browsers become instant. We will combine the canvas drawing, JSON data packing, and several techniques learned in previous chapters to build the draw-and-guess game.

In this chapter, we will learn the following topics:

- ◆ Trying an existing multiuser sketchpad which shows drawings from different connected users through WebSockets
- ◆ Installing a WebSockets server which is implemented by `node.js`
- ◆ Connecting the server from a browser
- ◆ Creating an instant chat room with WebSocket API
- ◆ Creating a multiuser drawing pad in Canvas
- ◆ Building a draw-and-guess game by integrating the chat room and drawing with game logic

The following screenshot shows the draw-and-guess game that we will create in this chapter:

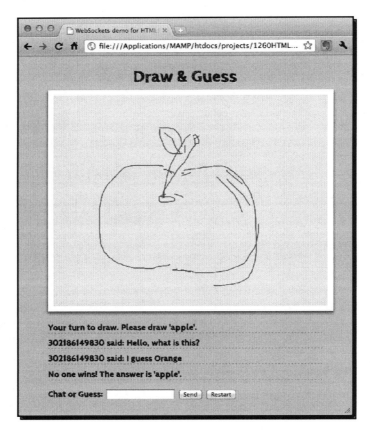

So, let's get on with it.

Trying an existing WebSockets web application

Before we start to build our WebSockets example, we will take a look at an existing multiuser sketchpad example. This example lets us know how the data is sent between browsers by using the WebSockets server instantly.

A browser's capability of using WebSockets

At the time of writing this book, only Apple Safari and Google Chrome supported the WebSockets API. Mozilla Firefox and Opera dropped support on WebSockets because of a potential security issue on the protocol. Google Chrome is also planning to drop WebSockets until the security hole is fixed.

The following link from Mozilla explains why they disabled WebSockets:

```
http://hacks.mozilla.org/2010/12/websockets-disabled-in-firefox-4/
```

Time for action – Trying the multiuser sketchpad

Carry out the following steps:

1. Open the following link in a web browser:

   ```
   http://www.chromeexperiments.com/detail/multiuser-sketchpad/
   ```

2. You will get an introduction page of the multiuser sketchpad. Right click on the **Launch Experiment** option and choose **Open link in new window**.

3. The browser prompts a new window with the sketchpad application. Then, we repeat the preceding step again to open another instance of the sketchpad.

4. Put the two browsers side by side on the desktop.

5. Try to draw something on either sketchpad. The drawing should appear on both sketchpads. In addition, the sketchpad is shared with everyone who is connecting. You may also see drawings from other users.

6. The following screenshot shows a cup drawn on the sketchpad by two users:

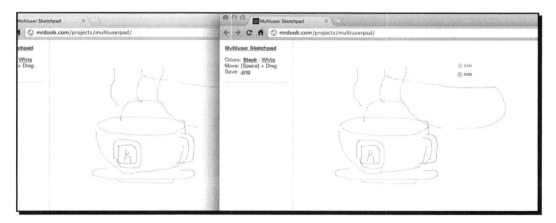

What just happened?

We have just seen how browsers can be connected together in real time. We draw something on the sketchpad and all other connected users can view the drawings. In addition, we can see what others are drawing too.

The example is made by using the HTML5 WebSockets feature with a backend server to broadcast drawing data to all connected browsers.

The drawing part is built on a canvas which we already covered in *Chapter 4, Building* the *Untangle Game with Canvas and Drawing API*. The WebSocket API enables browsers to establish a persistent connection with the server. The backend is an event-based server named node.js which we will install and use in this chapter.

Installing a WebSocket server

The HTML5, WebSockets provides a client-side API to connect a browser to a backend server. This server has to support WebSockets protocol in order to keep the connection persistent.

Installing the Node.JS WebSocket server

In this section, we will download and install a server named Node.JS on which we can install a WebSockets module.

Time for action – Installing Node.JS

Carry out the following steps:

1. Go to the following URL which contains the source code of the Node.JS server:

   https://github.com/joyent/node

2. Click on the **Downloads** button on the page. It prompts a dialog asking which format to download. Just select the ZIP format.

3. Unzip the ZIP file in a working directory.

4. In Linux or Mac OSX, use Terminal and change the directory to where the node.js file is located.

Node.JS works out of the box in Linux and Mac. The following link provides an installer for installing it on Windows:
http://node-js.prcn.co.cc/

5. Run the following command:
```
$ ./configure
$ sudo make install
```

The sudo make install command installs Node.JS with root ownership and also installs the required third party libraries with root access. The following link discusses how we can install the Node.JS without using sudo:
http://increaseyourgeek.wordpress.com/2010/08/18/
install-node-js-without-using-sudo/

6. The sudo make install command requires typing the password of the user in a system who has admin privileges. Type the password to continue the installation.

7. After the installation, we can check whether the node.js is installed by checking its version with the following command:
```
$ node --version
```

8. The preceding command should print a version number of the node.js. In my case, it is version 0.5 pre:
```
v0.5.0-pre
```

9. Next, we will install the WebSockets library for the Node.JS server. Go to the following URL in a browser:
```
https://github.com/miksago/node-websocket-server
```

10. Click on the **Downloads** button on the page and download the ZIP file.

11. Unzip the ZIP file in a directory. We will need the lib directory in this package later.

What just happened?

We just downloaded and installed the Node.JS server. We also downloaded the WebSockets library for the node.js server. We will build server logic on top of this server and the WebSockets library through the examples in this chapter.

> Node.js server installation runs well on Unix or Linux operating systems. However, it requires a few more steps to install and run the node.js server on Windows. The following link shows how we can install the node.js server on Windows:
>
> https://github.com/joyent/node/wiki/Building-node.js-on-Cygwin-(Windows)

Creating a WebSockets server to broadcast the connection count

We just installed the node.js server with the WebSockets library. Now, we will build something to test the WebSockets. Imagine now we want a server that accepts connections from browsers and then broadcasts the connection count to all users.

Time for action – Creating a WebSocket server that sends the total count of connections

Carry out the following steps:

1. Create a new directory named server.

2. Copy the entire lib folder in the node-websocket-server package in the server directory.

3. Create a new file named server.js under the server directory with the following content:

```
var ws = require(__dirname + '/lib/ws/server');
var server = ws.createServer();

server.addListener("connection", function(conn){
    // init stuff on connection
    console.log("A connection established with id",conn.id);
    var message = "Welcome "+conn.id+" joining the party.
      Total connection:"+server.manager.length;
    server.broadcast(message);
```

```
        });

        server.listen(8000);

        console.log("WebSocket server is running.");
        console.log("Listening to port 8000.");
```

4. Open the terminal and change to the server directory.

5. Type the following command to execute the server:

```
node server.js
```

6. We should get the following result if it works:

```
$ node server.js
WebSocket server is running.
Listening to port 8000.
```

What just happened?

We just created a simple server logic that initialized the WebSockets library and listened to the connection event.

Initializing the WebSockets server

In Node.JS, different functions are packed into modules. When we need a functionality in a specific module, we use require to load it. We load the WebSockets module and then initialize the server using the following code in the server logic:

```
var ws = require(__dirname + '/lib/ws/server');
var server = ws.createServer();
```

__dirname represents the current directory of the server JavaScript file that is being executed. We placed the lib folder under the same folder of our server logic file. Therefore, the WebSockets server is in **current directory | lib | ws | server**.

At last, we need to assign a port for the server to listen to by the following code:

```
server.listen(8000);
```

In the preceding code snippet, 8000 is the port number with which a client connects to this server. We may choose a different port number, but we have to ensure that the chosen port number is not overlapped by other common server services.

In order to get more information about the global scope objects and variables from the `node.js` server, please visit their official document at the following link:
`http://nodejs.org/docs/v0.4.3/api/globals.html`

Listening to the connection event on the server side

The `node.js` server is event-based. This means that most logic is executed when a certain event is fired. The following code we used in the example listens to the `connection` event and handles it:

```
server.addListener("connection", function(conn){
    console.log("A connection established with id",conn.id);
    …
});
```

The `connection` event comes with a connection argument. We have an `id` property in the connection instance that we can use to distinguish each connected client.

The following table lists two commonly used server events:

Server-side event for WebSockets node.js	Description
connection	Event fires when there is a new connection established by the client
close	Event fires when a connection closes

Getting a count of connected clients on the server side

We can get the count of connected clients in the WebSockets `node.js` server by accessing the server manager. We can get the count by using the following code:

```
var totalConnectedClients = server.manager.length;
```

Broadcasting a message to all connected browsers

Once the server gets a new `connection` event, we broadcast the updated count of the connection to all clients. Broadcasting a message to clients is easy. We just need to call the `broadcast` function in the `server` instance with a `string` argument as the message.

The following code snippet broadcasts a server message to all connected browsers:

```
var message = "a message from server";
server.broadcast(message);
```

Creating a client that connects to a WebSocket server and getting the total connections count

We built the server in the last example and now we will build a client that connects to our WebSocket server and receives messages from the server. The message will contain the total connection count from the server.

Time for action – Showing the connection count in a WebSocket application

Carry out the following steps:

1. Create a new directory named `client`.

2. Create an HTML file named `index.htm` in the `client` folder.

3. We will add a few markups in our HTML file. Put the following code in the `index.htm` file:

```
<!DOCTYPE html>
<html lang="en">
<head>
  <meta charset="utf-8">
  <title>WebSockets demo for HTML5 Games Development: A
    Beginner's Guide</title>
  <meta name="description" content="This is a WebSockets demo
    for the book HTML5 Games Development: A Beginner's Guide
    by Makzan">
  <meta name="author" content="Makzan">

</head>
<body>

<script src="js/jquery-1.6.min.js"></script>
<script src="js/html5games.websocket.js"></script>
</body>
</html>
```

4. Create a directory named `js` and put the jQuery JavaScript file inside.

5. Create a new file named `html5games.websockets.js` as follows:

```
var websocketGame = {
}
// init script when the DOM is ready.
$(function(){
```

```
// check if existence of WebSockets in browser
if (window["WebSocket"]) {

  // create connection
  websocketGame.socket = new WebSocket("ws://127.0.0.1:8000");

  // on open event
  websocketGame.socket.onopen = function(e) {
    console.log('WebSocket connection established.');
  };

  // on message event
  websocketGame.socket.onmessage = function(e) {
    console.log(e.data);
  };

  // on close event
  websocketGame.socket.onclose = function(e) {
    console.log('WebSocket connection closed.');
  };
}
});
```

6. We will test the code. First, we need to run the node server with our `server.js` code by node `server.js`.

7. Next, open the `index.htm` file in a client directory in a web browser twice.

8. Inspect the server terminal. There should be log messages similar to the following indicating the connection information and total connection count:

```
$ node server.js
WebSocket server is running.
Listening to port 8000.
A connection established with id 3863522640
A connection established with id 3863522651
```

9. Then, we inspect the console panel in a browser. We get the total connection count once we have loaded the page. The following screenshot shows the result on the client side:

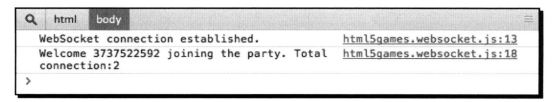

What just happened?

We just built a client that established a WebSockets connection to the server we built in the last section. The client then prints any message received from the server to the console panel in the Inspector.

Establishing a WebSocket connection

In any browser that supports WebSockets, we can establish a connection by creating a new WebSocket instance with the following code:

```
var socket = new WebSocket(url);
```

The url argument is a string with the WebSockets URL. In our example, we are running our server locally. Therefore, the URL we have used is ws://127.0.0.1:8000, where 8000 represents the port number of the server to which we are connecting. It is 8000 because the server is listening to the port 8000 when we built the server-side logic.

WebSockets client events

Similar to the server, we have several WebSockets events on the client side. The following table lists the events we will use to deal with WebSockets:

Event name	Description
onopen	Fired when a connection to the server is established
onmessage	Fired when any message from the server is received
onclose	Fired when the server closes the connection
onerror	Fired when there is any error in the connection

Building a chatting application with WebSockets

We now know how many browsers are connected. Suppose we want to build a chat room where users can type a message in their respective browsers and broadcast the message to all the connected users instantly.

Sending a message to the server

We will let the user input a message and then send the message to the node.js server. The server will then forward the message to all connected browsers. Once the browser receives the messages, it displays it in the chat area. In this case, the users are connected to the instant chat room once they load the web page.

Time for action – Sending a message to the server through WebSockets

Carry out the following steps:

1. First, code the server logic.

2. Open `server.js` and add the following highlighted code:

```
server.addListener("connection", function(conn){
    // init stuff on connection
    console.log("A connection established with id",conn.id);
    var message = "Welcome "+conn.id+" joining the party.
      Total connection:"+server.manager.length;
    server.broadcast(message);

    // listen to the message
    conn.addListener("message", function(message){
        console.log("Got data '"+message+"' from
          connection "+conn.id);
    });
});
```

3. Now move on to the `client` folder.

4. Open the `index.htm` file and add the following markup in the `body` section. It provides inputs for the user to type and send messages to the server:

```
<input type='text' id="chat-input">
<input type='button' value="Send" id="send">
```

5. Then, add the following code to the `html5games.websocket.js` JavaScript file. It sends the message to the server when the user clicks on the `send` button or presses the *Enter* key:

```
$("#send").click(sendMessage);

$("#chat-input").keypress(function(event) {
    if (event.keyCode == '13') {
        sendMessage();
    }
});

function sendMessage()
{
    var message = $("#chat-input").val();
    websocketGame.socket.send(message);
```

```
    $("#chat-input").val("");
}
```

6. Before testing our code, check the server terminal and see whether the node server is still running. Press *Ctrl+C* to terminate it and run it again by using the `node server.js` command.

7. Open `index.htm` in a web browser. You should see an input text field with a **Send** button as shown in the following screenshot:

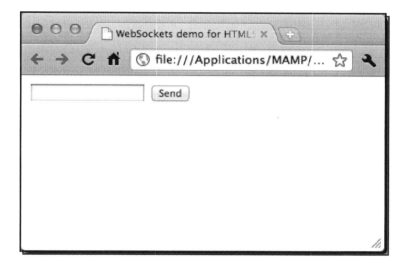

8. Try to type something in the input text field and then click on the **Send** button or press *Enter*. The input text is cleared.

9. Now, switch to the server terminal and we will see the server printing the text we just sent. You can also put the browser and server terminal side by side to see how instantly the message is sent from the client to the server. The following screenshot shows the server terminal with messages from two connected browsers:

```
WebSocket server is running.
Listening to port 8000.
A connection established with id 4391524340
A connection established with id 4391524351
Got data 'Testing message.' from connection 4391524340
Got data 'Hi, I'm a web browser connecting you with WebSocket.' from connection 4391524351
Got data 'We can send message to server now. cool.' from connection 4391524340
```

What just happened?

We just extended our connection example by adding an input text field for the users to type some text there and send it out. The text is sent as a message to the WebSockets server. The server will then print the received message in the terminal.

Sending a message from the client to the server

In order to send a message from the client to the server, we call the following send method in the WebSocket instance:

```
websocketGame.socket.send(message);
```

In the following code snippet from our example, we get the message from the input text field and send it to the server:

```
var message = $("#chat-input").val();
websocketGame.socket.send(message);
```

Receiving a message on the server side

On the server side, we need to handle the message we just sent from the client. We have an event named message in the connection instance in the WebSocket node.js library. We can listen to the connection message event to receive a message from each client connection.

The following code snippet shows how we use the message event listener to print the message and the unique connection ID on the server terminal:

```
conn.addListener("message", function(message){
    console.log("Got data '"+message+"' from connection "+conn.id);
});
```

 Only string is accepted when sending and receiving messages between the server and the client. We cannot directly send objects. However, we can convert the data into a JSON-formatted string before transmitting. We will show an example of sending data objects later in this chapter.

Broadcasting every received message on the server side to create a chat room

In the last example, the server could receive messages sent from browsers. However, the server does nothing except print the received messages in the terminal. Therefore, we will add some logic to the server to broadcast the messages out.

Time for action – Broadcasting the messages to all connected browsers

Carry out the following steps:

1. Open the `server.js` file for the server-side logic.

2. Add the following highlighted code to the message event listener handler:

```
conn.addListener("message", function(message){
    console.log("Got data '"+message+"' from connection "+conn.id);
    var displayMessage = conn.id + " says: "+message;
    server.broadcast(displayMessage);
});
```

3. That is it for the server side. Move on to the `client` folder and open the `index.htm` file.

4. We want to display the chat messages in the chat history area. Add the following code to the HTML file:

```
<ul id="chat-history"></ul>
```

5. Next, we need the client-side JavaScript to handle the received message from the server. We used it to print it out into the console panel, replace the `console.log` code by the following highlighted code in the `onmessage` event handler:

```
socket.onmessage = function(e) {
    $("#chat-history").append("<li>"+e.data+"</li>");
};
```

6. Let's test our code. Terminate any running node server by *Ctrl + C*. Then run the server again.

7. Open the `index.htm` file twice and put them side by side. Type something in the text field and press *Enter*. The message will appear on both opened browsers. If you open many instances of the HTML file, the message should appear on all browsers. The following screenshot shows two browsers displaying the chat history side by side:

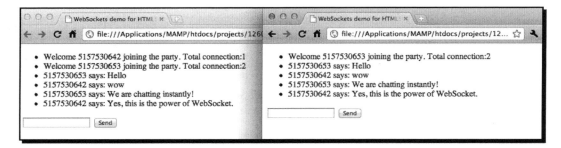

What just happened?

This is an extension of our previous examples. We discussed how a server broadcasts the connection count to all connected clients. We also discussed how the client sends a message to the server. In this example, we combine these two techniques to let the server broadcast the received messages to all connected users.

Comparing between WebSockets and polling approaches

If you have ever built a web page chat room by using a server-side language and a database, then you may wonder what is the difference between the WebSocket implementation and the traditional one.

The traditional chat room method is often implemented by using a **polling** approach. The client asks the server for an update periodically. The server responds to the client with either no update or updated data. However, the traditional approach has several problems. The client does not get new data updated from the server until the next time it asks the server. This means that the data update is delayed with the periodic time and the response is not instant enough. If we want to improve this issue by shortening the polling duration, then more bandwidth is utilized because clients need to keep sending requests to the server.

The following graph shows requests between the client and the server. It shows that many useless requests are sent, but the server responds to the client without any new data:

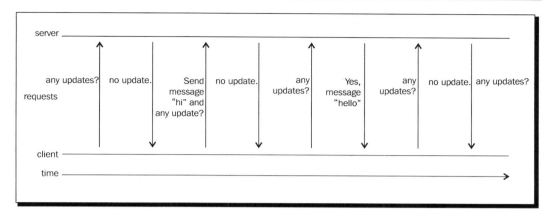

There is a better polling approach named **long polling**. The client sends a request to the server and waits for the response. Instead of the traditional polling approach where the server responds with "no update", the server does not respond at all until there is something that needs to be pushed to the server. In this approach, the server can push something to clients whenever there is an update. Once the client receives a response from the server, it creates another request and waits for the next server notification. The following graph shows the long polling approach where clients ask for updates and the server responds only when there is an update:

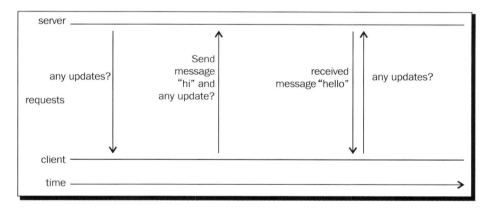

In the WebSockets approach, the number of requests are way less than the polling approach. It is because the connection between the client and server is persistent. Once the connection is established, a request from either the client side or the server side is sent only when there is any update. For instance, a client sends a message to the server when it wants to update something to the server. The server also sends messages to clients only when it needs to notify the clients of a data update. No other useless requests are sent during the connection. Therefore, less bandwidth is utilized. The following graph shows the WebSockets approach:

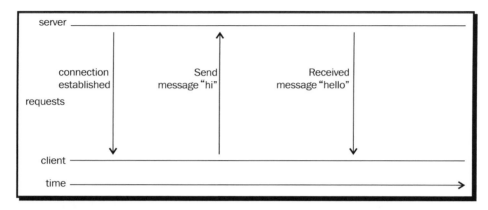

Pop quiz – The benefit of WebSockets verses the polling approach

What are the benefits of using an event-based WebSockets approach to implement the multiuser chat room? How do these benefits make the message-passing so instant?

Making a shared drawing whiteboard with Canvas and WebSockets

Suppose we want a shared sketchpad. Anyone can draw something on the sketchpad and all others can view it, just like the sketchpad example we played at the beginning of this chapter. We learned how messages are communicated between clients and servers. We will go further and send drawing data.

Building a local drawing sketchpad

Before we deal with the data sending and the server handling, let's focus on making a drawing whiteboard. We will use the canvas to build a local drawing sketchpad.

Time for action – Making a local drawing whiteboard with the Canvas

Carry out the following steps:

1. We will focus only on the client side in this section. Open the `index.htm` file and add the following `canvas` markup:

```
<canvas id='drawing-pad' width='500' height='400'>
</canvas>
```

2. We will draw something on the canvas and we will need the mouse position relative to the canvas. We did this in *Chapter 4, Building* an *Untangle Game with Canvas and Drawing API.* Add the following style to the canvas:

```
<style>
   canvas{position:relative;}
</style>
```

3. Then, we open the `html5games.websocket.js` JavaScript file to add the drawing logic.

4. Replace the `websocketGame` global object with the following variable at the top of the JavaScript file:

```
var websocketGame = {
   // indicates if it is drawing now.
   isDrawing : false,

   // the starting point of next line drawing.
   startX : 0,
   startY : 0,
}

// canvas context
var canvas = document.getElementById('drawing-pad');
var ctx = canvas.getContext('2d');
```

5. In the jQuery `ready` function, we add the following mouse event handler code. The code handles the mouse down, move, and up events:

```
// the logic of drawing on canvas
$("#drawing-pad").mousedown(function(e) {
   // get the mouse x and y relative to the canvas top-left point.
   var mouseX = e.layerX || 0;
   var mouseY = e.layerY || 0;
```

```
    startX = mouseX;
    startY = mouseY;

    isDrawing = true;
});

$("#drawing-pad").mousemove(function(e) {
    // draw lines when is drawing
    if (websocketGame.isDrawing) {
        // get the mouse x and y relative to the canvas
          top-left point.
        var mouseX = e.layerX || 0;
        var mouseY = e.layerY || 0;

        if (!(mouseX == websocketGame.startX &&
          mouseY == websocketGame.startY)) {
            drawLine(ctx, websocketGame.startX,
              websocketGame.startY,mouseX,mouseY,1);

            websocketGame.startX = mouseX;
            websocketGame.startY = mouseY;
        }
    }
});


$("#drawing-pad").mouseup(function(e) {
    websocketGame.isDrawing = false;
});
```

6. At last, we have the following function to draw a line on the canvas with the given starting and ending point:

```
function drawLine(ctx, x1, y1, x2, y2, thickness) {
    ctx.beginPath();
    ctx.moveTo(x1,y1);
    ctx.lineTo(x2,y2);
    ctx.lineWidth = thickness;
    ctx.strokeStyle = "#444";
    ctx.stroke();
}
```

7. Save all files and open the `index.htm` file. We should see an empty space where we can draw something by using the mouse. The drawings are not sent to the server yet, so others cannot view our drawings:

What just happened?

We just created a local drawing pad. This is like a whiteboard where the player can draw on the canvas by dragging the mouse. However, the drawing data is not sent to the server yet; all drawings are only displayed locally.

The `drawing line` function is the same that we used in *Chapter 4*. We also used the same code to get the mouse position relative to the canvas element. However, the logic of the mouse events is different from *Chapter 4*.

Drawing on the canvas

When we draw something on the computer, it often means that we click on the canvas and drag the mouse (or pen). The line is drawn until the mouse button is up. Then, the user clicks on another place and drags again to draw lines.

In our example, we have a Boolean flag named `isDrawing` to indicate if the user is drawing. The `isDrawing` flag is false by default. When the mouse button is down, we turn the flag to true. When the mouse is moving, we draw a line between the moved point and the last point when the mouse button is down. Then, we set the `isDrawing` flag to false again when the mouse button is up.

This is how the drawing logic works.

Have a go hero – Drawing with colors

Can we modify the drawing sketchpad by adding color support? How about adding five buttons with red, blue, green, black, and white color? The player can choose the color when drawing.

Broadcasting the drawing to all connected browsers

We will go further by sending our drawing data to the server and let the server broadcast the drawing to all connected browsers.

Time for action – Sending the drawing through WebSockets

Carry out the following steps:

1. First, we need to modify the server logic. Open the `server.js` file and replace the following code. It uses a JSON-formatted string for broadcasting, so we can send and receive data object:

```
// Constants
var LINE_SEGMENT = 0;
var CHAT_MESSAGE = 1;

var ws = require(__dirname + '/lib/ws/server');
var server = ws.createServer();

server.addListener("connection", function(conn){
    // init stuff on connection
    console.log("A connection established with id",conn.id);
    var message = "Welcome "+conn.id+" joining the party.
      Total connection:"+server.manager.length;
```

```
var data = {};
data.dataType = CHAT_MESSAGE;
data.sender = "Server";
data.message = message;

server.broadcast(JSON.stringify(data));

// listen to the message
conn.addListener("message", function(message){
    console.log("Got data '"+message+"' from connection
      "+conn.id);
    var data = JSON.parse(message);
    if (data.dataType == CHAT_MESSAGE) {
        // add the sender information into the message
          data object
        data.sender = conn.id;
    }
    server.broadcast(JSON.stringify(data));
});
});

server.listen(8000);

console.log("WebSocket server is running.");
console.log("Listening to port 8000.");
```

2. On the client side, we need the logic to respond to the server with the same data object definition. Open the `html5games.websocket.js` JavaScript file in the **client | js** directory.

3. Add the following constants to the `websocketGame` global variable. The same constants with the same values are also defined in the server side logic.

```
// Contants
LINE_SEGMENT : 0,
CHAT_MESSAGE : 1,
```

4. When handling the message event on the client-side, we convert the JSON formatted string back to the data object. If the data is a chat message, then we display it as chat history, otherwise we draw it on the canvas as a line segment. Replace the `onmessage` event handler with the following code:

```
socket.onmessage = function(e) {
    // check if the received data is chat message or line segment
    console.log("onmessage event:",e.data);
    var data = JSON.parse(e.data);
```

```
      if (data.dataType == websocketGame.CHAT_MESSAGE) {
          $("#chat-history").append("<li>"+data.sender+"
            said: "+data.message+"</li>");
      }
      else if (data.dataType == websocketGame.LINE_SEGMENT) {
          drawLine(ctx, data.startX, data.startY,
            data.endX, data.endY, 1);
      }

};
```

5. When the mouse is moving, we not only draw the line on the canvas but also send the line data to the server. Add the following highlighted code to the mouse move event handler:

```
$("#drawing-pad").mousemove(function(e) {
    // draw lines when is drawing
    if (websocketGame.isDrawing) {
        // get the mouse x and y relative to the canvas
          top-left point.
        var mouseX = e.layerX || 0;
        var mouseY = e.layerY || 0;

        if (!(mouseX == websocketGame.startX &&
          mouseY == websocketGame.startY)) {
            drawLine(ctx,startX,startY,mouseX,mouseY,1);

            // send the line segment to server
            var data = {};
            data.dataType = websocketGame.LINE_SEGMENT;
            data.startX = startX;
            data.startY = startY;
            data.endX = mouseX;
            data.endY = mouseY;
            websocketGame.socket.send(JSON.stringify(data));

            websocketGame.startX = mouseX;
            websocketGame.startY = mouseY;
        }

    }
});
```

6. Lastly, we need to modify the send message logic. We now pack the message in an object and format it as JSON when sending it to the server. Change the `sendMessage` function to the following code:

```
function sendMessage() {
    var message = $("#chat-input").val();

    // pack the message into an object.
    var data = {};
    data.dataType = websocketGame.CHAT_MESSAGE;
    data.message = message;

    websocketGame.socket.send(JSON.stringify(data));
    $("#chat-input").val("");
}
```

7. Save all files and re-launch the server.

8. Open the `index.htm` file in two browser instances.

9. First, try the chat room feature by typing some messages and sending them. Then, try drawing something on the canvas. Both browsers should display the same drawing as shown in the following screenshot:

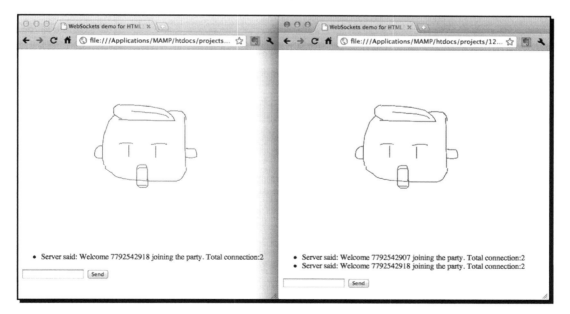

What just happened?

We have just built a multiuser sketchpad. This is similar to the sketchpad we tried at the beginning of this chapter. We extended what we learned when building a chat room by sending a complex data object as a message.

Defining a data object to communicate between the client and the server

In order to communicate correctly between the server and clients with several data packed into one message, we have to define a data object that both client and server understand.

There are several properties in the data object. The following table lists the properties with why we need them:

Property name	Why we need this property
dataType	This is an important property that helps us to understand about the entire data. The data is either a chat message or a drawing line segment data.
sender	If the data is a chat message, the client needs to know who sent the message.
message	When the data type is a chat message, we surely need to include the message content itself into the data object.
startX startY	When the data type is a drawing line segment, we include the x/y coordinate of the starting point of the line.
endX endY	When the data type is a drawing line segment, we include the x/y coordinate of the ending point of the line.

In addition, we have the following constants defined on both the client side and the server side. These constants are for the dataType property:

```
// Contants
LINE_SEGMENT : 0,
CHAT_MESSAGE : 1,
```

With these constants, we can compare the dataType by the following readable code instead of using the meaningless integer:

```
if (data.dataType == websocketGame.CHAT_MESSAGE) {…}
```

Packing the drawing lines data into JSON for broadcasting

We used the JSON.stringify function in the last chapter when storing a JavaScript object into a JSON-formatted string in the local storage. Now, we need to send the data in a string format between the server and the client. We used the same method to pack the drawing lines data into an object and send it as a JSON string.

The following code snippet shows how we pack the line segment data on the client side and send it to the server with a JSON-formatted string:

```
// send the line segment to server
var data = {};
data.dataType = websocketGame.LINE_SEGMENT;
data.startX = startX;
data.startY = startY;
data.endX = mouseX;
data.endY = mouseY;
websocketGame.socket.send(JSON.stringify(data));
```

Recreating the drawing lines after receiving them from other clients

The JSON parsing often comes as a pair of stringify. When we receive a message from the server, we have to parse it to the JavaScript object. The following code on the client side parses the data and either updates the chat history or draws a line based on the data:

```
var data = JSON.parse(e.data);
if (data.dataType == websocketGame.CHAT_MESSAGE) {
    $("#chat-history").append("<li>"+data.sender+" said:
      "+data.message+"</li>");
}
else if (data.dataType == websocketGame.LINE_SEGMENT) {
    drawLine(ctx, data.startX, data.startY, data.endX, data.endY, 1);
}
```

Building a multiplayer draw-and-guess game

We built an instant chat room earlier in this chapter. Moreover, we just built a multiuser sketchpad. How about combining these two techniques and building a draw-and-guess game? A draw-and-guess game is a game in which one player is given a word to draw. All other players do not know the word and guess the word according to the drawing. The one who draws and who correctly guesses the word earn points.

Time for action – Building the draw-and-guess game

We will implement the game flow of the draw-and-guess game as follows:

1. First, we will add the game logic on the client side.

2. Open the `index.htm` file in the client directory. Add the following restart button right after the *send* button:

    ```
    <input type='button' value="Restart" id="restart">
    ```

3. Open the `html5games.websocket.js` JavaScript.

4. We need a few more constants to determine different states during the game play. Add the following highlighted code to the top of the file:

    ```
    // Constants
    LINE_SEGMENT : 0,
    CHAT_MESSAGE : 1,
    GAME_LOGIC : 2,

    // Constant for game logic state
    WAITING_TO_START : 0,
    GAME_START : 1,
    GAME_OVER : 2,
    GAME_RESTART : 3,
    ```

5. In addition, we want a flag to indicate this player to in charge of drawing. Add the following Boolean global variable to the code:

    ```
    isTurnToDraw : false,
    ```

6. When the client receives a message from the server, it parses it and checks whether it is a chat message of line drawing. We have another type of message now for handling the game logic named `GAME_LOGIC`. The game logic message contains different data for different game states. Add the following code to the `onmessage` event handler:

    ```
    else if (data.dataType == websocketGame.GAME_LOGIC) {
      if (data.gameState == websocketGame.GAME_OVER) {
        websocketGame.isTurnToDraw = false;
        $("#chat-history").append("<li>"+data.winner+" wins!
          The answer is '"+data.answer+"'.</li>");
        $("#restart").show();
      }
      if (data.gameState == websocketGame.GAME_START) {
        // clear the canvas.
    ```

```
      canvas.width = canvas.width;

      // hide the restart button.
      $("#restart").hide();

      // clear the chat history
      $("#chat-history").html("");

      if (data.isPlayerTurn) {
        isTurnToDraw = true;
        $("#chat-history").append("<li>Your turn to draw.
          Please draw '"+data.answer+"'.</li>");
      }
      else {
        $("#chat-history").append("<li>Game Started. Get Ready.
          You have one minute to guess.</li>");
      }
    }
  }
}
```

7. We have added the game logic to the client side. There is some minor code on the client side containing the restart logic and preventing the non-drawing player to draw on the canvas. These codes can be found in the code bundle.

8. It is time to move on to the server side.

9. In the previous example, the server side is just in charge of broadcasting any incoming message to all connected browsers. This is not enough for a multiplayer game. The server will act as the game master that controls the game flow and winning determination. Therefore, delete the existing code in `server.js` and use the following code. The changes are highlighted:

```
// Constants
var LINE_SEGMENT = 0;
var CHAT_MESSAGE = 1;
var GAME_LOGIC = 2;

// Constant for game logic state
var WAITING_TO_START = 0;
var GAME_START = 1;
var GAME_OVER = 2;
var GAME_RESTART = 3;

var ws = require(__dirname + '/lib/ws/server');
var server = ws.createServer();
```

```
// the current turn of player index.
var playerTurn = 0;


var wordsList = ['apple','idea','wisdom','angry'];
var currentAnswer = undefined;


var currentGameState = WAITING_TO_START;


var gameOverTimeout;


server.addListener("connection", function(conn){
  // init stuff on connection
  console.log("A connection established with id",conn.id);
  var message = "Welcome "+conn.id+" joining the party.
    Total connection:"+server.manager.length;
  var data = {};
  data.dataType = CHAT_MESSAGE;
  data.sender = "Server";
  data.message = message;
  server.broadcast(JSON.stringify(data));

  // send the game state to all players.
  var gameLogicData = {};
  gameLogicData.dataType = GAME_LOGIC;
  gameLogicData.gameState = WAITING_TO_START;
  server.broadcast(JSON.stringify(gameLogicData));

  // start the game if there are 2 or more connections
  if (currentGameState == WAITING_TO_START &&
    server.manager.length >= 2)
  {
    startGame();
  }

  // listen to the message
  conn.addListener("message", function(message){
    console.log("Got data '"+message+"' from connection
      "+conn.id);
    var data = JSON.parse(message);
    if (data.dataType == CHAT_MESSAGE)
    {
      // add the sender information into the message data object.
      data.sender = conn.id;
    }
```

```
    server.broadcast(JSON.stringify(data));

    // check if the message is guessing right or wrong
    if (data.dataType == CHAT_MESSAGE)
    {
      if (currentGameState == GAME_START && data.message ==
        currentAnswer)
      {
        var gameLogicData = {};
        gameLogicData.dataType = GAME_LOGIC;
        gameLogicData.gameState = GAME_OVER;
        gameLogicData.winner = conn.id;
        gameLogicData.answer = currentAnswer;
        server.broadcast(JSON.stringify(gameLogicData));

        currentGameState = WAITING_TO_START;

        // clear the game over timeout
        clearTimeout(gameOverTimeout);
      }
    }


    if (data.dataType == GAME_LOGIC && data.gameState ==
      GAME_RESTART)
    {
      startGame();
    }
  });
});

function startGame()
{
  // pick a player to draw
  playerTurn = (playerTurn+1) % server.manager.length;

  // pick an answer
  var answerIndex = Math.floor(Math.random() * wordsList.length);
  currentAnswer = wordsList[answerIndex];

  // game start for all players
  var gameLogicData1 = {};
  gameLogicData1.dataType = GAME_LOGIC;
  gameLogicData1.gameState = GAME_START;
```

```
    gameLogicData1.isPlayerTurn = false;
    server.broadcast(JSON.stringify(gameLogicData1));

    // game start with answer to the player in turn
    var index = 0;
    server.manager.forEach(function(connection){
      if (index == playerTurn)
      {
        var gameLogicData2 = {};
        gameLogicData2.dataType = GAME_LOGIC;
        gameLogicData2.gameState = GAME_START;
        gameLogicData2.answer = currentAnswer;
        gameLogicData2.isPlayerTurn = true;
        server.send(connection.id, JSON.stringify(gameLogicData2));
      }
      index++;
    });

    // game over the game after 1 minute.
    gameOverTimeout = setTimeout(function(){
      var gameLogicData = {};
      gameLogicData.dataType = GAME_LOGIC;
      gameLogicData.gameState = GAME_OVER;
      gameLogicData.winner = "No one";
      gameLogicData.answer = currentAnswer;
      server.broadcast(JSON.stringify(gameLogicData));

      currentGameState = WAITING_TO_START;
    },60*1000);

    currentGameState = GAME_START;
}


server.listen(8000);

console.log("WebSocket server is running.");
console.log("Listening to port 8000.");
```

10. We will save all files and re-launch the server. Then, launch the index.htm file in two browser instances. One browser gets a message from the server informing the player to draw something. The other browser, on the other hand, informs the player to guess what the other is drawing within one minute.

11. The player who is told to draw something can draw on the canvas. The drawings are broadcasted to other connected players. The players who are told to guess cannot draw anything on the canvas. Instead, players type what they guess in the text field and send to the server. If the guessing is correct, then the game ends. Otherwise, the game continues until the one-minute countdown finishes.

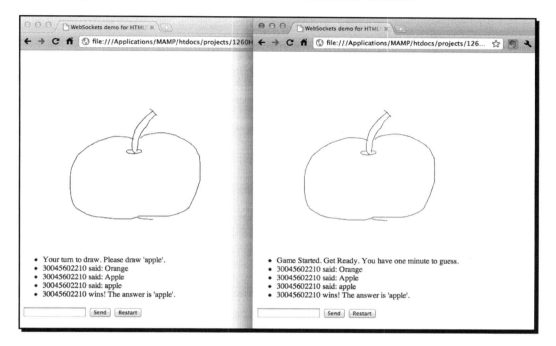

What just happened?

We just created a multiplayer draw-and-guess game in WebSockets and Canvas. The main difference between the game and the multiuser sketchpad is that the server now controls the game flow instead of letting all users draw.

Controlling the game flow of a multiplayer game

Controlling the game flow of a multiplayer game is much more difficult than a single game. We can simply use a few variables to control the game flow of a single game, but we have to use message passing to inform each player of specific updated game flow.

First, we require the following highlighted constant GAME_LOGIC for dataType. We use this dataType to send and receive a message which is related to the game logic control:

```
// Constants
var LINE_SEGMENT = 0;
```

```
var CHAT_MESSAGE = 1;
var GAME_LOGIC = 2;
```

There are several states in the game flow. Before the game starts, the connected players are waiting for the game to start. Once there are enough connections for the multiplayer game, the server sends a game logic message to all players to inform them to start the game.

When the game is over, the server sends a game over state to all players. Then, the game finishes and the game logic halts until any player clicks on the restart button. Once the restart button is clicked, the client sends a game restart state to the server instructing the server to prepare a new game. Then, the game starts again.

We declare the four game states as the following constants in both client and server, so they understand them:

```
// Constant for game logic state
var WAITING_TO_START = 0;
var GAME_START = 1;
var GAME_OVER = 2;
var GAME_RESTART = 3;
```

The following code on the server side holds an index to indicate which player is in turn now:

```
var playerTurn = 0;
```

The data which is sent to the player (whose turn it is) is different from the data that is sent to other players. The other players receive the following data with only a game start signal:

```
var gameLogicData1 = {};
gameLogicData1.dataType = GAME_LOGIC;
gameLogicData1.gameState = GAME_START;
gameLogicData1.isPlayerTurn = false;
```

On the other hand, the player (who is in turn to draw) receives the following data with the word information:

```
var gameLogicData2 = {};
gameLogicData2.dataType = GAME_LOGIC;
gameLogicData2.gameState = GAME_START;
gameLogicData2.answer = currentAnswer;
gameLogicData2.isPlayerTurn = true;
```

Enumerating connected clients on the serverside

We can enumerate all connected clients by using the `forEach` method in the `server manager` class. The following code shows the usage. It loops through each connection and calls the given `callback` function as follows:

```
server.manager.forEach(function);
```

For example, the following code snippet prints all connections ID on the server terminal:

```
server.manager.forEach(function(connection){
    console.log("This is connection",connection.id);
}

}
```

Sending a message to a specific connection on the server side

We used broadcast in our previous examples to send a message to all connected clients. Besides sending the message to everyone, we can send it to a specific connection by using the send method as follows:

```
server.send(connectionID, message);
```

The send method requires two arguments. The connectionID is the unique ID of the target connection and message is the string that we want to send.

In the following code extracted from our draw-and-guess game, we send special data to the player's browser who now has to draw something. We use the forEach function to loop through the connections and check whether the connection is in turn to draw. Then, we pack the answer and send this data to this target connection as follows:

```
server.manager.forEach(function(connection){
    if (index == playerTurn)
    {
        var gameLogicData2 = {};
        gameLogicData2.dataType = GAME_LOGIC;
        gameLogicData2.gameState = GAME_START;
        gameLogicData2.answer = currentAnswer;
        gameLogicData2.isPlayerTurn = true;
        server.send(connection.id, JSON.stringify(gameLogicData2));
    }
    index++;
});
```

Improving the game

We just created a multiplayer game which is playable. However, there is still lots to improve. In the following sections, we list two possible improvements in the game.

Storing drawn lines on each game

In the game, the drawer draws lines and other players guess the drawing. Now, imagine that two players are playing and the third player joins. As there is no storage for the drawn lines anywhere, the third player cannot see what the drawer has drawn. This means that the third player has to wait until the game ends to play.

Have a go hero

How can we let a player who has joined late continue the game without losing those drawn lines? How can we reconstruct the drawing for a newly connected player? How about storing all drawing data of the current game on the server?

Improving the answer checking mechanism

The answer checking on the server side compares the message with the `currentAnswer` variable to determine whether a player guessed correctly. The answer is treated as incorrect if the case does not match. It looks strange when the answer is "apples" and the player is told wrong when guessing "apple".

Have a go hero

How can we improve the answer checking mechanism? How about improving the answer checking logic to treat the answer as correct when using a different case or even similar words?

Decorating the draw-and-guess game with CSS

The game logic is basically finished and the game is playable already. However, we forgot to decorate the game to make it look appealing. We will use CSS styles to decorate our draw-and-guess game.

Time for action – Decorating the game

Carry out the following steps:

1. The decoration only applies to the client side. Open the `index.htm` file.

2. Add the following CSS style link in the head:

```
<link href='http://fonts.googleapis.com/css?family=Cabin+Sketch:
    bold' rel='stylesheet' type='text/css'>
<link rel="stylesheet" type="text/css" media="all"
    href="css/drawguess.css">
```

3. We put all markups in the `body` inside `section` with `id=game`. Also, we add an `h1` title for the game as follows:

```
<section id="game">
    <h1>Draw & Guess</h1>
    ...
</section>
```

4. Add a wording **Chat or Guess:** in front of the text field input, so the player knows where to type their guessing words.

5. Next, create a directory named `css` inside the `client` folder.

6. Create a new file named `drawguess.css` and save it in the `css` directory.

7. Put the following styles in the CSS file:

```css
body {
    background: #ccd6e1;
    font-family: 'Cabin Sketch', arial, serif;
}

#game {
    width: 500px;
    margin: 0 auto;
}

#game h1 {
    text-align: center;
    margin-bottom: 5px;
    text-shadow: 0px 1px 0px #fff;
}

#drawing-pad {
    border: 10px solid #fffeff;
    background: #f1f3ef;
    box-shadow:0px 3px 5px #333;
}

#chat-history {
    list-style: none;
    padding: 0;
}

#chat-history li {
    border-bottom: 1px dashed rgba(20,20,20,.2);
    margin: 10px 0;
}
```

8. Save all files and open the `index.htm` file again in two browsers to play the game. As we only changed the decoration code, the game should look better now as shown in the following screenshot:

What just happened?

We just applied styles to our game and embedded a font from the **Google Font Directory** that looks like sketching text. The canvas is now styled to look more like a canvas with a thick border and subtle shadow.

Summary

We learned a lot in this chapter about connecting browsers to WebSockets. The messages and events from one browser are broadcasted to another browser in almost real time.

Specifically, we:

◆ Learned how WebSockets provide real-time events by drawing on an existing multiplayer sketchpad. It shows drawings from other users who are connected.

◆ Installed a Node.js server with the WebSocket library. By using this server, we can easily build an event-based server to handle WebSocket requests from browsers.

◆ Discussed the relationship between the server and a client.

◆ Built an instant chat room application. We learned how to implement a server script to broadcast incoming messages to other connected browsers. We also learned how to display a received message from the server on the client side.

◆ Built a multiuser drawing board. We learned how to pack data in the JSON format to pass a message between the server and browsers.

◆ Built a draw-and-guess game by integrating the chatting and drawing pad. We also learned how to create the game logic in a multiplayer game.

Now that we have learned to build a multiplayer game, we are ready to build physics games with the help of the physics engine in the next chapter.

9
Building a Physics Car Game with Box2D and Canvas

2D Physics Engine is a hot topic in game development. With the help of a physics engine, we can easily create a playable game by just defining an environment and a simple rule. Taking existing games as examples, players in the Angry Birds game fly birds to destruct the enemy's castle. In Cut the Rope, candy drops into the monster's mouth to progress to the next level.

In this chapter, we will learn the following topics:

◆ Installing the Box2D JavaScript library
◆ Creating a static ground body in the physics world
◆ Drawing the physics world on the Canvas
◆ Creating a dynamic box in the physics world
◆ Advancing the world time
◆ Adding wheels to the game
◆ Creating the physics car
◆ Adding force to the car with a keyboard input
◆ Checking a collision in the Box2D world
◆ Restarting the game
◆ Adding a level support to our car game
◆ Replacing the Box2D outline drawing with graphics
◆ Adding a final touch to make the game fun to play

The following screenshot shows what we will get by the end of this chapter. It is a car game in which a player moves the car towards the destination point:

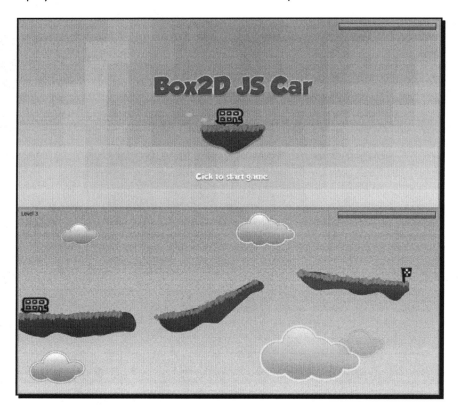

So, let's get on with it.

Installing the Box2D JavaScript library

Now, suppose that we want to create a car game. We apply force to the car to make it move forward. The car moves on a ramp and then flies through the air. Afterwards, the car falls on the destination ramp and the game finishes. Every collision in every part of the physics world counts on this movement. If we have to make this game from scratch, then we have to calculate at least the velocity and angle of each part. Luckily, the physics library helps us to handle all these physical problems. All we have to do is to create the physics model and present it in the canvas.

Time for action – Installing the Box2D physics library

Carry out the following steps:

1. We will get the Box2D JavaScript library. The original Box2D JavaScript library is based on the prototype JavaScript library. The prototype library provides similar functions from jQuery but with a little different API. Thanks to KJ (http://kjam. org/post/105) who ported it into the jQuery capable version, we can use the jQuery library on which we have based our whole book. The Box2D library with the starting code can be found from the code bundle named box2d_game.

2. Now, we should have the following setup:

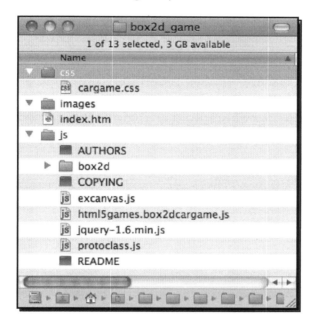

 We have already imported the essential JavaScript files. It is worth remembering that if you want to later use this base to create another physics game, Box2D JS recommends copying the JavaScript import codes in exactly the same order because there are dependencies between files.

3. Now, we will create an empty world to test our Box2D library installation. Open the html5games.box2dcargame.js JavaScript file and put the following code in the file to create the world:

```
// the global object that contains the variable needed for the car
game.
```

```
var carGame = {
}

var canvas;
var ctx;
var canvasWidth;
var canvasHeight;

$(function() {

    carGame.world = createWorld();

    console.log("The world is created. ",carGame.world);

    // get the reference of the context
    canvas = document.getElementById('game');
    ctx = canvas.getContext('2d');
    canvasWidth = parseInt(canvas.width);
    canvasHeight = parseInt(canvas.height);
});

function createWorld() {

    // set the size of the world
    var worldAABB = new b2AABB();
    worldAABB.minVertex.Set(-4000, -4000);
    worldAABB.maxVertex.Set(4000, 4000);

    // Define the gravity
    var gravity = new b2Vec2(0, 300);

    // set to ignore sleeping object
    var doSleep = false;

    // finally create the world with the size, gravity,
        and sleep object parameter.
    var world = new b2World(worldAABB, gravity, doSleep);


    return world;
}
```

4. Open the `index.html` file in a web browser. We should see a grey canvas with nothing there.

We have not presented the physics world in the canvas yet. That is why we only see a blank canvas on the page. However, we have printed the newly created world in the console log. The following screenshot shows the console tracing the world object with many properties beginning with `m_`. These are the physical states of the world:

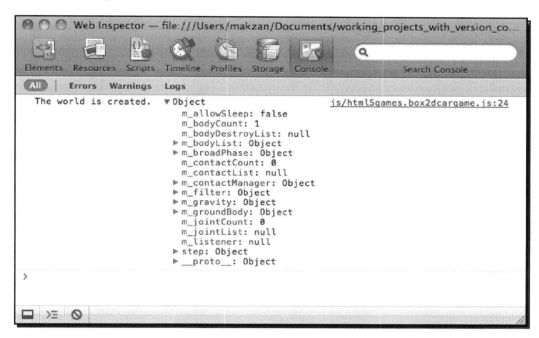

What just happened?

We have just installed the Box2D JavaScript library and created an empty world to test the installation.

Using b2World to create a new world

The `b2World` is a core class in the Box2D environment. All our physics bodies, including the ground and car, are created in this world. The following code shows how to create a world:

```
var world = new b2World(worldAABB, gravity, doSleep);
```

The `b2World` class takes three arguments to initialize, which are listed in the following table with their description:

Arguments	Type	Discussion
worldAABB	b2AABB	Represents the bounding area of the world
gravity	b2Vec2	Represents the gravity of the world
doSleep	Bool	Defines whether the world ignores slept objects or not

Using b2AABB to define a bounding area

In the physics world, we need a lot of bounding area. The first bounding we need is for the world. All things within the world bounding will be calculated and things outside the bounding area will be destroyed.

We can treat `b2AABB` as a rectangle with the lowest bounding point and highest bounding point. The following code snippet shows how to use the `b2AABB` class. The `minVertex` is the top left-most point of the bound while `maxVertex` is the bottom right-most point. The following world defines a world with 8000x8000:

```
var worldAABB = new b2AABB();
worldAABB.minVertex.Set(-4000, -4000);
worldAABB.maxVertex.Set(4000, 4000);
```

 The unit in the Box2D mathematics model is different from what we commonly use in the computer world. The length unit is in meters instead of pixels. Moreover, the rotation unit is in radians.

Setting the gravity of the world

We have to define the gravity of the world. The gravity is defined by `b2Vec2`. The `b2Vec2` is a vector with a 1x2 matrix. We can treat it as a vector of X and Y-axis. Therefore, the following code defines the gravity with 300 units downwards:

```
var gravity = new b2Vec2(0, 300);
```

Setting the Box2D to ignore the slept object

A slept body is a dynamic body that does not move or change states anymore.

The physics library calculates the mathematical data and collision of all bodies in the world. The performance will slow down when there are more bodies in the world to get calculated in every frame. When creating the physics world, we need to set the library to either ignore slept bodies or calculate all of them.

In our game, there are only a few bodies, so the performance is not yet a problem. Moreover, if later our created bodies get into an idle or sleep state, we cannot interact with them anymore. Therefore, we set this flag to false in this example.

 At the time of writing this book, only Google Chrome runs the Box2D JavaScript library in canvas smoothly. Therefore, it is suggested to test the game in Google Chrome until other web browsers can run it smoothly.

Creating a static ground body in the physics world

The world is empty now. If we are going to place objects there, those objects will fall and finally leave our sight. Now suppose that we want to create a static ground body in the world, so that objects can stand there. We can do this in Box2D.

Time for action – Creating a ground in the world

Carry out the following steps:

1. Open the `html5games.box2dcargame.js` JavaScript file.

2. Add the following function to the end of the JavaScript file. It creates a fixed body as the playground:

```
function createGround() {
    // box shape definition
    var groundSd = new b2BoxDef();
    groundSd.extents.Set(250, 25);
    groundSd.restitution = 0.4;

    // body definition with the given shape we just created.
    var groundBd = new b2BodyDef();
    groundBd.AddShape(groundSd);
    groundBd.position.Set(250, 370);
    var body = carGame.world.CreateBody(groundBd);

    return body;
}
```

3. Call the `createGround` function after creating the world as follows:

```
createGround();
```

4. As we are still defining the logic and have not yet presented the physics world visually, we will see nothing if we open the browser. However, it is a good habit to try it and inspect the console window for an error message if there is any.

What just happened?

We have created a ground body with the shape and body definitions. This is a common process we will use a lot to create different kinds of physical bodies in the world. So, let's get into details on how we made it.

Creating a shape

A shape defines the geometrical data. In the JavaScript port of Box2D, a shape also defines material properties such as density, friction, and restitution. The shape can be a circle, rectangle, or a polygon. The following code that we used in the preceding example defines a box shape definition. In the box shape, we have to define the size of the box by setting the `extents` property. The `extents` property takes two arguments: half width and half height. It is a half value, so the final area of the shape is four times the value:

```
// box shape definition
var groundSd = new b2BoxDef();
groundSd.extents.Set(250, 25);
groundSd.restitution = 0.4;
```

Creating a body

After defining the shape, we can then create a body definition with the given shape definition. Then, we set the initial position of the body and finally ask the world instance to create a body from our body definition. The following code shows how we create a body in the world with the given shape definition:

```
var groundBd = new b2BodyDef();
groundBd.AddShape(groundSd);
groundBd.position.Set(250, 370);
var body = carGame.world.CreateBody(groundBd);
```

A body set without a mass is considered as a static body, or fixed body. These bodies are immovable and will not have collisions with other static bodies. Therefore, these bodies can be used as a ground or walls to become the level environment. On the other hand, a dynamic body will move following the gravity and collision with other bodies. We will create a dynamic box body later.

Drawing the physics world in the canvas

We have created a ground but it is only in the mathematics model. We do not see anything in the canvas because we have not drawn anything on it yet. In order to show what the physics looks like, we have to draw something according to the physics world.

Time for action – Drawing the physics world into the canvas

Carry out the following steps:

1. First, open the `html5games.box2dcargame.js` JavaScript file.

2. Add a `drawWorld` function call to the page loaded event handler as the following code:

```
$(function() {

  // create the world
  carGame.world = createWorld();

  // create the ground
  createGround();

  // get the reference of the context
  canvas = document.getElementById('game');
  ctx = canvas.getContext('2d');
  canvasWidth = parseInt(canvas.width);
  canvasHeight = parseInt(canvas.height);

  // draw the world
  drawWorld(carGame.world, ctx);
});
```

3. Next, open the `draw_world.js` JavaScript file from the Box2D JavaScript example code. There are two functions named `drawWorld` and `drawShapes`. Copy the entire file, which is shown in the following code, to the end of our JavaScript file:

```
// drawing functions
function drawWorld(world, context) {
  for (var b = world.m_bodyList; b != null; b = b.m_next) {
    for (var s = b.GetShapeList(); s != null; s = s.GetNext()) {
      drawShape(s, context);
    }
  }
}
```

```
// drawShape function directly copy from draw_world.js in Box2dJS
library
function drawShape(shape, context) {
  context.strokeStyle = '#003300';
  context.beginPath();
  switch (shape.m_type) {
  case b2Shape.e_circleShape:
    var circle = shape;
    var pos = circle.m_position;
    var r = circle.m_radius;
    var segments = 16.0;
    var theta = 0.0;
    var dtheta = 2.0 * Math.PI / segments;
    // draw circle
    context.moveTo(pos.x + r, pos.y);
    for (var i = 0; i < segments; i++) {
      var d = new b2Vec2(r * Math.cos(theta),
        r * Math.sin(theta));
      var v = b2Math.AddVV(pos, d);
      context.lineTo(v.x, v.y);
      theta += dtheta;
    }
    context.lineTo(pos.x + r, pos.y);

    // draw radius
    context.moveTo(pos.x, pos.y);
    var ax = circle.m_R.col1;
    var pos2 = new b2Vec2(pos.x + r * ax.x, pos.y + r * ax.y);
    context.lineTo(pos2.x, pos2.y);
    break;
  case b2Shape.e_polyShape:
    var poly = shape;
    var tV = b2Math.AddVV(poly.m_position,
      b2Math.b2MulMV(poly.m_R, poly.m_vertices[0]));
    context.moveTo(tV.x, tV.y);
    for (var i = 0; i < poly.m_vertexCount; i++) {
      var v = b2Math.AddVV(poly.m_position,
        b2Math.b2MulMV(poly.m_R, poly.m_vertices[i]));
      context.lineTo(v.x, v.y);
    }
    context.lineTo(tV.x, tV.y);
    break;
  }
  context.stroke();
}
```

4. Now re-open the game in a browser and we should see the outline of the ground body in the canvas, as shown in the following screenshot:

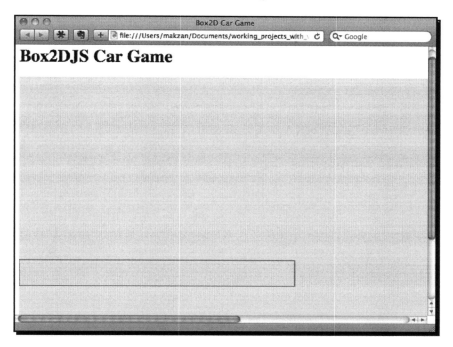

What just happened?

We have just created a function to draw every shape in the world as a box with a dark green outline.

The following code shows how we loop through each shape in the world to draw it:

```
function drawWorld(world, context) {
    for (var b = world.m_bodyList; b != null; b = b.m_next) {
        for (var s = b.GetShapeList(); s != null; s = s.GetNext()) {
            drawShape(s, context);
        }
    }
}
```

There is the drawJoint function and related code from the Box2D JS library too. This joint drawing function is optional for our example. Adding the joint drawing function can let us see the invisible joint connected between two bodies.

Now we will take a look at the `drawShape` function.

On every shape, we want to draw the outline of the object in the canvas to present it. We set the line style to dark green before drawing anything. Then, we check whether the shape is a circle, rectangle box, or a polygon. If it is a circle, then we use the pole coordinate to draw the circle with the given radius of the shape. If it is a polygon, then we draw each side of the polygon as follows:

```
function drawShape(shape, context) {
   context.strokeStyle = '#003300';
   context.beginPath();
   switch (shape.m_type) {
   case b2Shape.e_circleShape:
      // Draw the circle in canvas bases on the physics object shape
      break;
   case b2Shape.e_polyShape:
      // Draw the polygon in canvas bases on the physics object shape
      break;
   }
   context.stroke();
}
```

Creating a dynamic box in the physics world

Imagine now we drop a box into the world. The box falls from the air and finally hits the ground. The box bounces up a little and finally stops on the ground. This is different from what we created in the last section. In the last section, we created a static ground which is immovable and will not be affected by gravity. Now we will create a dynamic box.

Time for action – Putting a dynamic box in the world

Carry out the following steps:

1. Open our JavaScript logic file and add the following box creation code to the page loaded event handler. Place the code after the `createGround` function:

```
// create a box
var boxSd = new b2BoxDef();
boxSd.density = 1.0;
boxSd.friction = 1.5;
boxSd.restitution = .4;
boxSd.extents.Set(40, 20);

var boxBd = new b2BodyDef();
```

```
boxBd.AddShape(boxSd);
boxBd.position.Set(50,210);
carGame.world.CreateBody(boxBd);
```

2. Now we will test the physics world in a browser. We should see that a box is created at the given initial position. However, the box is not falling down; it is because we still have something to do to make it fall:

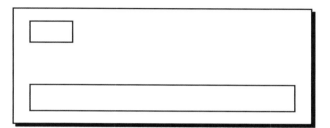

What just happened?

We have just created a dynamic body in the world. In contrast to the ground body that is immovable, this box is affected by the gravity and the velocity changes during a collision. When a body contains a shape with any mass or density, it is a dynamic body. Otherwise, it is static. Therefore, we define a density to our box. Box2D will make it dynamic and calculate the mass according to the density and the size of the body automatically.

Setting the bouncing effect with the restitution property

The restitution value is between 0 and 1. In our case, the box is falling down on the ground. When the restitution value is 0 on both the ground and the box, the box does not bounce at all. When either the box or ground has restitution value 1, the collision is perfectly elastic.

 When two bodies collide, the restitution value of that collision is the maximum value between both restitution values of the bodies. Therefore, if a box with a restitution of 0.4 drops on the ground with restitution 0.6, this collision uses 0.6 to calculate the bouncing velocity.

Advancing the world time

The box is dynamic but it does not fall down. Are we doing anything wrong here? The answer is no. We have setup the box correctly, but we forget to advance the time in the physics world.

In the Box2D physics world, all calculations are done in a systematic iteration. The world calculates the physical transformation of all things according to the current step. When we move the `step` to the next level, the world calculates again as the new state.

Time for action – Setting up the world step loop

We will make the world time advance by carrying out the following steps:

1. In order to advance the world step, we have to call the `step` function in the world instance periodically. We used `setTimeout` to keep calling the `step` function. Put the following function in our JavaScript logic file:

```
function step() {
    world.Step(1.0/60, 1);
    ctx.clearRect(0, 0, canvasWidth, canvasHeight);

    drawWorld(carGame.world, ctx);

    setTimeout(step, 10);
}
```

2. Next, we will kick-start the world by calling the first `step` function in the document ready event handler. Add the following highlighted code to the loaded handler function:

```
$(function() {
    ...

    // start advancing the step
    step();
});
```

3. We will again simulate the world in a browser. The box is created at the initialized position and falls on the ground correctly. The following screenshot shows the sequence of a box dropping on the ground:

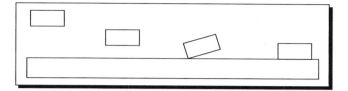

What just happened?

We have advanced the time of the world. Now the physics library simulates the world every 10 milliseconds.

The `step` function is similar to our `gameloop` function in *Chapter 2, Getting Started with DOM-based Game Development*. It executes periodically to calculate the new state of the game.

Adding wheels to the game

Now we have a box in the game. Imagine now we create two circular shaped bodies as the wheels. Then, we will have the basic component of a car, the body, and the wheels.

Time for action – Putting two circles in the world

We will add two circles to the world by carrying out the following steps:

1. Open the `html5games.box2dcargame.js` JavaScript file to add the wheel bodies.

2. Add the following code after the box creation code. It calls the `createWheel` function which we will write to create a circular shaped body:

```
// create two wheels in the world
createWheel(carGame.world, 25, 230);
createWheel(carGame.world, 75, 230);
```

3. Now let's work on the `createWheel` function. We design this function to create a circle shaped body in the given world at the given x and y coordinates in the world. Put the following function in our JavaScript logic file:

```
function createWheel(world, x, y) {
    // wheel circle definition
    var ballSd = new b2CircleDef();
    ballSd.density = 1.0;
    ballSd.radius = 10;
    ballSd.restitution = 0.1;
    ballSd.friction = 4.3;
```

```
// body definition
var ballBd = new b2BodyDef();
ballBd.AddShape(ballSd);
ballBd.position.Set(x,y);
return world.CreateBody(ballBd);
}
```

4. We will now reload the physics world in a web browser. This time, we should see the result similar to the one shown in the following screenshot with a box and two wheels falling down from the air. These bodies collide with others and bounce away when they hit the wall:

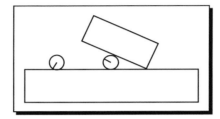

What just happened?

When simulating the physics world, both the box and wheels drop and collide with each other and the ground.

Creating a circular body is similar to creating a box body. The only difference is that we use a CircleDef class instead of the box shape definition. In the circle definition, we define the circle size by using the radius property instead of the extents property.

Creating a physical car

We have prepared the car box body and two wheel bodies. We are just one step away from making a car. Imagine now we have a glue to glue the wheels to the car body. Then, the car and wheels will not separate anymore and we will have a car. We can use **joint** to achieve that. In this section, we will use joint to stick the wheels and the car body together.

Time for action – Connecting the box and two circles with revolute joint

Carry out the following steps:

1. We are still working only on the logic part. Open our JavaScript logic file in a text editor.

2. Add the following global variable at the top of the document to reference the car body:

```
var car;
```

3. Create a function named `createCarAt` which takes the coordinate as arguments. Then, we move the body and the wheel creation code in this function. Afterwards, add the following highlighted Joint creation code. At last, return the car body:

```
function createCarAt(x, y) {
    // the car box definition
    var boxSd = new b2BoxDef();
    boxSd.density = 1.0;
    boxSd.friction = 1.5;
    boxSd.restitution = .4;
    boxSd.extents.Set(40, 20);

    // the car body definition
    var boxBd = new b2BodyDef();
    boxBd.AddShape(boxSd);
    boxBd.position.Set(x,y);
    var carBody = carGame.world.CreateBody(boxBd);

    // creating the wheels
    var wheelBody1 = createWheel(carGame.world, x-25, y+20);
    var wheelBody2 = createWheel(carGame.world, x+25, y+20);

    // create a joint to connect left wheel with the car body
    var jointDef = new b2RevoluteJointDef();
    jointDef.anchorPoint.Set(x-25, y+20);
    jointDef.body1 = carBody;
    jointDef.body2 = wheelBody1;
    carGame.world.CreateJoint(jointDef);

    // create a joint to connect right wheel with the car body
    var jointDef = new b2RevoluteJointDef();
    jointDef.anchorPoint.Set(x+25, y+20);
```

```
        jointDef.body1 = carBody;
        jointDef.body2 = wheelBody2;
        carGame.world.CreateJoint(jointDef);

        return carBody;

    }
```

4. Then, all we need to do is to create a car with the initial position. Add the following code to the page loaded event handler after the world creation:

```
// create a car
car = createCarAt(50, 210);
```

5. It is time to save the file and run the physics world in a browser. At this time, the wheels and the car body are not separate pieces. They glue together as a car and drop on the ground correctly, as shown in the following screenshot:

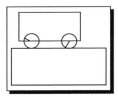

What just happened?

Joint is useful to add constraint between two bodies (or between a body and the world). There are many kinds of joints and what we used in this example is called **revolute joint**.

Using a revolute joint to create an anchor point between two bodies

The revolute joint sticks two bodies together with a common anchor point. The two bodies are then glued together and are only allowed to rotate based on the common anchor point. The left hand side of the following screenshot shows that two bodies are connected with an anchor. In our code example, we set the anchor point to be exactly the center point of the wheel. The right hand side of the following screenshot shows how we set the joint. The wheel rotates as a wheel because the rotation origin is at the center. This setup makes the car and wheels look real:

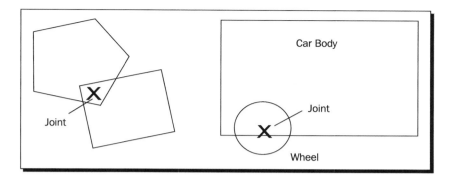

There are other types of joints which are useful in different ways. Joints are useful in creating a game environment and as there are several types of joints, each joint type is worth a try and you should think how to use them. The following link is the Box2D manual which explains each type of joint and how we can use them on different environment setups:

`http://www.box2d.org/manual.html#_Toc258082974`

Adding force to the car with a keyboard input

We have the car ready now. Let's move it with our keyboard.

Time for action – Adding force to the car

Carry out the following steps:

1. Open the `html5games.box2dcargame.js` JavaScript file in a text editor.

2. In the page loaded event handler, we add the following `keydown` event handler to the beginning. It listens to the *X* key and *Z* key to apply force in different directions:

```
// Keyboard event
$(document).keydown(function(e) {
  switch(e.keyCode) {
    case 88: // x key to apply force towards right
      var force = new b2Vec2(10000000, 0);
      carGame.car.ApplyForce
        (force, carGame.car.GetCenterPosition());
      break;
    case 90: // z key to apply force towards left
      var force = new b2Vec2(-10000000, 0);
      carGame.car.ApplyForce
        (force, carGame.car.GetCenterPosition());
      break;
```

```
    }
});
```

3. That is all. Save the files and run our game in the browser. When you press the *X* or *Z* key, the car starts moving. If you keep pressing the key, the world will keep adding force to the car and make it fly away:

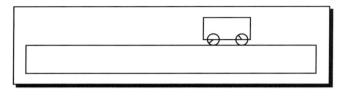

What just happened?

We just created an interaction with our car body. We can move the car left and right by pressing the *Z* and *X* keys. It seems like the game is getting interesting now.

Applying force to a body

We can apply force to any body by calling the `ApplyForce` function in that body. The following code shows the usage of the function:

```
body.ApplyForce(force, point);
```

This function takes two arguments, which are listed in the following table:

Arguments	Type	Discussion
force	b2Vec2	The force vector to apply to the body
point	b2Vec2	The point where the force applies

Understanding the difference between ApplyForce and ApplyImpulse

Besides the ApplyForce function, we can also move any body by using the ApplyImpulse function. Both functions move the body, but they move them in a different approach. If we want to change the instance velocity of a body, then we use ApplyImpulse once on the body to change velocity to our target value. On the other hand, we need to constituently apply force to a body to increase the speed.

For example, we want to increase the velocity of the car like stepping on the pedal. In this case, we apply force to the car. If we are creating a ball game that needs to kick-start the ball, we may use the ApplyImpulse function to add an instance impulse to the ball body.

Have a go hero

Can you think about a different situation where we will need to apply force or impulse to the body?

Adding ramps to our game environment

Now we can move the car. However, the environment is not interesting enough to play. Imagine now there are some ramps for the car to jump, and there is a gap between two platforms that a player has to fly the car over. It will become more interesting to play with different ramp setups.

Time for action – Creating the world with ramps

Carry out the following steps:

1. We will open the game logic JavaScript file.

2. Move the current ground creation code into a new function named createGround. Then, change the code to use the four given arguments as follows:

```
function createGround(x, y, width, height, rotation) {
    // box shape definition
    var groundSd = new b2BoxDef();
    groundSd.extents.Set(width, height);
    groundSd.restitution = 0.4;

    // body definition with the given shape we just created.
    var groundBd = new b2BodyDef();
    groundBd.AddShape(groundSd);
    groundBd.position.Set(x, y);
```

```
groundBd.rotation = rotation * Math.PI / 180;
var body = carGame.world.CreateBody(groundBd);

return body;
}
```

3. Now we have a function to create the ground body. We will now replace the ground creation code in the page loaded handler function with the following code:

```
// create the ground
createGround(250, 270, 250, 25, 0);
// create a ramp
createGround(500, 250, 65, 15, -10);
createGround(600, 225, 80, 15, -20);
createGround(1100, 250, 100, 15, 0);
```

4. Save the file and preview the game in a browser. We should see a ramp now and a destination platform as shown in the following screenshot. Try to control the car, jump over the ramp, and reach the destination without falling down. Refresh the page to restart the game if you fail:

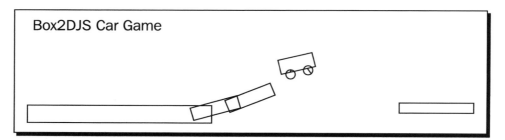

What just happened?

We just wrapped the ground box creating code into a function, so that we can easily create a combination of ground bodies. These ground bodies composite the level environment of the game.

In addition, this is the first time we are rotating a body. We set the rotation of the body by using the `rotation` property which takes a value in radian. Most people may get used to the degree unit; we can get the radian value from degree by using the following formula:

```
groundBd.rotation = degree * Math.PI / 180;
```

By setting the rotation of a box, we can have a ramp of varying slope setup in our game.

Have a go hero – Creating different environments with different joints

We have a ramp setup now and we can play with the car within the environment. How about using different kinds of joints to setup the playground? For example, how about a pulley joint to act as a lift? On the other hand, how about including a dynamic board with a joint at the center?

Checking collisions in the Box2D world

The Box2D physics library calculates all collisions automatically. Imagine now we setup a ground body as the destination. Players win when they successfully move the car to hit the destination. As Box2D already calculates all collisions, all we have to do is get the detected collision list and determine whether our car has hit the destination ground.

Time for action – Checking a collision between the car and the destination body

Carry out the following steps:

1. Again, we start from our game logic. Open the `html5games.box2dcargame.js` JavaScript file in a text editor.

2. We setup a destination ground in the ground creation code and assign it to our `gamewinWall` reference inside the `carGame` global object instance as follows:

```
carGame.gamewinWall = createGround(1200, 215, 15, 25, 0);
```

3. Next, we move on to the `step` function. In each step, we get the complete contact list from the world and check whether any two colliding objects are car and the destination ground:

```
function step() {
  carGame.world.Step(1.0/60, 1);
  ctx.clearRect(0, 0, canvasWidth, canvasHeight);
  drawWorld(carGame.world, ctx);
  setTimeout(step, 10);

  //loop all contact list to check if the car hits the
    winning wall
  for (var cn = carGame.world.GetContactList(); cn != null;
      cn = cn.GetNext()) {
    var body1 = cn.GetShape1().GetBody();
    var body2 = cn.GetShape2().GetBody();
    if ((body1 == carGame.car && body2 == carGame.gamewinWall) ||
```

```
                    (body2 == carGame.car && body1 == carGame.gamewinWall))
        {
           console.log("Level Passed!");
        }
     }
  }
```

4. We will now save the code and open the game in a browser again. This time, we have to open the console window to track if we get the **Level Passed!** output when the car hits that wall. Try to finish the game and we should see the output in the console once the car hits the destination:

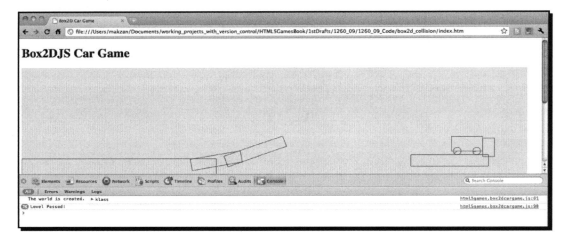

What just happened?

We just created the game winning logic by checking the collision contacts. The player wins when the car successfully reaches the destination ground object.

Getting the collision contact list

In each step, Box2D calculates all collisions and puts them into a **contact list** in the `world` instance. We can get the contact list by using the `carGame.world.GetContactList()` function. The returned contact list is a **link list**. We can travel through the entire link list by using the following for-loop:

```
for (var cn = carGame.world.GetContactList(); cn != null; cn =
cn.GetNext()) {
    // We have shape 1 and shape 2 of each contact node.
    // cn.GetShape1();
    // cn.GetShape2();
}
```

When we get the collided shapes, we check whether the body of that shape is a car or the destination body. As the car shape may be in shape 1 or shape 2, and the same applies to the `gamewinWall`, we use the following code to check both combinations:

```
var body1 = cn.GetShape1().GetBody();
var body2 = cn.GetShape2().GetBody();
if ((body1 == carGame.car && body2 == carGame.gamewinWall) ||
    (body2 == carGame.car && body1 == carGame.gamewinWall))
{
    console.log("Level Passed!");
}
```

Have a go hero

We created a game over dialog in *Chapter 7, Using Local Storage to Store Game Data*. How about using that technique here to create a dialog showing the player passed the level when hitting the winning wall? It will also be useful as level transition later when we add different level setups to the game.

Restarting the game

You may have already tried refreshing the page several times in the last example to make the car successfully jump to the destination. Imagine now we can press a key to re-initialize the world. Then, we can follow the trial-and-error method until success.

Time for action – Restarting the game while pressing the R key

We will assign the *R* key as the restart key for our game:

1. Again, we only need to change the JavaScript file. Open the `html5games.box2dcargame.js` JavaScript file in a text editor.

2. We move the create world, ramp, and the car code into a function named `restartGame`. They were originally in the page loaded handler function:

```
function restartGame() {
    // create the world
    carGame.world = createWorld();

    // create the ground
    createGround(250, 270, 250, 25, 0);

    // create a ramp
    createGround(500, 250, 65, 15, -10);
```

```
        createGround(600, 225, 80, 15, -20);
        createGround(1100, 250, 100, 15, 0);

        // create a destination ground
        carGame.gamewinWall = createGround(1200, 215, 15, 25, 0);

        // create a car
        carGame.car = createCarAt(50, 210);
    }
```

3. Then, in the page loaded event handler, we call the `restartGame` function to initialize the game as follows:

```
restartGame();
```

4. Finally, we add the following highlighted code to the `keydown` handler to restart the game when the *R* key is pressed:

```
$(document).keydown(function(e) {
  switch(e.keyCode) {
    case 88: // x key to apply force towards right
      var force = new b2Vec2(10000000, 0);
      carGame.car.ApplyForce
        (force, carGame.car.GetCenterPosition());
      break;
    case 90: // z key to apply force towards left
      var force = new b2Vec2(-10000000, 0);
      carGame.car.ApplyForce
        (force, carGame.car.GetCenterPosition());
      break;
    case 82: // r key to restart the game
      restartGame();
      break;
  }
});
```

5. How about restarting the game when the player passes the level? Add the following highlighted code to the game win logic:

```
if ((cn.GetShape1().GetBody() == carGame.car &&
     cn.GetShape2().GetBody() == carGame.gamewinWall) ||
    (cn.GetShape2().GetBody() == carGame.car &&
     cn.GetShape1().GetBody() == carGame.gamewinWall))
{
    console.log("Level Passed!");
    restartGame();
}
```

6. It is time to test the game in a browser. Try playing the game and press the *R* key to restart the game.

What just happened?

We refactor our code to create a `restartGame` function. The world is destroyed and initialized again each time we call this function. We can destroy the existing world and create a new empty one by creating a new world instance of our world variable as follows:

```
carGame.world = createWorld();
```

Have a go hero – Creating the game over wall

Now the only way to restart the game is by pressing the restart key. How about creating a ground at the bottom of the world that checks any falling car? When the car drops and hits the bottom ground, we know that the player has failed and then restart the game.

Adding a level support to our car game

Imagine now we can level up to the next environment setup when finishing each game. We will need several environment setups for each level.

Time for action – Loading game with levels data

We will refactor our code to support loading the static ground bodies from a levels data structure. Let's work on it by carrying out the following steps:

1. Open the `html5games.box2dcargame.js` JavaScript file in a text editor.

2. We will need each ground setup on each level. Put the following code at the top of the JavaScript file. It is an array of levels. Each level is another array of objects with the position, dimension, and rotation of the static ground body:

```
carGame.levels = new Array();
carGame.levels[0] = [{"type":"car","x":50,"y":210,"fuel":20},
{"type":"box","x":250, "y":270, "width":250,
  "height":25, "rotation":0},
{"type":"box","x":500,"y":250,"width":65,"height":15,
  "rotation":-10},
{"type":"box","x":600,"y":225,"width":80,"height":15,
  "rotation":-20},
{"type":"box","x":950,"y":225,"width":80,"height":15,
  "rotation":20},
{"type":"box","x":1100,"y":250,"width":100,"height":15,
```

```
        "rotation":0},
    {"type":"win","x":1200,"y":215,"width":15,"height":25,
        "rotation":0}];

    carGame.levels[1] = [{"type":"car","x":50,"y":210,"fuel":20},
    {"type":"box","x":100, "y":270, "width":190,
        "height":15, "rotation":20},
    {"type":"box","x":380, "y":320, "width":100, "height":15,
        "rotation":-10},
    {"type":"box","x":666,"y":285,"width":80,"height":15,
        "rotation":-32},
    {"type":"box","x":950,"y":295,"width":80,"height":15,
        "rotation":20},
    {"type":"box","x":1100,"y":310,"width":100,"height":15,
        "rotation":0},
    {"type":"win","x":1200,"y":275,"width":15,"height":25,
        "rotation":0}];

    carGame.levels[2] = [{"type":"car","x":50,"y":210,"fuel":20},
    {"type":"box","x":100, "y":270, "width":190,
        "height":15, "rotation":20},
    {"type":"box","x":380, "y":320, "width":100,
        "height":15, "rotation":-10},
    {"type":"box","x":686,"y":285,"width":80,"height":15,
        "rotation":-32},
    {"type":"box","x":250,"y":495,"width":80,"height":15,
        "rotation":40},
    {"type":"box","x":500,"y":540,"width":200,"height":15,
        "rotation":0},
    {"type":"win","x":220,"y":425,"width":15,"height":25,
        "rotation":23}];
```

3. Then, we use the following variable in the carGame object instance to store the current level:

```
var carGame = {
    currentLevel: 0
}
```

4. Replace the `restartGame` function with the following code. It changes the function to accept a `level` argument. Then, create the ground or car by the level data:

```
function restartGame(level) {
   carGame.currentLevel = level;

   // create the world
   carGame.world = createWorld();

   // create a ground in our newly created world
   // load the ground info from level data
   for(var i=0;i<carGame.levels[level].length;i++) {
      var obj = carGame.levels[level][i];

      // create car
      if (obj.type == "car") {
         carGame.car = createCarAt(obj.x,obj.y);
         continue;
      }

      var groundBody = createGround(obj.x, obj.y,
        obj.width, obj.height, obj.rotation);

      if (obj.type == "win") {
         carGame.gamewinWall = groundBody;
      }
   }
}
```

5. In the page loaded handler function, we change the `restartGame` function calling by providing `currentLevel` as follows:

```
restartGame(carGame.currentLevel);
```

6. We also need to provide the `currentLevel` value in the restart key handler:

```
case 82: // r key to restart the game
   restartGame(carGame.currentLevel);
   break;
```

7. Lastly, we change the following highlighted code in the game win logic. We level up the game when the car hits the destination:

```
if ((body1 == carGame.car && body2 == carGame.gamewinWall) ||
   (body2 == carGame.car && body1 == carGame.gamewinWall))
{
   console.log("Level Passed!");
```

```
        restartGame(carGame.currentLevel+1);
    }
```

8. We will now run the game in the web browser. Finish the level and the game should restart at the next level:

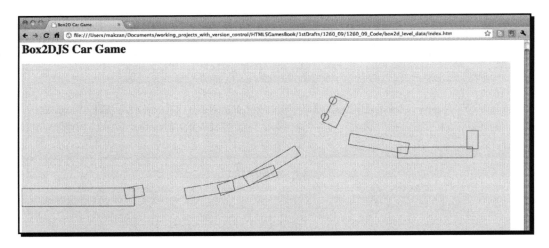

What just happened?

We just created a data structure to store the levels. Then, we created the game with the given level number and constructed the world with the level data.

Each level data is an array of objects. Each object contains properties of each ground body in the world. This includes basic properties such as position, size, and rotation. There is also a property named `type`. It defines whether the body is a normal box body, car data, or the destination winning ground:

```
carGame.levels[0] = [{"type":"car","x":50,"y":210,"fuel":20},
{"type":"box","x":250, "y":270, "width":250, "height":25,
"rotation":0},
{"type":"box","x":500,"y":250,"width":65,"height":15,"rotation":-10},
{"type":"box","x":600,"y":225,"width":80,"height":15,"rotation":-20},
{"type":"box","x":950,"y":225,"width":80,"height":15,"rotation":20},
{"type":"box","x":1100,"y":250,"width":100,"height":15,"rotation":0},
{"type":"win","x":1200,"y":215,"width":15,"height":25,"rotation":0}];
```

When creating the world, we use the following code to loop through all objects in the level array. We then create the car and ground bodies and reference the game winning ground according to the type:

```
for(var i=0;i<carGame.levels[level].length;i++) {
```

```
var obj = carGame.levels[level][i];

// create car
if (obj.type == "car") {
  carGame.car = createCarAt(obj.x,obj.y);
  continue;
}

var groundBody = createGround(obj.x, obj.y, obj.width,
  obj.height, obj.rotation);

if (obj.type == "win") {
  carGame.gamewinWall = groundBody;
}
}
```

Have a go hero – Creating more levels

Now we have several levels setup for our game. How about duplicating the level data to create more interesting levels to play? Create your own levels and play with them. It is just as if a kid builds blocks and plays with them.

Replacing the Box2D outline drawing with graphics

We have created the game that is at least playable with several levels. However, they are just some outline boxes. We cannot even distinguish between the destination body and other ground bodies in the game. Imagine now the destination is a racing flag and there is a car graphic to represent it. It will make the game purpose clearer.

Time for action – Adding a flag graphic and a car graphic to the game

Carry out the following steps:

1. We will first download the graphics we need for this example. Go to the following link to download the graphics:

    http://gamedesign.cc/html5games/1260_09_example_graphics.zip

2. Extract the ZIP file in the images folder.

3. Now it is time to edit the `index.htm` file. Add the following HTML markup to the body:

```
<div id="asset">
    <img id="flag" src='images/flag.png'>
    <img id="bus" src="images/bus.png">
    <img id="wheel" src="images/wheel.png">
</div>
```

4. We want to hide the asset DIV that contains our `img` tags. Open the `cargame.css` file and add the following CSS rule to keep the asset DIV out of our sight:

```
#asset {
    position: absolute;
    top: -99999px;
}
```

5. We will now move on to the logic part. Open the `html5games.box2dcargame.js` JavaScript file.

6. In the `createGround` function, we add a new argument named `type` to pass in the type. Then, we add the highlighted code to assign the reference of the `flag` image to the ground shape user data if it is a winning destination ground:

```
function createGround(x, y, width, height, rotation, type) {
    // box shape definition
    var groundSd = new b2BoxDef();
    groundSd.extents.Set(width, height);
    groundSd.restitution = 0.4;
    if (type == "win") {
        groundSd.userData = document.getElementById('flag');
    }

    ...

}
```

7. When creating the ground, we need to pass the `type` property now. Replace the ground creation code with the following one:

```
var groundBody = createGround(obj.x, obj.y, obj.width,
    obj.height, obj.rotation, obj.type);
```

8. Next, we assign the reference of the `bus` image tag to the user data in the car shape. Add the following highlighted code to the car box definition creation:

```
// the car box definition
var boxSd = new b2BoxDef();
```

```
boxSd.density = 1.0;
boxSd.friction = 1.5;
boxSd.restitution = .4;
boxSd.extents.Set(40, 20);
boxSd.userData = document.getElementById('bus');
```

> We used to get the reference of an element by the jQuery $ (selector) method. The jQuery selector returns an array of the element objects with additional jQuery data wrapped. If we want to get the original document element reference, then we can either use the document.getElementById method or $ (selector).get(0). As $ (selector) returns an array, get(0) gives the first original document element in the list

9. Then, we need to handle the wheels. We assign the wheel image tag to the wheel body's userData property. Add the following highlighted code to the createWheel function:

```
function createWheel(world, x, y) {
    // wheel circle definition
    var ballSd = new b2CircleDef();
    ballSd.density = 1.0;
    ballSd.radius = 10;
    ballSd.restitution = 0.1;
    ballSd.friction = 4.3;
    ballSd.userData = document.getElementById('wheel');

    ...
}
```

10. Finally, we have to draw the images in the canvas. Replace the drawWorld function with the following code. The highlighted code is the changed part:

```
function drawWorld(world, context) {
  for (var b = world.m_bodyList; b != null; b = b.m_next) {
    for (var s = b.GetShapeList(); s != null; s = s.GetNext()) {
      if (s.GetUserData() != undefined) {
        // the user data contains the reference to the image
        var img = s.GetUserData();

        // the x and y of the image.
        // We have to substract the half width/height
        var x = s.GetPosition().x;
        var y = s.GetPosition().y;
        var topleftX = - $(img).width()/2;
        var topleftY = - $(img).height()/2;

        context.save();
        context.translate(x,y);
```

```
            context.rotate(s.GetBody().GetRotation());
            context.drawImage(img, topleftX, topleftY);

            context.restore();
        } else {
            drawShape(s, context);
        }
    }
  }
}
```

11. Finally, save all files and run the game in a web browser. We should see a yellow bus graphic, two wheels, and a flag as the destination. Play the game now and the game should move on to the next level when the bus hits the flag:

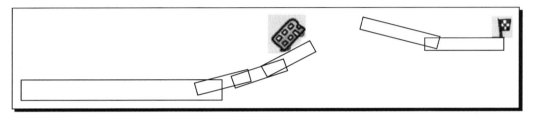

What just happened?

We are now presenting our game with minimal graphics. At least, players can easily know what they are controlling and where they should go.

The Box2D library uses a canvas to render the physics world. Therefore, all techniques that we learned about a canvas can be applied here. In *Chapter 5*, *Building a Canvas Games Masterclass*, we learned the use of the `drawImage` function to display an image in the canvas. We used this technique to draw the flag graphic in the canvas of the physics world.

Using userData in shape and body

How do we know which physics body needs to be displayed as the flag image? There is a property named `userData` in every Box2D shape and body. This property is used to store any custom data related to that shape or body. For example, we may store the filename of the graphic file or we just directly store the reference to the image tag.

We have a list of image tags referencing the graphic assets that we need in the game. However, we do not want to display the image tags, they are just for the purpose of loading and referencing. We hide those asset image tags by setting their position out of the HTML bound with the following CSS style. We do not use `display:none` because we cannot get the width and height of the element that is not displayed at all. We need the width and height to position graphics correctly in the physics world:

```
#asset {
    position: absolute;
    top: -99999px;
}
```

Drawing graphics every frame according to the state of its physics body

The drawing from Box2D is just for development use before we replace it with our graphics.

The following code checks whether the shape has a user data assigned. In our example, the user data is used for referencing the `image` tag of that graphics asset. We get the image tag and pass it to the canvas context `drawImage` function to draw.

All box and circle shapes in Box2D have the origin point at the center. However, the image drawing in the canvas needs the top-left point. Therefore, we have both x/y coordinates and offset of top-left x/y points which is a negative half width and height of the image:

```
if (s.GetUserData() != undefined) {
    // the user data contains the reference to the image
    var img = s.GetUserData();

    // the x and y of the image.
    // We have to substract the half width/height
    var x = s.GetPosition().x;
    var y = s.GetPosition().y;
    var topleftX = - $(img).width()/2;
    var topleftY = - $(img).height()/2;

    context.save();
    context.translate(x,y);
    context.rotate(s.GetBody().GetRotation());
    context.drawImage(img, topleftX, topleftY);
    context.restore();
}
```

Rotating and translating an image in the canvas

We used the `drawImage` function to draw an image directly with the coordinate. However, the situation is different here. We need to rotate the drawn image. This is done by rotating the context before drawing and then restoring the rotation afterwards. We can do this by saving the context state, translating it, rotating it, and then calling the `restore` function. The following code shows how we draw an image at a given position and rotation. The `topleftX` and `topleftY` are the offset distances from the image center origin to the top left point:

```
context.save();
context.translate(x,y);
context.rotate(s.GetBody().GetRotation());
context.drawImage(img, topleftX, topleftY);
context.restore();
```

We do not need to make the physics body area exactly the same as its graphics. For example, if we have a round circle chicken, we can represent it in the physics world by just a ball body. Using a simple physics body can improve the performance a lot.

Have a go hero – Applying the previously learned technique to the car game

We have learned using CSS3 transition to animate a scoreboard. How about applying it to this car game? Moreover, how about adding some engine sounds to the car? Just try applying what we have learned through this book to give players a complete game experience.

Adding a final touch to make the game fun to play

Imagine now we want to publish the game. The game logic is basically here, but it looks quite ugly with the black and white environment. In this section, we will add some final touches to the game so it is much more attractive. We will also apply some constraints to limit the time of ApplyForce. This constraint makes the game more fun because it requires a player to think before he applies too much force to the car.

Time for action – Decorating the game and adding a fuel limitation

Carry out the following steps:

1. First, we need some background images for the starting screen, game winning screen, and environment backgrounds for each level. These graphics can be found from the code bundle named `box2d_final_game`. The following screenshot shows the graphics we need in this section:

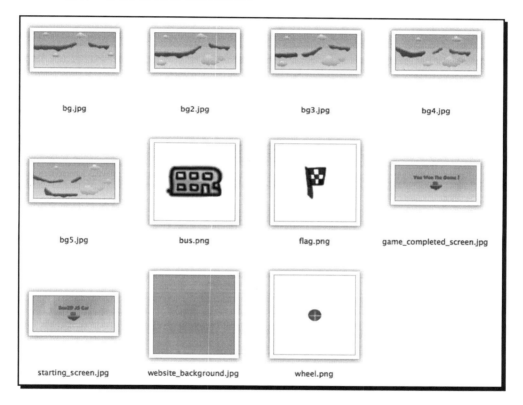

2. Open the `index.htm` file and replace the canvas element with the following markup. It creates two more game components named current level and fuel remaining, and groups the game components into a `game-container` DIV:

```
<section id="game-container">

    <canvas id="game" width='1300' height='600'
      class="startscreen"></canvas>
```

```html
<div id="fuel" class="progressbar">
  <div class="fuel-value" style="width: 100%;"></div>
</div>

<div id="level"></div>
</section>
```

3. Next, we will copy the `cargame.css` file from the code bundle. It contains several class style definitions for the game. The game should look similar to the one shown in the following screenshot when we have applied the new stylesheet:

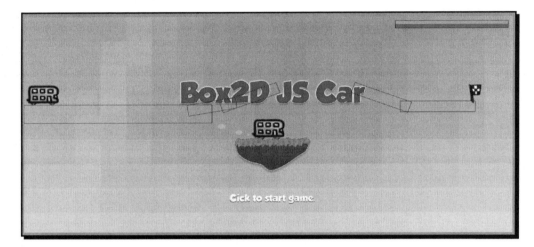

4. Now we will move on to the JavaScript part. Open the `html5games. box2dcargame.js` file.

5. Update the `carGame` object declaration with the following additional variable:

```javascript
var carGame = {
    // game state constant
    STATE_STARTING_SCREEN : 1,
    STATE_PLAYING : 2,
    STATE_GAMEOVER_SCREEN : 3,

    state : 0,

    fuel: 0,
    fuelMax: 0,

    currentLevel: 0
}
```

6. Now we have the starting screen. Instead of starting the game once, the page is loaded. We show the starting screen and wait for the player to click on the game canvas. Add the following logic to the page `ready` function:

```
// set the game state as "starting screen"
carGame.state = carGame.STATE_STARTING_SCREEN;

// start the game when clicking anywhere in starting screen
$('#game').click(function(){
    if (carGame.state == carGame.STATE_STARTING_SCREEN)
    {
        // change the state to playing.
        carGame.state = carGame.STATE_PLAYING;

        // start new game
        restartGame(carGame.currentLevel);

        // start advancing the step
        step();
    }
});
```

7. We need to remove the original `step()` function calling at the end of the page `ready` function because we are calling it on a mouse click.

8. Next, we need to handle the game winning screen when the player passes all levels. In the winning flag collision checking logic, we replace the original `restartGame` function calling with the following logic which checks whether we show the next level or the ending screen:

```
if (currentLevel < 4)
{
    restartGame(currentLevel+1);
}
else
{
    // show game over screen
    $('#game').removeClass().addClass('gamebg_won');

    // clear the physics world
    world = createWorld();

}
```

9. Then, we will handle the game playing background. We prepared each game background for each level setting. We will switch the background in the `restartGame` function which responds to reconstruct the world:

```
$("#level").html("Level " + (level+1));

// change the background image to fit the level
$('#game').removeClass().addClass('gamebg_level'+level);
```

10. With the game graphics now, we do not need the physics object outline drawing any more. We can remove the `drawShape(s, context);` code in the `drawWorld` function.

11. Finally, let's add some constraints. Remember that in our level data, we include a mystery fuel data to the car. It is an indicator indicating how much fuel the car contains. We will use this fuel to limit the player's input. The fuel reduces each time a force is applied to the car. The player cannot apply any additional force once the fuel runs out. This limitation makes the game more fun to play:

12. Update the *x* and *z* `keydown` function with the following logic:

```
case 88: // x key to apply force towards right
  if (carGame.fuel > 0)
  {
    var force = new b2Vec2(10000000, 0);
    carGame.car.ApplyForce
      (force, carGame.car.GetCenterPosition());
    carGame.fuel--;
    $(".fuel-value").width(carGame.fuel/carGame.fuelMax *
      100 +'%');
  }
  break;
case 90: // z key to apply force towards left
  if (carGame.fuel > 0)
  {
    var force = new b2Vec2(-10000000, 0);
    carGame.car.ApplyForce
      (force, carGame.car.GetCenterPosition());
    carGame.fuel--;
    $(".fuel-value").width(carGame.fuel/carGame.fuelMax *
      100 +'%');
  }
  break;
```

13. In addition, in the car creating logic in the restart game function, we initialize the fuel as follows:

```
// create car
if (obj.type == "car")
{
    carGame.car = createCarAt(obj.x,obj.y);
    carGame.fuel = obj.fuel;
    carGame.fuelMax = obj.fuel;
    $(".fuel-value").width('100%');
    continue;
}
```

14. Now, run the game in a browser. We should get five graphic levels. The following screenshot shows how the last four levels look:

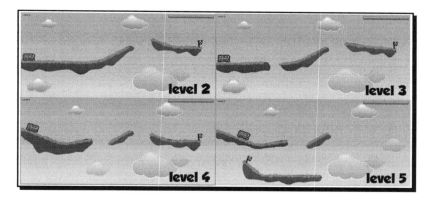

15. After passing all levels, we get the following winning screen:

What just happened?

We just decorated our game with more graphics. We also draw each level environment a background image. The following screenshot illustrates how the visual ground represents the logical physics boxes. Unlike the car and the winning flag, the ground graphics are not associated with the physics ground. It is just a background image with the graphics in their respective positions. We can use this approach because those boxes will never move:

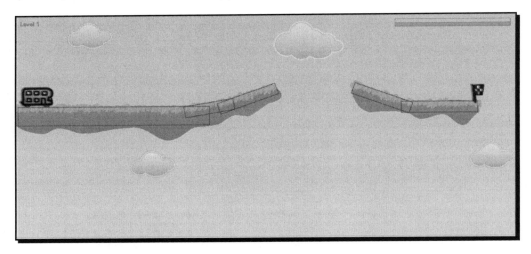

We can then prepare several CSS styles for each level with the level number in the class name, such as .gamebg_level_1 and .gamebg_level_2. With each class linked with each level background, we can change the background when switching a level in the following code:

```
$('#game').removeClass().addClass('gamebg_level'+level);
```

Adding fuel to add a constraint when applying force

Now we limit the player's input by providing limited fuel to use. The fuel decreases when players apply force to the car. We used the following keydown logic to decrease the fuel and prevent additional force when running out of fuel:

```
case 88: // x key to apply force towards right
  if (carGame.fuel > 0)
  {
    var force = new b2Vec2(10000000, 0);
    carGame.car.ApplyForce(force, carGame.car.GetCenterPosition());
    carGame.fuel--;
    $(".fuel-value").width(carGame.fuel/carGame.fuelMax * 100 +'%');
  }
```

Presenting the remaining fuel in a CSS3 progress bar

In our game, we present the remaining fuel as a progress bar. The progress bar is actually a DIV inside another DIV. The following markup shows the structure of the progress bar. The outer DIV defines the maximum value and the inner DIV shows the actual value:

```
<div id="fuel" class="progressbar">
    <div class="fuel-value" style="width: 100%;"></div>
</div>
```

The following screenshot illustrates the structure of the progress bar:

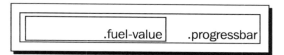

With this structure, we can show a specific progress by setting the width as a percentage value. We use the following code to update the progress bar according to the percentage of the fuel:

```
$(".fuel-value").width(carGame.fuel/carGame.fuelMax * 100 +'%');
```

This is the basic logic to setup a progress bar and control it with the width style. Furthermore, we give the progress bar's background a nice gradient as shown in the following screenshot:

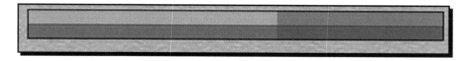

It is done in the stylesheet with the following CSS3 gradient background definition:

```
.progressbar {
  background: -webkit-gradient(linear, left top, left bottom,
    color-stop(0%,#8C906F), color-stop(48%,#8C906F),
    color-stop(51%,#323721), color-stop(54%,#55624F),
    color-stop(100%,#55624F));
}


.progressbar .fuel-value {
  background: -webkit-gradient(linear, left top, left bottom,
    color-stop(0%,#A8D751), color-stop(48%,#A8D751),
    color-stop(51%,#275606), color-stop(54%,#4A8A49),
    color-stop(100%,#4A8A49));
}
```

Summary

We learned a lot in this chapter about using the Box2D physics engine to create a car adventure game in canvas.

Specifically, we covered the following topics:

◆ Installing the JavaScript ported physics engine

◆ Creating static and dynamic bodies in the physics world

◆ Setting up the car by using joints to constrain bodies and wheels

◆ Getting a keyboard input with the prototype library

◆ Interacting with the car by adding force to it

◆ Checking collisions in the physics world as the level destination

◆ Drawing an image to replace the outline of our physical game objects

We also discussed adding a fuel bar to limit the player's input to give some constraint and add more fun to the game play.

We have now learned about using the Box2D physics library to create a canvas-based physics game.

We discussed different aspects of making HTML5 games with CSS3 and JavaScript through all nine chapters. We learned building a traditional Ping Pong game in DOM, we built a card matching game in CSS3, and an Untangle puzzle game with the canvas. Then, we explored adding sounds to the game and created a mini piano musical game around it. Next, we discussed saving and loading game statuses by using the local storage. Moreover, we tried building a draw-and-guess real-time multiplayer game with WebSockets. Finally, we created a car game with a physics engine in this chapter.

Throughout the book, we built different types of games and learned some essential techniques that we need to make HTML5 games. The next step is to go on and deploy your own games. To help develop your own games, there are some resources that can help. The following list gives some useful links for HTML5 games development:

HTML5 game engines

◆ Impact (http://impactjs.com/)

◆ Rocket Engine (http://rocketpack.fi/engine/)

◆ LimeJS (http://www.limejs.com/)

Game sprites, and textures

- Lost Garden (`http://lunar.lostgarden.com/labels/free%20game%20graphics.html`)
- Some free sprites from The_Protagonist's Domain (`http://www.freewebs.com/teh_pro/sprites.htm`)
- HasGraphics sprites, textures, and tilesets (`http://hasgraphics.com/category/sprites/`)
- CG Textures (`http://cgtextures.com/`)

Sound effects

- PacDV (`http://www.pacdv.com/sounds/`)
- FlashKit Sound Effects (`http://www.flashkit.com/soundfx/`)
- FlashKit Sound Loops (`http://www.flashkit.com/loops/`)

Pop Quiz Answers

Chapter 2: Getting Started with DOM-based Game Development

Running our code after the page is ready

1	d

Understanding the behavior of absolution position

1	c

Chapter 3: Building Memory Match Game in CSS3

Storing internal custom data with HTML5 custom data attribute

1	c or d

Accessing custom data attribute with jQuery

1	a and d

Chapter 4: Building Untangle Game with Canvas and Drawing API

Using startAngle and endAngle

1	c

Using closePath with fill command only

1	b

Accessing shapes in canvas

1	b
2	d

Clearing drawn shapes in canvas

1	a
2	b

Chapter 5: Building Canvas Games Masterclass

Drawing text in canvas

1	c
2	b

Styling canvas background

1	b

Chapter 6: Adding Sound Effects to your Games

Using the audio tag

1	b
2	Please the fallback content between \<canvas\> and \</canvas\>

Chapter 7: Using Local Storage to Store Game Data

Using local storage

1	False
2	True
3	True

Chapter 8: Building Multiplayer Draw-and-Guess Game with WebSockets

1	Referring to the content related to Web Sockets section In the WebSockets approach, the amount of requests is much less than the polling approach. It is because the connection between the client and server is persistence. Once the connection is established, a request from either client-side or server-side is only sent when there is any update. For instance, a client sends a message to server when it wants to update something to server. The server also sends messages to clients only when it needs to notify the clients for data update. No other useless requests are sent during the connection. Therefore much less bandwidth is used. The following graph shows the WebSockets approach.

Index

CSS sprite sheet 78
CSS transform functions 61
currentLevel variable 129
currentTime property 171
custom data attribute 84

D

data-custom-name attribute 86
data-href attribute 85
data-score attribute 85
data storage
  HTML5 local storage, using 206
data storage, HTML5 local storage used
  game over dialog, creating 206-209
  game scores, saving 210, 211
  local storage, benefits 212
  local storage, limitations 213
  local storage, treating as associated array 213
  setItem function, using 211
dataType property 258
development environment
  preparing 26
dim class 156
document.getElementById method 305
Document Object Model. *See* **DOM**
DOM 7
DOM-based game development
  collision detection, beginning 49
  DOM object moving, JavaScript Interval used
    47
  HTML documents, preparing 26
  keyboard input, getting from player 37
  manipulating, jQuery used 35
  multiple keyboard input, supporting 43
  Ping Pong game elements, setting 30
  text in HTML, displaying 53
DOM object moving, JavaScript Interval used
  dball, moving 47- 49
  collision detection, starting 49
draw-and-guess game
  about 234
  chatting application building, WebSockets used
    243
  decorating, CSS used 268-270
  message broadcasting 247
  multiplayer game building 259

  shared drawing whiteboard, making 250
  WebSocket server, installing 236
  WebSockets web application, trying 234
drawBackground function 175
drawCricle function 107
drawImage function 148, 149, 308
drawJoint function 283
drawLayerBG function 158
drawLayerUI function 160
drawWorld function 281, 312

E

endX property 258
endY property 258
event
  audio 203
  ended 203
  pause 203
  play 203
  progress 203
  timeupdate 203
  TransitionEnd 83
existing WebSockets web application
  about 234
  multiuser sketchpad, trying 235, 236

F

fadeout class 156
features, CSS3
  about 11
  animation 14, 15
  transform 13, 14
  transition 12, 13
features, HTML5
  audio 8
  canvas 8
  GeoLocation 8
  local storage 10
  offline application 11
  WebGL 9
  WebSocket 10
fill command 103
fill function 102
fillText function 141

M

N

O

WebSockets server installation
  client events 243
  connected clients count, determining 240
  connection, establishing 243
  connection client, creating 241, 242
  connection event listening, on server side 240
  initializing 239
  message, broadcasting 240
  Node.JS WebSocket server, installing 236
  WebSockets server, creating for connection
    count broadcast 238
Web SQL Database
  URL 220
which function 39

world time
  about 286
  world step loop, setting 286

X

x keydown function 312

Z

Z-index property 67
z keydown function 312

Thank you for buying
HTML5 Games Development by Example
Beginner's Guide

About Packt Publishing

Packt, pronounced 'packed', published its first book "Mastering phpMyAdmin for Effective MySQL Management" in April 2004 and subsequently continued to specialize in publishing highly focused books on specific technologies and solutions.

Our books and publications share the experiences of your fellow IT professionals in adapting and customizing today's systems, applications, and frameworks. Our solution-based books give you the knowledge and power to customize the software and technologies you're using to get the job done. Packt books are more specific and less general than the IT books you have seen in the past. Our unique business model allows us to bring you more focused information, giving you more of what you need to know, and less of what you don't.

Packt is a modern, yet unique publishing company, which focuses on producing quality, cutting-edge books for communities of developers, administrators, and newbies alike. For more information, please visit our website: www.PacktPub.com.

Writing for Packt

We welcome all inquiries from people who are interested in authoring. Book proposals should be sent to author@packtpub.com. If your book idea is still at an early stage and you would like to discuss it first before writing a formal book proposal, contact us; one of our commissioning editors will get in touch with you.

We're not just looking for published authors; if you have strong technical skills but no writing experience, our experienced editors can help you develop a writing career, or simply get some additional reward for your expertise.

Flash Game Development by Example

ISBN: 978-1-84969-090-4   Paperback:328 pages

Build 10 classic Flash games and learn game development along the way

1. Build 10 classic games in Flash. Learn the essential skills for Flash game development.

2. Start developing games straight away. Build your first game in the first chapter.

3. Fun and fast paced. Ideal for readers with no Flash or game programming experience.Topic

4. The most popular games in the world are built in Flash.

Flash Development for Android Cookbook

ISBN: 978-1-84969-142-0   Paperback: 372 pages

Over 90 recipes to build exciting Android applications with Flash, Flex, and AIR

1. The quickest way to solve your problems with building Flash applications for Android

2. Contains a variety of recipes to demonstrate mobile Android concepts and provide a solid foundation for your ideas to grow

3. Learn from a practical set of examples how to take advantage of multitouch, geolocation, the accelerometer, and more

Please check **www.PacktPub.com** for information on our titles

HTML5 Multimedia Development Cookbook

ISBN: 978-1-84969-104-8   Paperback:288 pages

Recipes for practical, real-world HTML5 multimedia driven development.

1. Use HTML5 to enhance JavaScript functionality. Display videos dynamically and create movable ads using JQuery.

2. Set up the canvas environment, process shapes dynamically and create interactive visualizations.

3. Enhance accessibility by testing browser support, providing alternative site views and displaying alternate content for non supported browsers

XNA 4.0 Game Development by Example: Beginner's Guide

ISBN: 978-1-84969-066-9   Paperback: 428 pages

Create your own exciting games with Microsoft XNA 4.0

1. Dive headfirst into game creation with XNA

2. Four different styles of games comprising a puzzler, a space shooter, a multi-axis shoot 'em up, and a jump-and-run platformer

3. Games that gradually increase in complexity to cover a wide variety of game development techniques

4. Focuses entirely on developing games with the free version of XNA

Please check **www.PacktPub.com** for information on our titles

Printed in Great Britain
by Amazon.co.uk, Ltd.,
Marston Gate.